Resistance

Resistance

The Essence of the Islamist Revolution

ALASTAIR CROOKE

PLUTO PRESS
www.plutobooks.com

First published 2009 by Pluto Press
345 Archway Road, London N6 5AA
175 Fifth Avenue, New York, NY 10010

www.plutobooks.com

Distributed in the United States of America exclusively by
Palgrave Macmillan, a division of St. Martin's Press LLC,
175 Fifth Avenue, New York, NY 10010

British Library Cataloguing in Publication Data
A catalogue record for this book is available from the British Library

ISBN   978 0 7453 2886 7   Hardback
ISBN   978 0 7453 2885 0   Paperback

Library of Congress Cataloging in Publication Data applied for

10   9   8   7   6   5   4   3

Designed and produced for Pluto Press by
Chase Publishing Services Ltd, Sidmouth, England
Typeset from disk by Stanford DTP Services, Northampton, England
Printed and bound in the European Union by
CPI Antony Rowe, Chippenham and Eastbourne

CONTENTS

ACKNOWLEDGEMENTS

To Usama from whom I have learned so much.

And with thanks also to Nawaf and Chafiq; and particularly to those particular people, Aisling and others, without whose contributions and practical support, tolerance and encouragement it would never have seen the light of day: they know who they are, and have been thanked more personally. I thank also Pluto for being sufficiently intrepid to have a go.

POLITICAL MOVEMENTS

Deobandi is a conservative Sunni Wahhabist-type movement named after the town, Deoband, in India where a seminary Darul Uloom was founded in 1866. Its ideology was influenced by Wahhabism – as brought to India. It is now the second largest centre of learning in the Muslim world after al-Azhar University in Cairo. In 1857, Muslims had joined Hindus in the Sepoy mutiny against Britain. The British responded by deposing the last Mughal emperor Bahadur Shah Zafar – ending 400 years of Muslim rule on the Indian subcontinent. In its place the British established direct rule of India. They also shut down Muslim schools. Deobandism arose as an anti-colonialist movement opposed to the British colonial rule in India. It became politically active in opposing the abolition of the Caliphate in 1924, and in the era of President Zia ul-Haq of Pakistan, became politically influential in Pakistan. It has been a long-standing ideological supporter of the Taliban, who follow a simplistic version of Deobandi thinking, tempered by tribal custom.

DFLP or the Democratic Front for the Liberation of Palestine was formed in 1969 as a breakaway fraction of the PFLP led by Newef Hawatmeh, who has been described as leader of the Maoist faction of the PFLP. Its original programme was based on the view that Palestinian national goals could only be achieved through revolution by the masses. It is now a very small movement.

FATEH, literally 'opening', stands as a reverse acronym for 'Palestinian National Liberation Movement'. Fateh was founded in 1954 by members of the Palestinian diaspora – principally refugees from Palestine who were professionals working in the Gulf states. Among its founders was Yasir Arafat. It is one of the two principal Palestinian movements. It is a broad tent nationalist movement that has dominated the PLO with a policy, since the 1990s, of seeking to negotiate a settlement with Israel.

HAMAS: The letters that form the name are an acronym in Arabic that stands for Islamic Resistance Movement. It was formed in 1987 in Gaza, Palestine, by members of the Sunni Muslim Brotherhood in response to the Israeli occupation of Gaza. In 2006 it won comfortably the Palestinian parliamentary elections; but was unable to govern effectively as Israel interned many of its parliamentarians; and the EU and US isolated and imposed sanctions on the movement. It has formed the vanguard of Palestinian resistance to Israeli occupation since the second Palestinian Intifada, literally the 'shaking-off' or uprising that began in 2000, and stands as a respected symbol for Sunni Muslims everywhere.

Hesballah, literally the 'Party of God', emerged in 1982 as a Shi'i resistance fighting the Israeli invasion of south Lebanon; but its roots go back to the Shi'i 'awakening' in Lebanon of the 1950s and 1960s. It was influenced by Hesb al-Da'wa resistance movement formed in 1957 in Iraq, 'Imam' Musa Sadr, 'Imam' Khomeini and the Iranian Revolution. It is represented in the Lebanese Parliament; and it and its leader, Sayyed Hassan Nasrallah, are acknowledged to be among the most prominent influences in the contemporary Muslim world.

Hesb al-Da'wa or Islamic 'call' party was founded in 1957 at Najaf in Iraq. It represented the first Islamist resistance movement. Initially it comprised both Sunni and Shi'i and had members who were also affiliated with the Muslim Brotherhood and Hesb al-Tahrir. Saddam Hussein waged a relentless war of persecution against its members, including its leading ideologue, Mohammad Baqir Sadr, who was cruelly murdered together with his sister: Baqir Sadr's writings on politics, sociology and economics had a profound influence on the Iranian Revolution.

Hesb al-Tahrir, literally the 'party of liberation', was established in Jerusalem in 1954 by Sheikh al-Nabahani. It is an international

Sunni political party whose goal is to combine all Muslim countries in a unitary Islamic state or caliphate, ruled by Islamic law and with a Caliph head of state elected by Muslims.

Isma'ili sect of Shi'i Islam takes its name from a dispute over the succession in the Shi'i imamate. Isma'ilis accept with other Shi'i the initial Shi'i Imams, but believe that the Imamate ended with the occultation of Muhammad bin Ismail in the eighth century. From the eighth century CE, the teachings of Isma'ilism further transformed into the belief system as it is known today, with an explicit concentration on the deeper, esoteric meaning of Islam. Isma'ilism rose at one point to become the largest branch of Shi'ism, and was at the height of political power during the Fatimid Empire in the tenth through twelfth centuries.

al-Manar is not a movement, but is the satellite television channel belonging to Hesballah. It has a wide audience throughout the Middle East and is influential. The European Union and the United States have tried to prevent its broadcasts into their territories. The US has designated the entire television enterprise as a 'terrorist entity'.

Muslim Brotherhood or 'The society of the Muslim Brothers', its full title, is a transnational Sunni movement and one of the world's oldest and largest Islamist movements in the Arab world, founded by an Egyptian schoolteacher, Hassan Banna, in 1928.

Palestinian Islamic Jihad is a Palestinian resistance movement that was formed in Gaza by members of the Muslim Brotherhood during the 1970s initially as a branch of the Egyptian Islamic Jihad. Although a Sunni movement, its inspiration derived from the Iranian Revolution through the writings of one of its co-founders, Fathi Shaqaqi (1951–95), who wrote key texts on the ideas of Imam Khomeini and the Iranian Revolution. It is a smaller movement than Hamas, and its focus lies principally in resistance to the Israeli occupation.

PFLP or Popular Front for the Liberation of Palestine is a Marxist-Leninist secular nationalist party founded in 1967. In the first Palestinian Intifada or uprising, the PFLP was one of the most militarily active resistance movements. It was initially opposed to the Oslo Accords but by 1999 had acquiesced to Fateh's negotiations with Israel.

PLO or Palestinian Liberation Organisation is the political confederation of Palestinian movements which has, since 1974, been recognised by the Arab League as 'sole Representative of the Palestinian People'. In effect it has been a fiefdom of the Fateh movement. Technically legal agreements between Israel and Fateh have been signed under the auspices of the PLO.

Al-Qae'da, literally 'The Base', is a global Sunni movement that was founded in 1988 in the wake of the Soviet withdrawal from Afghanistan and subsequent political implosion. Its aim has been to cause a similar wider western implosion – similar to that suffered by the USSR – by provoking the West to overreact, and to overextend itself both militarily and financially in the pattern of the Soviet Union, thereby exposing its internal contradictions. Its ideology has been influenced by Wahhabism and Egyptian Islamic Jihad, although its ideology cannot be neatly categorised in this way. Its significance has always been exaggerated in the West.

Salafism, literally 'pious ancestors', is a very early Sunni movement dating to the twelfth century CE. Salafis see the first three generations of Muslims, who are known as 'The Prophet's Companions', and the two succeeding generations after them, as the Tabi'in, as examples of how Islam should be practised.

Taliban, literally 'students', is a conservative Sunni movement associated with ethnic Pashtoons, which ruled Afghanistan from 1996 until the 2001 US-led attack on Afghanistan in the wake of the 9/11 attack on the World Trade Center in New York. Centred around the conservative mullahs of Khandahar, and brought into existence by the Pakistani intelligence service, the Taliban are not so much a true Islamist movement as a tribal movement espousing Pakhtoonwali – the conservative tribal practice, law and customs of south Afghanistan and the neighbouring areas of Pakistan, which is far from synonymous with Islamism.

Wahhabism is a conservative and reformist orientation of Sunni Islam that was founded by Mohammad ibn abd-al Wahhab (1703–92) in the eighteenth century in what is now Saudi Arabia. Abd-al Wahhab, influenced by Ibn Taymiyya sought to purify Islam from its later accretions by a return to the practices of the first three generations of the companions of the Prophet. Wahhabism is the dominant form of Islam in Saudi Arabia and is popular in Kuwait and in Qatar. 'Wahhabism' is often used interchangeably with the term Salafism; but Wahhabism is more correctly viewed as a current within Salafism. Salafists reject the suggestion that abd-al Wahhab established a new school of thought.

Young Turks were a coalition formed in the 1880s of various Turkish political movements advocating western-style reform of the Ottoman Empire. Many were explicitly atheist and followed the positivist ideology of Auguste Comte. At the centre of the Young Turks' revolution was the Committee of Union and Progress (CUP) that came to office in 1908 and which espoused a form of secular and unitary nationalist thinking which was xenophobic and exclusive. The policies pursued by the CUP prepared the way for Mustafa Kemal known as 'Ataturk'.

PROMINENT FIGURES MENTIONED IN THE TEXT

Jamal al-din al-Afghani (1838–97) is an early Islamic reformer whom many regard as a pioneer of Islamist thinking in the late nineteenth century. Born an Iranian Shi'i, he called himself 'the Afghan', which is thought to suggest a Sunni background. He held that Muslims should unify to face the threat from the West by taking their destiny into their own hands. Throughout his career, he showed a remarkable ability to become all things to all men. At different times he presented himself as a revolutionary, a secular freethinker, a Shi'i martyr and a parliamentarian.

Imam Ali ibn Abi Talib (d. 661) was a cousin of the Prophet and married to his daughter and father of the Prophet's two grandsons Hasan and Hussein. After the Prophet's death the companions were divided on who should lead the Muslim community. One current that believed Ali should become Caliph were to become the Shi'i or 'partisans of Ali'; whilst others held that the succession must be decided according to tradition: hence the Sunnah or 'followers of tradition'. Ali became the fourth Caliph; but the first Shi'i Imam after the schism. His son Hussein – Imam Hussein – was martyred at Karbala in Iraq in 680, an event commemorated annually at the Ashura ceremony.

Yasir Arafat (1929–2004) was born in Cairo to Palestinian parents. His father was from Gaza and his mother, who died when he was four years of age, came from a Jerusalem family. His father worked as a textile merchant, but after his wife's death was unable to manage the children alone and sent Yasir to family in Jerusalem. He lived with his uncle in the Old City for four years. During the 1948 war Arafat fought alongside the Muslim Brotherhood forces, but did not join them. After the war, he returned to university to study civil engineering. In 1957 he moved to Kuwait and together with friends from the Muslim Brotherhood founded Fateh in or around 1959. He later became chairman of the PLO and President of the Palestinian National Authority.

Hassan al-Banna (1906–49) was the son of a respected local imam (prayer leader). He became politically active in opposing British rule by the age of 13. He became a Sufi in 1922 and attended al-Azhar University in 1923. He was a social and political reformer, best known for founding the Muslim Brotherhood in 1928, one of the largest and most influential twentieth-century Muslim revivalist organisations. Al-Banna's leadership was critical to the growth of the brotherhood during the 1930s and 1940s.

Abolhassan Bani-Sadr (b. 1933–) Bani-Sadr had participated in the anti-Shah student movement in Iran during the early 1960s, was imprisoned twice, and was wounded during an uprising in 1963. He then fled to France where he collaborated with Ali Shariati in translating the works of Frantz Fanon into Farsi. He returned to Iran together with Khomeini as the revolution was beginning in February 1979 and became the first President of Iran following the Revolution.

Grand Ayatollah Mohammad Hussein Fadlallah (b. 1935–) was born in Najaf, Iraq. His father had come to Najaf from Lebanon in order to pursue his studies. In Najaf, Fadlallah was in the circle of Mohammad Baqir Sadr and Da'wa; but held aloof from too overt an involvement in the movement. He returned to Lebanon in 1966. He is regarded as one of the foremost scholars and philosophers of this era, with a large following stretching throughout the Middle East to Pakistan. He has also been a long-standing activist on behalf of the Shi'i of Lebanon, and a supporter of the resistance against Israeli occupation.

Imam Hussein (626–680) was the son of Imam Ali and Fatima, the daughter of the Prophet. At the Battle of Karbala in 680, he and his small band were hopelessly outnumbered by the forces of the

Governor of Damascus, and Hussein was killed and beheaded. The anniversary of his martyrdom is called Ashura and it is a day of mourning and religious observance for all Shi'i Muslims. Hussein's willingness to face almost certain death against overwhelming odds in the cause of justice and the fight against tyranny has been a continuing source of inspiration to Shi'i Muslims over the centuries.

Ibn Arabi (1165–1240) was an Arab of Andalus (Spain), whose father was a friend of Ibn Rushd and who also met with the celebrated philosopher and was present at his funeral. A 'mystical' philosopher in the tradition of Suhrawardi's theosophy, his emphasis was on the true potential of the human being and the path to realising that potential. He was a seminal influence on both Sayyid Qutb and Imam Khomeini.

Ibn Mubarak (d. 797) was an early example of a fighting scholar, an Iranian who tried to recreate the early community of the Prophet for his band of warriors with his accounts of martyrdom of those early heroes of the early wars of Islam. He also placed the emphasis on the collective norms of the fighters' intention in jihad as well as the striving, sacrifice and volunteering of the many individuals who comprised it.

Ibn Rushd (1126–98), also known as Averroes, was born in Andalus (Spain). His thinking remained of central importance in religious as well as in philosophic thought. He asserted that rational explanation must underlie the articulation of God and that a logical structure should be the approach to defend and explain the revelations of the Qur'an.

Ibn Sinna (980–1037), also known as Avicenna, was a Persian philosopher whose influence on Islamic culture was to be profound. He wrote 450 treatises on a range of subjects of which 240 have survived. He was scientist and philosopher who believed that human reason working according to Aristotle's rules of logic could lead to the attainment of truth. Ibn Sinna found the answer in the Neo-platonic version of Greek philosophy.

Ibn Taymiyya (1263–1328), born in Syria, was a key Sunni writer and ideologue. In reaction to the Mongol rule in Iraq and Iran – whose leaders he believed had converted out of expediency rather than belief – he argued that they should be viewed as no more than the heathens they always had been. He asserted a rigid literalism: like Ibn Hanbal, he held that the Qur'an was to be understood obediently and literally. Beyond that, a Muslim must look for truth to the Hadith and then to the Companions of the Prophet only. He issued a ruling against the study of philosophy; and condemned Sufism as heretical. Taymiyya preached a jihad which was largely about the suppression of heretics, by which he meant mainly the Shi'i. He has become important today as the main source of authority for Sunni hostility towards the Shi'i for validating jihad against Muslim 'heathen' leaders.

Mustafa Kemal (1881–1938), also known as Ataturk, was an army officer and the first President of the Republic of Turkey. A successor in ideological terms to the Young Turks, he completed the process of building an exclusionary secular Turkish nationalism. He abolished the Islamic Caliphate in 1924.

'Imam' Ruhollah Khomeini (1902–89) was an Iranian scholar, philosopher and religious figure, and the political leader of the Iranian Revolution. Following the Revolution, Imam Khomeini became the Supreme Leader of Iran until his death in 1989.

Usama bin Laden (b. 1957–) was born to a prominent and prosperous Yemeni father and Syrian mother. His father was a construction magnate with ties to the Saudi royal family. He joined the jihad in Afghanistan against the Soviet occupation, following a period of political involvement with the Muslim Brotherhood in the late 1970s, and in 1984 established the Services Bureau with Abdullah Azzam in Peshawar, Pakistan. During this time he met his future collaborator Ayman al-Zawahiri. They established al-Qae'da in 1988 in Afghanistan.

Khaled Mesha'al (b. 1956–) was born in Silwad in Palestine where he lived until his family moved to Kuwait during the 1967 Six Day

War. He took a degree in physics at Kuwait University and during this period became politically active in the Palestinian cause. He taught at schools in Kuwait from 1978 to 1984. He was involved in the foundation of Hamas, in 1987, from its outset. In 1997 he was the subject of a failed assassination attempt by the Israeli Mossad intelligence service, who attempted to introduce poison into his ear while he resided in Jordan. An angry King Hussein demanded the antidote from Mossad, which saved his life – and as part of the deal Israel agreed to release Sheikh Ahmad Yasin. Mesha'al has been the head of the Hamas political committee since 1996.

Sayyed Hassan Nasrallah (b. 1960–) was born in East Beirut; but with the outbreak of civil war in 1975, the family moved back to its family home in the south. With a keen interest in Islam, he was encouraged by a senior cleric to continue his studies in Najaf. It was during this period in Najaf that he first met Sheikh Abbas Mousawi, who was to become Hesballah's first Secretary General in 1991. In 1978, he and Abbas Mousawi – together with several hundred other Lebanese students – were expelled from Iraq. On their return to Lebanon Mousawi established a theological school in the Beqa'a Valley at which Nasrallah studied and taught. The college followed the teachings of Mohammad Baqir Sadr who had founded Da'wa. Nasrallah was one of the founders of Hesballah in 1982 and became its Secretary General in 1992 after Mousawi's assassination by Israel.

Sayyid Qutb (1906–66) was a leading ideologue of the Muslim Brotherhood whose writings influenced a generation of Muslims. His writings became increasingly critical of Muslim leaders, and of the social injustice associated with contemporary society. He advocated armed vanguardism to bring about radical social change. He was hanged in Cairo in 1966.

Mohammad Baqir Sadr (1935–80) hailed from a celebrated clerical family noted for its intelligence. He was the son of an Ayatollah, the father-in-law of Muqtada Sadr, the present leader of the 'Mahdi Army' in Iraq, and cousin to Imam Musa Sadr who was the seminal influence in the Shi'i mobilisation in Lebanon that led to the forming of Hesballah. He founded the Hesb al Da'wa in Najaf in 1957 and became a leading Islamist philosopher and thinker whose ideas helped shape the future Iranian constitution.

Musa Sadr (1928–78) from the same celebrated family as Mohammad Baqir Sadr, his father was an Ayatollah. Originally planning a more secular profession, he was persuaded by his father to pursue his clerical studies. Asked to come to Lebanon in 1958, he proved to be a new kind of leader for the Shi'i of south Lebanon: an activist cleric involved in the life of the community. He became a principal catalyst in the Shi'i mobilisation in Lebanon and founded the Amal movement. He and two colleagues travelled to Libya in 1978 and were never seen again. Following his still unexplained disappearance, Musa Sadr became known as the 'Vanished Imam'.

Mulla Sadra (1571–1640) born at Shiraz in Iran, the son of a notable Shirazi family, he completed his education at Isfahan. He was a philosopher and scholar who led the Iranian cultural renaissance in the seventeenth century. Mulla Sadra is regarded as arguably the single most important philosopher in the Muslim world in the last 400 years. His philosophy had a profound influence on Imam Khomeini.

Ali Shariati (1933–77) was an Iranian sociologist and revolutionary, well known and respected for his work in the field of sociology of religion. He is known as one of the most original and influential Iranian social thinkers of the twentieth century, and as the ideologue of the Iranian Revolution.

Abd-al Wahhab (1703–92) articulated a conservative and reformist orientation of Sunni Islam in the eighteenth century in what is now Saudi Arabia. Influenced by Ibn Taymiyya, Abd-al Wahhab sought to purify Islam from its later accretions by a return to the practices of the first three generations of the companions of the Prophet. Wahhabism is the dominant form of Islam in Saudi Arabia and is popular in Kuwait and Qatar. 'Wahhabism' is often used interchangeably with the term 'Salafism'; but Wahhabism is more correctly viewed as a current within Salafism. Salafists reject the suggestion that abd-al Wahhab established a new school of thought.

Sheikh Ahmad Yasin (1937–2004) a quadriplegic who was nearly blind, he was confined to a wheelchair after a sporting accident at the age of 12. He was born in the village of Majdal that was destroyed in the 1948 war and became a refugee in Gaza. Despite his physical handicap, he studied at al-Azhar University in Cairo. It was in Cairo that he joined the Muslim Brotherhood. In 1997 he was released from Israeli imprisonment as part of an arrangement with Jordan following a failed Israeli assassination attempt on Khaled Mesha'al. In 2004 he was assassinated in an Israeli helicopter attack on his daily journey to pray at the mosque.

Ayman al-Zawahiri (b. 1951–) grew up in the Egyptian town of Maadi as the product of an unusually strict and illustrious Muslim family. His father's uncle was grand imam of Cairo's al-Azhar University – the pre-eminent seminary in the Sunni Muslim world and his mother's family was equally renowned as Muslim scholars. In spite of their lofty social credentials, his family refused to participate in Maadi social life – viewing it as morally reprehensible. He qualified as a surgeon, but from the age of 15 years was politically active in movements seeking to overthrow President Nasser, ultimately becoming the head of Egyptian Islamic Jihad. He met Usama bin Laden in Peshawar, Pakistan, in 1980, and joined with him in forming al-Qae'da following his release from a period of imprisonment in Egypt in 1981.

INTRODUCTION

The Iranian cleric, dressed in dun coloured robes, a tall, bearded, white-turbaned, 'Hojat al-Islam', a position nudging on that of Ayatollah, a man deeply engaged in thinking about the next stages of the Iranian Revolution quietly sat at a table in a cafe in Qom. This is the small city, surrounded by desert, of 146 seminaries and religious institutes that lies 80 kilometres from Tehran. It is the city 'think tank' of the Shi'i Muslims of Iran. The cleric, who is one of the most eminent scholars in Iran, who holds doctorates in both western and Islamic philosophy, came to explain the nature of the conflict between Islamism and the West. This struggle, he said, at its core was a dispute about the 'essence of man'.

He may be a philosopher, but he is a practical man too, with personal experience of revolution and war, and at the forefront of key political and theological disputes in his own country. Yet he did not give the answer that this conflict was all about a tussle over power or sovereignty, as many westerners instinctively assume; nor did he mention foreign policy as such as its immediate cause; and most certainly, he did not attribute it to 'envy' at western 'achievements'.

The West, the cleric was about to tell me, is curiously sightless as to how its ideas – and the consequences that have flowed from these ideas – have affected others: it had induced a form of collective western amnesia concerning the dark side of its contribution to history. It was not just the content of the ideas, which generally had been espoused with the best of intentions; nor was it innate to all western thinking. Western civilisation had produced intellectual giants who transcended the label 'western': Surprisingly, he was about to tell me, the core of the problem lay rather in the western process of thinking – how it 'thinks about thinking'.

1

It was this thinking, and how this had come to distort its view of the human being; and how, from this, the West had lost the centrality of the human as a guide to how we should live in the future. 'Only from such introspection can we begin to address what went wrong', the cleric suggested.

It is to this dark side to history – the complex strands of western thinking that stand behind the last 200 years of events – that I look for an explanation of why Muslims, suddenly, at a particular moment in history, began to feel the need to mobilise and to embrace resistance and revolution. I try to bring out and trace the essence and the spirit of the ideas that lie behind this rising resistance to the West – rather than to attempt a historical survey of Islamism in all its diversity. I attempt to show why these new ideas and this new thinking seemed so energising and liberating for Muslims; and I explore what it was that happened in the Iranian Revolution that was so important that Shi'i influence has become so significant throughout the Middle East – and therefore also such a feared new guest at the table of the waning Arab regimes.

Resistance is the story of how the Muslim world embarked on a journey to find a new confidence and self-esteem; and to uncover a 'solution' to their feelings of having become victims of a catastrophe; to rediscover a 'self' that is not in shock, cut off from its past, and humiliated by being exposed to contempt and demonisation. Not surprisingly, it has responded to its circumstances in ways that are different to those of Christians – as we shall see later. Its 'solution' to its problems however challenges in a fundamental way western thinking about politics, economics and the principles around which society is organised.

Westerners find it difficult to comprehend the reasons why parts of the Muslim world have adopted a resistance against the West; and why a small minority have become attached to more apocalyptic violence. Westerners also find it hard to understand what the nature of this disaster that has overtaken Islam might be; and why this disaster – whatever it may be – should be held to justify armed resistance.

The reasons why westerners should have a blind spot to a challenge by Islamists on the plane of ideas, rather than on the battlefield, the reasons why so many Muslims embarked upon revolution, and the meaning of this revolution, are questions that Resistance attempts to answer. For some, even the suggestion that there is in the West such a blind spot will be shocking: they believe that to entertain such concepts is tantamount to appeasement of those harbouring irrational hostility towards the West.

The Islamist armed resistance did not emerge in a vacuum however. I argue that its emergence in the last century was neither irrational nor motivated by divinely inspired whimsy; but is capable of a clear and reasoned historical explanation. It is an explanation that addresses the mythical and deep emotional roots that stand behind flawed western policies, and which attempts to expose their still highly relevant Christian antecedents – even in today's 'secular' world. This forms the first part of Resistance. In the subsequent section, I try to show how the western preferred explanations for Islamist violence are intended to curtail debate and critical thought, rather than offer true explanations. I look for the underlying reasons why the West has been so fixated in its denial of rationality in Islamism.

I attempt to show how the western response of demonising Islamism bears no relation to the human reality; but has been a projection of long-standing western anxieties and worries about their vulnerability to nihilism 'infecting' their own societies via liberalism. I try to show that the fear of the inherent weaknesses of western societies – epitomised by the Weimar Republic in Germany – caused American policy-makers deliberately to contrive a 'fear' of Islamism. This was done as much to build defences against the 'dangers' from liberalism and a 'lack of patriotism' as from any objective analysis of Islamism.

It was, in other words, a reaction to, and conditioned by, buried fears about western society to its own inherent flaws. The 'threat' from Islamism merely served as an opportune peg for conservatives to restructure western societies in way that would weaken and undermine liberal and social democratic support.

But paradoxically – in view of the European enthusiasm to follow this US lead – its ultimate target always was multicultural liberalism, more than Islamism per se. It was conceived to strike at the very principles and identity by which Europe defines itself. Europe's readiness to embrace policies and an intolerance at odds with its own liberal self-image – in pursuit of national 'resolve' to fight terrorism – sets up internal conceptual contradictions that will divide and embitter European politics.

Resistance will argue – contrary to the overwhelming settled western opinion – that the conflict between Islam and the West is at core a religious one – even if the policies pursued by the West are avowedly secular. The key ideas and processes that underlie western policy can be traced as a linear continuum from the Protestant and puritan struggle with another sacral community, namely Roman Catholicism. The same processes, and even the same language used against Catholics, later were to be extended to Islam. But it cannot be held to be an exclusively Protestant creation, however, as many of these themes such as seeing history as a teleological process, apocalyptic expectations, and the belief in a transformation and redemption that can be brought about by human action alone, go to the roots of Christianity. But, at the heart of all this, as the Iranian cleric suggested, is a fundamental cleavage in what we mean when we talk about the 'essence of man'.

Western Modernity and the 'Essence of Man'

To begin this story, let us now return to the Iranian cleric with whom we began, and revert to his account of The Essence of the Islamist Revolution. His analysis foreshadows key themes that we will explore in subsequent chapters.

For the Iranian cleric, it was this:

... transgression against the essence of man that was the tragedy that the West had brought upon the world. There had been, in past history, huge afflictions and disasters; there had been wars, discrimination between classes and races, and famine – all of these things – but none of these compared with the disasters of today: what is different today is that science and knowledge, the most sacred things man has, have been abused. And, more gravely, that all these terrible afflictions of today: domination, control and war, have been rationalised and justified; and are all claimed by the West to be done in the 'interests of mankind'.

He continued:

In my opinion, any serious discussion about the state of the world has to start from this point. I strongly reject the belief that today's conflicts – its system of governance and the present world order – are solely the product of political rivalry, economic disagreements or of national interests. The crises in today's world, be they spiritual, moral or environmental, arise out of the thinking of the past two or three centuries: And the especial tragedy of our situation is not just that we face these crises; but that this flawed thinking has taken root in politicians who have acted in the belief that what they do is right and for the betterment of mankind.

Our present conflicts have to be distinguished – within Islam they are minor and mainly historical – but those with the West centre on Islam itself, and are essential. That's why I feel that the conflict between Islam and the West is the main root of all the conflicts that we witness throughout the world.

When we talk about Islam and the West we do not mean the peoples inhabiting the western countries or the Islamic peoples, but rather the conflict between two universal thoughts and visions. We don't want to change the basis of this dialogue to one about Iran versus America or between Shi'i and others. I do not condone that in any way.

I view the world's present condition somewhat like a patient who is sick. There are two aspects to this sickness; there are the external symptoms, and there is the internal cause of the illness which runs more deeply. If we are truly aware, and we want to get rid of this sickness, then first we have to separate between the presentation of symptoms and its underlying causes. One may imagine that part of the cause is related to those external symptoms: wars, injustice and the current conditions. Nevertheless, the job of defining the original roots and raison d'être for these problems has to be done by the world's great thinkers.

In reality, what we are facing is a conflict between two civilisations; between two views about living. Recognising these two different ways of living is the main task facing us in terms of thinking and learning ... However, if we can really awaken the peoples together with true leadership, we will be able to overcome these dangers and threats; and those differences will not be an obstacle to the future course of the Islamic Umma [the Muslim community of believers].

Thus the message of the Iranian Revolution to today's world lies in hoisting up the banner of the essence and the truth of man ... and to show that the concepts upon which Islam is based are identical with human objectives throughout history, but from which we have diverged under the influence of the modern world ... Throughout the revolutionary phase of the Islamic revolution, Imam Khomeini never saw the revolution as the property of a certain specific sect or to be the reflection of specifically Sunni or Shi'i thought; he always recognised its value to all Islam and linked the values of the revolution directly to the Qur'an and to the human values that are embedded in the Qur'an.

Over the past decades we have witnessed many manifestations of western resort to power: culture, ethics and morality – all have been used as instruments of power, a means of domination by the West. We have to try to relinquish this attachment to power, and to revert to what is human. On the one hand, we need to reinvest culture with its rationality; and on the other hand, to humanise politics; to make politics humane. Only in this way can we limit abuse of power, and prevent the domination of man over man, and man over humanity.

The main idea and message of the Islamic revolution therefore is to present this new way of living and a new vision of modernity emerging for today's world. It is one that fundamentally differs from what the West terms 'modernity'.[1]

The cleric's comments derive from what is often overlooked in the West: that the Prophet Mohammad did not see himself as founding a new religion. The Qur'an did not put forward any philosophical arguments for monotheism, but insisted that its message was simply a 'reminder' of truths that everybody knew. In fact, the Qur'an has a negative view of theological speculation, which it calls 'Zannah', a self-indulgent caprice about ineffable matters that nobody can ascertain one way or another ... far more crucial than theological speculation, the Qur'an states, is the 'striving' (jihad) to live in the way that God had intended for human beings.[2] Islam is all about activism. It is centred on direct social and political struggle to achieve the correct way of living – a commitment to struggle that is seen as appropriate today as it was in the time of the Prophet.

When an Iranian revolutionary speaks of transgressions against the essence of man, and calls on mankind to try to relinquish concepts of power and revert to the human, he is re-stating the Qur'anic grand narrative of a world then beset by malaise, inequality and warfare and its practical remedy of a 'reminder' of truths that everybody knew[3] – the need to recuperate 'old truths' – the essential human values that were known to all religions.

Islam as a Revolutionary Vision

The Prophet Mohammad's new sect would eventually be called Islam (surrender): a Muslim was a man or woman who had made this submission of his or her entire being to Allah and his demand that human beings behave to one another with justice, equity and compassion.[4]

The radicalism of Islam therefore lay in the command to build a community in which men and women behaved with compassion, with respect for others – whatever their standing in life – and in which there was a fair distribution of wealth. In short, Islam is about the experience of daily living in such a society. It was a revolutionary social and political vision of the future with far-reaching implications. Muslims are commanded actively and literally to fight daily for justice and for human respect and compassion. It is the revival of this radical message of social justice that lies at the centre of the Islamist revolution.

But when the cleric points to the 'essence of man' as the root of the divergence between Islam and the West, he was, as we shall see later, looking beyond a simple re-statement of Islam. He was also hinting that, behind the importance of the identification of this underlying cause to the dispute, it might be possible to go beyond this initial insight to perceive the beginnings of a 'solution' too.

By 'solution' I mean that when faced with a disaster, or an overwhelming problem, peoples and nations – and individuals too

– often try to recoup a collapsed morale, and to 'find themselves' again in a new and more effective way. Sometimes this takes the form of a symbolic journey or an exile that marks a clean break with the past – such as the Jewish exile in Babylon, 589–538 BCE; or it comes from a new insight, perhaps occasioned by people seeing a new significance or meaning in old symbols and myths. And because old myths resonate at such a profound level of human emotion and imagination, any change to their interpretation and their meaning can have a powerful impact on people's thinking – often incomparably more potent than political argument: it can begin a process of redefining and journeying towards a new 'self' for a people.

As an example of what I mean, by journeying towards a new 'self', the troubled period known as the European 'Dark Ages' came within a whisker of precipitating the end of Christianity in Western Europe. As these Europeans looked around them, the only evidence of 'civilisation' were the few remnants lingering on from the once great Roman Empire: these lay only in its collapsed buildings, whose guiding inspiration must have seemed as remote to the local communities as if it derived from aliens from another world. It symbolised a lost era of cultural achievement. Roman skills and knowledge had been forgotten, and so completely lost – under the pressures of constant invasion and the battle just to survive – that the inhabitants had also let slip the ability to think and reason as they once had been able to do. They barely retained skills enough from the earlier civilisation even to farm adequately.

Their frail settlements were wiped out by an apparently endless cycle of famine, flood and disease. It was a demoralising and brutal existence; and it seemed that this frail culture of western Christianity eventually must succumb and be overwhelmed by the 'pagan' onslaught of constant 'barbarian' raids. In the south of Europe, Christianity precariously hung on by its fingernails in a few fortress monasteries; but in the northern provinces of the old empire, it seemed that Christianity might simply slip away from the people's grasp.

Yet faced with imminent catastrophe, their own past ravaged by continual foreign raids and overwhelmed by an alien culture, the western Christian church found the meagre resources to rediscover itself. It did this in a new way that not only ensured its survival, but provided it with a confidence and vision that enabled the West to rise to new power.

The new 'insight' was to re-imagine the life of Jesus as an affirmation of the ideals of monasticism as the vision by which men and women should aspire to live their lives. Monks saw their monasteries as idealised fortresses from which they ventured forth to prosecute a Holy War against demons and the forces of evil, much as the secular knights and feudal lords fought the worldly threat from Viking raiders. Initially, this Holy War was a figurative struggle waged by the people adopting penitential pilgrimage, monastic ideals and a dedication to the poor and vulnerable. In this way people looked to the monasteries for their vision of the future.

The practicality for ordinary Christians to live out their daily grind in the spirit of the elitist monks was beside the point: It was an 'imagined' solution that re-energised people and restored their confidence; and as stability began to return to the north of Europe, Christians began to feel that they could actually force a change on history through mass human action. They marched on Jerusalem in a mass pilgrimage in 1009 in the hope of compelling the 'anti-Christ' to emerge in the Temple – and to suffer his inevitable defeat that would bring about final redemption – the return of Jesus, and the triumph of Christianity across the world.

In 1095 Pope Urban II transformed pilgrimage into crusade; and Christians found 'renewal' by means of a journey and by crusading. Some monastical orders actually became disciplined, armed militia – now literally, as opposed to figuratively, fighting 'evil' by the sword – seeing death on the battlefield, killing Muslims, to be a blessed martyrdom. For over 200 years huge numbers of Christians voyaged to the 'Holy Land' on crusade. On eight separate occasions, the Pope and the monarchs of Europe, without any provocation, declared war on Islam. 'Christian soldiers marching as to war', which Christians still sing today in their churches, was their rediscovery of a new 'self' – and the consequences that flowed from it still shape the world in which we live today. The crusades rooted both anti-Semitism and demonisation of Islam deep into the European psyche. Pope Urban, as Karen Armstrong has noted, 'had made violence central to the religious experience of the Christian layman and western Christianity had acquired an aggression which it never entirely lost'.[5]

The 'solution' to the catastrophe of the 'Dark Ages' was successful in creating the myths – through re-writing the story of Charlemagne – that allowed western Europeans to imagine themselves as the muscular and aggressively powerful successors to Charlemagne: they created a new western European 'self' that was the polar opposite of the hated – and envied – eastern Byzantine court. Western heroes were strong, practical rather than clever, men trained to war, full of faith and charity; whereas the Byzantines may have been more intelligent and cultured; but they also were soft, effeminate, idlers and liars.

The Longevity of Myth and Religious Emotivity

One key theme that runs throughout Resistance is the power and longevity of emotion fuelled by myths and by deep-seated religious insights, which far from being mere ancient curiosities and relics, still condition the way people – including secular people – think today: the image projected of the Byzantines by western Christians was little more than a converse mirroring of western anxieties; but the latter's cultivation of its self-image of 'tough-minded aggression', presented as a more honest virtue than Byzantine cleverness and duplicity, has proved an enduring legacy: societies can become prisoners to their own history – until grave misfortune leaves them no option, but to re-imagine themselves afresh.

Christians again found the resources in the wake of the seventeenth century Religious Wars that ravaged Europe to journey towards a new 'self'. Protestants had read a new significance into the ancient story of the patriarch Abraham and his readiness to sacrifice his son Isaac. A new meaning and significance had emerged from an old tradition – a new 'solution' that had arisen for Protestants out of the disaster of religiously inspired European civil war. It was a solution that was later to take Europe and America to an unparalleled power. This also is a principal theme of Resistance, and is pursued further in subsequent chapters.

The consequences of that new definition of the Protestant 'self' lie at the heart of the cleric's perhaps surprising suggestion that ultimately what is in contention between Islamism and the West is the 'essence of man'. This may seem unexpected and shocking to many in the West who see 'human values' as the universal 'truths' on which all the world can agree; whereas the cleric, as we shall see, is pointing to the Islamists' own journey to a re-discovery of 'self', and the essence of its revolution, as hanging upon their insight into the 'essence of man', from which he believes the West has strayed.

Shi'i thinkers, such as this Iranian cleric, who frame the conflict between Islam and the West as a difference of view about humans – and therefore of the purpose and end of society and the meaning of politics – are taking the issue back to the bedrock of our common political and philosophical inheritance: to the tension that has always existed between the purpose of politics and the desires and needs of the individual as reflected in western democracy.

Philosophy's claims in respect of politics – from the times of ancient Athens – can be readily summed up as an imperative: to shield politics from the perils that are innate to it. And when these lures to which politics is prone capsize it; when it becomes the captive to a domineering elite; when it degrades and tries to suppress and control humans – it is the task of philosophy, Islamic and western, and of all activists and thinkers to try to haul politics back onto the solid ground of knowledge and critical thinking (as the Iranian cleric suggested), and to examine how it capsized and what is to be done to re-found it.

The whole political project of Platonism – our common root in both Islam and the West – can be conceived as an attempt to recuperate the human community to 'telos' (rationality and purpose) from the darker side of human passions; and as a remedy for the sheer fact of social division – 'the turbulence of collections of individuals who are always at odds with themselves, living rent by passion and at the mercy of desire'.[6]

Jacques Rancière, the contemporary French philosopher, has suggested that the entire political project of Platonism can be conceived as an 'anti-maritime project'[7] – a shorthand term that has come to describe not only the port of Athens, but also the modern western tradition of 'maritime' largely English-speaking politics that dates back to the late seventeenth century.

Since 1688, the maritime powers of Britain and America have been winning every military conflict, it has been argued by Walter Russell Mead in *God and Gold*.[8] Both societies came from a culture that was uniquely well positioned to develop and harness the forces of capitalism, to tolerate the stresses, uncertainty and inequalities associated with the free market, he suggests. It heralded a new kind of religious equilibrium in which individualism became the organisational principle around which society, politics and economics were organised – and in which individualism and constant change came to be accepted as good things.[9]

This loosely has been termed the 'maritime project' from its growth out of the geopolitical power strategy adopted by the English-speaking world and described as the rise of an 'overwhelming power destined to be used selfishly, as aggressively, although not as cruelly, and much more successfully than any that had preceded it. This was the power of the sea.'[10] It symbolised free trade, open markets and rugged insistence on the right of the individual to pursue his personal interests unencumbered by social or religious constraints.

Religion, the puritan variant of England, far from imposing social constraints in the interests of managing social division as the Catholic Church did, instead became a major actor in an intensifying and accelerating process of social change and capitalist development, accepting constant transformation as the normal and desirable human state.[11] It opened the 'maritime project' to the criticism that the Anglo-Saxon ethos, with its pursuit of business, efficiency and the ever-rising standard of living, was unconnected to any deeper vision of life or meaning: in other words it lacked Plato's 'telos' (rationality and purpose).

What Constitutes Democracy?

Rancière quotes from the Gorgias Plato's insistence that Athens has a disease that comes from its port, from the predominance of maritime enterprise governed entirely by profit and survival. Empirical politics, that is to say the fact of democracy, is identified by Plato with the maritime lust for possession.[12] The port became a symbol of the dark side of human nature: of the brutality of a maritime enterprise that was associated with violence, exploitation and domination, a lust for possession, and with a libidinous 'democracy' centred around the predations of drunken, pleasure-seeking sailors from the triremes.

The distance of 80 stadia that separated the Clinias' city[13] from its port, was in the Athenians' eyes, barely distance enough to quell this maritime bad smell of sailors and its degraded democracy. For Plato, the port of Athens symbolised the tensions between two very different visions: the wish to do 'truly political things' – for example, striving for a community based on justice, equity and compassion – against the latent violence, sensuality and avarice of maritime Athens.

Reverting again to our Shi'i cleric from Iran, what he is saying is that the issue is not the plethora of minor conflicts that exist between Islamism and the West:

> The current condition of the world is partly contingent on the politicians of today; and, as we can see, our current problems are aggravating. Today, there are various problems among Islamic societies; some have historic aspects and are fuelled by scholastic theological debates. These include sectarian differences; divergences among various Islamic schools of the Sunni and the Shi'i, or those that may be related to ethnicity within the Islamic World.
>
> But we believe the proper way to [resolve] these issues is by avoiding becoming entangled in these detailed conflicts that express only the symptoms of the malaise, and to return to the origins of Islam – to

return to the genuine resources and thoughts of the Qur'an – instead of enmeshing ourselves in the sectarian and ethnic aspects of the present circumstances.

This in effect is echoing Plato's call for a return to 'telos' (rationality and purpose). This reassertion, out of the heart of the Iranian Revolution, of the tensions between 'telos' and 'demos', carries huge implications for what is meant by 'democracy' – is democracy that of the Athenian port; or is it a higher project of justice, equity and compassion? The Iranian Revolution, by insisting on the latter, re-opened an ancient debate: the proper ends of democracy and what that means for how a nation-state functions.

Our Hojat al-Islam is suggesting that the causes of this 'essential' conflict with Islamism stem from a certain way of thinking in the West that has evolved over the last two to 300 years, and which has tipped even further in that direction during the last 20 to 30 years:

. In the West, values have metamorphosed into mere social contracts. The attractiveness of social contracts can vary at any time – depending on how they meet a person's prevalent desires and needs of the moment – and can be discarded as they see fit. In western thinking, the primary motivation for man is pleasure and pain; and these two impulses shape the outward and material characteristics of man. In western thought, rationality has lost its position. Instead of being directed to perceive truth and values – rationality has turned into a tool to accomplish man's psychological and materialistic needs. Instead of seeking out the realities of society, western thinking has been channelled into the construction of a desire-seeking and materialistic society.

By eliminating God from society they have eliminated also the values and structures which enable man to advance and to aspire to perfection. The separation of faith from reason was contrived deliberately – to eliminate from our minds the potential to know the values and realities of the world. This severance facilitated man's materialistic mind to dedicate itself to the 'management of society' – without intrusion from God – and without ethical values. Faith then became confined only to the personal corners of man's solitude with his Lord. The omission of God from this universal view is an omission of the ladder of values and ethics that man was destined to search out – in order to reach perfection.

Rationality therefore assumed a materialistic cast; and faith became no more than an individual's private connection with God. In this vision, values are only a means to obtain power, and to satiate personal desires and pleasures. It is important to understand what the substitution of these values of appetite signifies: it has led to the ethics of domination coming to the fore. Justice and human rights have been reduced to mere tools for those in power to maintain their rule. This is why justice in some cases is applied fully, and in others it is ignored totally. This comes about because values interpreted in this way are divorced from their true meaning and significance. Justice and rights in the West are degraded and no longer represent any meaningful criteria by which to define a man's 'welfare'. Man's 'welfare' is greater than the mere power of enjoyment. In this western ideology it is the individual's 'right' to pursue his or her own personal welfare – but its attainment is a purely personal attainment; he or she is not expected to consider the welfare of his or her community.

In face of this, how do Islam and the Islamic revolution describe man and his values, and what is the message of the Islamic revolution? First of all, the human being is part of the reality of existence; and there is no separation between him and existence. The system of existence, of which we are a part, is a moral one. Moral values are a part of this existence, and of this world. The ethical values within the order of existence are also real. Values such as justice, love and freedom are things within existence, and no one has the right to transgress or breach them. When Islam talks about God and the values of existence – an existence that is dependent on God, God is no abstract concept.

In the West, such Islamic concepts often have been muddled with, and not correctly distinguished, from Christian doctrine. The belief in God in Islam is, before anything, a belief in an invariable order of values and ethics – in the sense that the reality which created the world is also the reality that created the order of values and ethics for the world. The human being has the potential to elevate himself to perfection by understanding and following this ethical order. As for what is today called man's personal needs, these are not capable of providing for true human happiness.

Thus, in contrast with secularism which believes that values are contained within man, and are made by man, Islam believes that these values are more sublime than man, and are the point of perfection and happiness for man.

Therefore acting justly and wanting peace and observing the rights of others as well as the rights of the environment are all duties of man himself; and they cannot be neglected. There is another message in the belief in God – that man, whichever race or tribe he may come from, is a creation of God and that all are equal. This is in contrast with the western view that separates man from his 'being'. Islam sees that man is a harmonious being that cannot be partitioned. These unchanging human values may be perceived and accessed via a man's conscience; a man can, through his innate essence, perceive these values anywhere, and at any time.

Reason in Islamic thought is the guide by which man may obtain knowledge of the values of existence, and from which he may build a sound society. The concepts of governance and politics in Islam do not permit of the notion of one man dominating another, or of man's domination over nature. In Qur'anic thought, man is the criterion around which all revolves.[14]

The Challenge From Islam:
Reason and the Nature of Being

It is clear from this lucid account by one leading revolutionary thinker that there is a huge misunderstanding in the West about the nature of the Islamist revolution. The Islamists are disputing the essential claim that western secular 'modernity' does bring real human welfare. They are rejecting a particular process of instrumental western thinking – and the abuses of power to which it has given rise. The significance of this should become clearer in the next chapter. It represents a difference of view that is significant and which needs to be fully understood. In effect it presages a re-opening of the debates from which the classical foundations of western politics emerged.

Islamism is indeed challenging the West. But, apart from a small minority of Muslims who see the struggle in eschatological terms or in terms of 'burning the system, to build it afresh' as al-Qae'da does, the revolution is a struggle – a resistance – centred not on killing; but on ideas and principles. In Part III of Resistance we examine in detail the reasons for Islamist resistance from the perspective of two leading Islamist movements, one Sunni and one Shi'i, Hesballah and Hamas. The West, from the time of the crusades, has viewed Islam as a failed form of their own religion; and so too – even when the evidence to the contrary is overwhelming – finds it impossible to see Islam as anything other than a violent religion.

The Muslim had from the eleventh century been firmly established as the Christian 'enemy', and as such was both necessary and integral to the emerging identity of western Christendom. He was made to carry the burden of western anxiety about Christian violence during the crusades; but the persistence of the stereotyping of Islam as the 'religion of the sword' suggests that it touches on deeply buried myths and apocryphal currents underlying contemporary Christian attitudes.

In Resistance, I argue that this stereotyping is not true; armed Islamist resistance is not, as parodied in the western press, a reactionary violence directed against a modernity to which Islamists are either resistant or incapable of assimilating. Neither is it a mirror of crusader violence: when King Louis VII of France left for the crusade he wrote saying that he hoped to kill as many Muslims as Moses (sic) and as Joshua killed Amorites and Canaanites. The Iranian cleric supports resistance unequivocally; but its purpose is to force the West to change its behaviour – not to exterminate westerners as the crusaders sought to do to Muslims in the Holy Land. The wider issues surrounding the use of violence are explored in Chapter 8.

The cleric was outlining in our conversation an attempt to found a different politics, a politics of conversion that turns its back on contemporary western norms. Islamists charge that the West is guilty of distorting its own foundational concept of the Enlightenment. Their criticism of its subsequent distortion must be understood to be distinct from any criticism of the Enlightenment per se. 'The first step', the cleric suggested, 'must be [for westerners] to review and re-think the concepts that began with the Enlightenment – or even to step further back in history to the ideas of the Renaissance.'

Were this to be done, the West will find that it has distorted these key human concepts. The original Enlightenment represents ideas and a resource that has been used through human history; but it has been the subsequent misuse and distortion of these concepts that has paved the way for the western domination over the other parts of the world.

Today's West has evolved a different concept of rational human beings, society and the individual from that of its own Enlightenment, and indeed, one that is separated from the legacy of cumulated human experience. Given this western manipulation of these foundational concepts, I see it as far-fetched to think that talking to western political leaders can bring them to the type of dialogue that will resolve their flawed perspective of Islam.

The note of pessimism on which he concludes is notable, but perhaps is not unwarranted. But Islamists are not unique in making such criticisms. Nor can they be described as 'extremist' or 'anti-western' for such criticisms. Islamist political and philosophical thinking – at least in Tehran – parallels western critical theory in some aspects of its analysis, and perhaps it is no surprise that a leading German critical theorist, Jürgen Habermas, is so widely read in Tehran.

Critical Thinking: the Islamists and the Secularists

The Frankfurt 'School', of which Habermas was the leading light of its second generation, was a group of philosophers, sociologists, social psychologists and cultural critics who worked in the period before and after the second European war, initially in Frankfurt, but with the outbreak of war, were obliged to move first to Geneva and then to the United States.

The Frankfurt School were among the first to approach questions of morality, religion, science, reason and rationality simultaneously from a variety of perspectives. This led them to mirror the Islamists in challenging the widespread assumption of the time that the empirical approach was the only valid one.

Like the Islamists, they argued that by the eighteenth century, western instrumental rationality – that is thinking based on an often spurious 'scientific' experimental approach, which excluded other forms of thinking – had so tipped the balance of western thinking that it had allowed knowledge derived in this way to claim a false unassailability. From this position, like the Shi'i cleric, they would claim that this 'scientificity' had become so distorted that it had transformed into a means to dominate and control the environment, Nature and man himself. It had become a covert form of means/ends reasoning.

The School insisted that the empirical approach rested on the 'positivist' illusion that 'theory' is nothing more than finding the correct mirroring of some independent realm of facts. They rejected this approach in favour of a view that sees theory, and the way the world appears, as reciprocally determining each other. (Islamists however hold to a different philosophical view of reality.)

But it was the shock of the encounter with the consumer society in the United States that brought about a fundamental critique of western thinking that has left its lasting impression on modern western philosophy. Initially, the leaders of the School focused on the way American culture had been taken over by large corporations that exerted subtle techniques of manipulation and control. The corporate heavy hand on mass culture had the effect of making people accept and even affirm a social system that, behind their backs, thwarted and suppressed their fundamental interests – reinforcing continually upon them an illusion of contentment and happiness to be found in the status quo. Instead of being critical of social conditions that prevented them finding true happiness, they vicariously experienced the fictional happiness of their screen idols. Corporate America had de-politicised culture – and turned it into formaldehyde to de-sensitise people's critical faculties.[15]

Max Horkheimer and Theodor Adorno argued that what had happened in the take-over of the culture industry by corporate interests was illustrative of the capacity of modern western society to create and transform people's needs and desires to the extent that they became self-pacified and docile in pursuit of the lifestyle aspirations paraded before them – to the extent that they ceased wanting to lead fulfilling and worthwhile lives: lifestyle became an end in itself. The arrival of this induced docility effectively marked the de-politicisation of politics. Culture survived, but privatised – as a way of life, and not as a public network of norms and rules.

It represented the triumph of perfectly de-politicised politics: politics lived as a lifestyle – no longer positing struggle and sacrifice for justice or equity as a Muslim is commanded to do – in sharp contradiction to the pleasures of a tolerant lifestyle and a relaxed and light-hearted attitude to choice itself. A world where everything is permitted – so long as it is on offer as an individual pleasure, and where, in the harmony of pleasures offered, social division and injustice is de-tensioned in a false sense of equity of access to 'entertainment'. It is a world of self-pacified docility.

In a culture in which choice is the only undisputed value, and wants primary, relationships become revocable and provisional – as desires change and as the individual pursues his or her 'right' to choose. Community self-governance and cohesion is severed in an individualised society, and what emerges is exclusion and alienation.

Frankfurt School theorists called this a 'false state of reconciliation'. False in the sense that it was underpinned by the optimistic view that the social world was rational, conducive to human freedom and happiness, and that it was pursuing its linear progress towards ever greater human progress and 'welfare'. Whereas the reality was the opposite. Ever since the eighteenth century, Anglo-American writers have wrongly foreseen, over and over again, a lasting system of liberal prosperity and free trade bringing stability and contentment.

They were completely wrong. A century earlier Hegel also had argued that true reconciliation already had been reached: social and political conditions were such, he argued, that all things considered, they satisfied the rational man or woman's deepest interests. This utopian optimism was such that we were told recently that, following the collapse of the Soviet Union, political divisions had come to an end, together with history. It marked the apparent triumph of neo-liberalism. There were no realistic alternatives. Political leaders were required to do no more than provide effective and efficient administration and to deliver ever rising personal prosperity.

The De-politicisation of Politics and Culture

The leaders of the Frankfurt School, like our Shi'i cleric of today, had become increasingly pessimistic about the prospects of hauling politics back to a different conclusion – a conversion to a different set of values achieved through critical thinking and the stimulation of the public's critical facilities. The problem that both the Islamists and the critical theorists faced, and still face, was that the de-politicisation of politics is simultaneously a suppression of philosophy too.

They, like our Iranian interlocutor, disagreed with western claims for 'modernity' profoundly: western politics was not satisfying man's deepest needs – far from it. Like the Athenians, it seems that eighty stadia were barely sufficient to separate him – and his modern counterparts – from the bad smell emanating from the degraded 'demos' of the port.

Adorno and Horkheimer believed that the public's faculty of reason had atrophied to a mere calculus of the most efficient means to a given end. Instead of liberating man as the Enlightenment intended, the processes of modern society were de-humanising men and women and subjecting them to ever more pervasive networks of administrative discipline and control. Change, they believed, could only be attained through rational critical thinking … and yet, and yet … atrophied and distorted rationality was itself at the heart of the problem. For Adorno, ultimately, if rationality could not rescue the situation owing to its atrophied state, the only response to this dilemma was 'resistance'. He meant a resistance to the established order; the capacity to say 'no'; to refuse to adjust or adapt to the current social order.[16]

Jürgen Habermas, who leads the second generation of critical theorists, took a slightly more optimistic view. The critiquing and exposing of the prevailing western ideology – he defined ideology as being those false beliefs that are very widely assumed to be true, because members of society are somehow made to believe them

– could, he hoped, serve a purpose: Criticism that exposed these socially constructed illusions for what they are – illusions – could serve to make the social structures more fluid and susceptible to change, he believed.

Habermas, in order to overcome the difficulty of mounting a critique in an era categorised as 'the end of politics',[17] sought to identify, where possible, those social and institutional conditions under which some form of autonomy could be found and which might lead to the creation of truly democratic institutions – in the Platonic meaning – capable of withstanding the onslaught of neo-liberalism and the corporate media.

This secular western philosophic approach of critical theory, coming from a very different perspective to that of the Islamists, mirrors that of our Shi'i cleric:

> I believe that we have to have a combination of dialogue and resistance. Resistance on its own, without dialogue, without any theoretical underpinning, will give rise only to the emergence of movements like al-Qaeda. But dialogue, on its own, will also result in nothing: this is because the political leadership in the West largely refuses to accord others the respect as equal interlocutors that genuine dialogue and free exchange of ideas demands.

Of course these strictures are not intended by the cleric to suggest that there are none in the West capable of critical thought. This would represent a huge misreading of the West. His point however is to endorse the pessimism of modern western philosophy that rational discussion with well-intended westerners can – in itself – shift the paradigm in the West or open the ears of its political leaders to a critique threatening to their 'grand narrative'.

Theirs is an Anglo-American narrative that offers an all-embracing synthesis of the Abrahamic narrative with the story of capitalism. It links capitalist development to the unfolding will of God, reconciling those who accept it to the changes and upheavals of capitalist life, even as it promotes the ideas – the primacy of individualism – that tend to make capitalism successful, but these ideological forces that propelled first the British and then the Americans to world power have still another dimension:

Americans generally believe they are on a mission from God – and that the well-being of the United States depends on how faithful Americans are to their mission.[18] 'We Americans are the peculiar chosen people – the Israel of our time; we bear the ark of the liberties of the world', Herman Melville wrote.[19]

From the time that the first colonists arrived, America has viewed itself through a lens of a Christianity heavily influenced by the Puritan tradition of England. Christianity injected the belief that human history is a teleological process – that history represents a linear progress to a pre-determined end, and Christianity also brought with it the idea of the possibility of an inner transformation, a new age that comes about through human action and an effort of will. The Manichaeanism of St Augustine however, who saw evil as a permanent feature of the world and, following Mani, a Persian sage and the founder of Manichaeanism, introduced the idea that God's will could be resisted by the power of evil. Later Christians reformulated this as a cosmic war between good and evil – and the idea that good could ultimately prevail through human intervention was established.

The 'Redeemer Nation' and its Mission From God

With the rise in religiosity in the United States over the last 20 years, the enthusiasm for bringing about transforming events through American power in the world has come to the forefront of foreign policy. However, instead of looking for a redeemer to bring about this anticipated 'clean break' with history, a severance with past sins and wrong-doing, the US has redefined its 'mission from God' under President Bush as that of becoming the 'redeemer nation', as Professor John Gray has termed it.[20]

The certainty of an American special destiny, formulated in the mid-nineteenth-century, underpinned the evolution from the general call for a messianic saviour to implement a transfiguration of the world, which was at the core of early Christianity, to one of seeing America, the nation, as that saviour – the 'redeemer nation' – and the idea of America as the land of a 'chosen people' to which Melville gave expression.

Conrad Cherry, in his book God's New Israel: Religious Interpretations of American Destiny notes:

> ... the belief that America has been elected by God for a special destiny
> in the world has been the focus of American sacred ceremonies, the
> inaugural addresses of our presidents, the sacred scriptures of the civil
> religion. It has been so pervasive a motif in the national life that the word
> 'belief' does not really capture the dynamic role that it has played for the
> American people.[21]

US diplomacy in the Bush era, with the Europeans in tow,
reflected this redemptive approach and language: Syria and Iran
were urged to 'come clean' about past sins; states were to face
'a choice': either they were to modify their past 'disruptive'
behaviour, make a clean break with the past, or accept the
consequences that a disapproving 'redeemer nation' might visit
upon them; states had to 'step up' to the modern world – by which
was meant the western vision of free market liberal capitalism,
or face isolation. The 'axis of evil' would be overcome by the
forces of 'freedom'. 'Bad actors' were being required to redeem
themselves publicly, or face a violent redemption at the hands
of American forces.

The idea of forcing a discontinuity in history in this fashion
may be implausible; but the idea of violence harnessed in the
interests of 'progress' was not new in the West. An Enlightenment
thinker such as the Marquis de Codorcet, who died in prison a day
after his arrest by Robespierre's Committee of Public Safety, may
have been horrified by the manner in which his belief in human
progress came to fuel political terror. Yet the fact that both terror
and military force came to be used to promote Enlightenment
ideals was not surprising. It followed from the secularisation of
the Christian belief that human life could undergo an apocalyptic
inner transformation by a human act of will: a Christian eschatological theme had resurfaced in the US as a utopian project of
universal emancipation.

The point is clear: this is not a trend susceptible to rational
critique by western critical theorists or postmodernists – let

alone by Islamist thinkers relegated to the 'forces of evil'. Conrad Cherry's point was that to describe this redemptive drive as 'belief' was to understate its power over Americans. It is something that must run its course; and perhaps it may have already done so. But apocalyptic transformation is a Christian impulse that in the US has been buttressed by its confluence with political theory emanating from a very different standpoint – the economic theories of Milton Friedman.

Friedman was an advocate of a secular form of economic redemption, by which he believed that 'shock therapy' – as a communal equivalent to the electric shock treatment given to psychiatric patients – could serve to erase past patterns of patient behaviour, and to bring about a 'tabula rasa' of the patient's mind onto which more socially acceptable patterns of new behaviour could be imprinted.

Friedman argued that the economic equivalent of shock therapy – a traumatic event sufficient to produce prolonged communal shock to an economy – might be necessary to clean the social terrain of past patterns of (bad) behaviour and all forms of past social solidarity in order to prepare for a new neo-liberal economic structure to be built around the organisational principle of individualism.

The theory was trialled in Chile, where Friedman acted as the economic adviser, and more recently was attempted in Iraq, where Paul Bremmer sought to implement new neo-liberal economic structures onto the 'clean slate' of a disorientated and traumatised Iraq immediately after its occupation. Both in terms of psychiatry and economics, the idea of profound shock acting as agent for creating a tabula rasa onto which new patterns of behaviour could be written has proved to be a myth. It also carries the whiff of the 'scientific' experiments conducted on humans in Germany in the name of 'progress' – an example of the 'instrumental rationality' in western thinking that creating 'trauma', turning upside down the lives so many, was a part of their mission to increase human 'welfare'.

Recognising Resistance

Against this background, our Iranian revolutionary's pessimism about dialogue with the West seems mild. His insistence that resistance to western 'redemption', to the instrumental thinking of the established political and economic elite, and to their promotion of a docile and de-politicised society below them, is the only answer. Paradoxically, it is this resistance that may finally open the path to a genuine dialogue between Islam and the West – in due time.

But this is not the end of the story. Not too long ago, most European and American intellectuals lived in a mental world where there was just one grand narrative alive: the narrative of western 'progress'. That narrative survives among the elite and European and American political leaderships; but the postmodernist philosophers are certainly right to suggest that the western grand narrative is in collapse. But those who claim that all grand narratives have collapsed could not be more wrong. The grand narrative of Islam has not collapsed. It is revived and in the ascendant.

One of the most significant critical thinkers in today's world who saw this was the French philosopher Michel Foucault. He visited Tehran during its first revolutionary phase, and understood the energies and potential for radical change that the Iranian Revolution promised; but he was pilloried for his efforts by the Left, who have always shown themselves to be uncomfortable with religiously inspired thinking and politics.

Foucault's insight was the understanding that the West needed to find the means to refresh its own narrative if it was to step beyond the constraints of its fast-fading 'vision' – fast fading, at least for a majority of Muslims, and the world's population. It is not our purpose here to promote, or to argue for dialogue between western politicians and Islamists – and, from the regional standpoint, it is perhaps the resistance around the world towards the West that may prove yet to be the better catalyst for change in Europe and America.

We share our Iranian cleric's pessimism on this score; but we also believe that Adorno's and the Frankfurt School's separate pessimism about the prospects for westerners to bring about real change in their own societies reflects the circumstances of an earlier age. It seems that, in the heady aftermath of the implosion of the Soviet Union, the West has pushed its ideological pendulum too far: it is plain that the political, social and economic components of the free market neo-liberal vision are unravelling. Foucault's belief that the Iranian Revolution contained within it important insights for western thinkers, too, was emptied of its impact by both the hostility he encountered from the left and the aspects of the revolution that were either misunderstood or which excited strong western aversion. The message got lost in the resulting brouhaha.

It is perhaps time, however, to revisit Foucault's meta-thesis: that is, his insight on how societies that face a narrative of decline, step over and beyond this constraint, to renew their thinking and their values. The two routes to doing this, he suggested, are to re-think a society's foundational principles – in other words to re-examine the Enlightenment and to adjust to a fresh look at what it stood for – or to look outside the society for others' insights.

Clearly the Iranian Revolution, at this time, cannot be the specific inspiration for such insights – as Foucault had hoped. Iran has been too thoroughly demonised. And nor should there be any moral duty on Islamists in the region to do this job – at least until, perhaps, the conditions for real dialogue re-emerge.

If Iran is not presently available as a source of new thinking, or of recalibrating values – then Adorno's 'resistance' of mounting a 'critical' critique to the existing order, mounted within the West by westerners and Muslims living in the West, can at least be conducted from the already constructed platform of the ideas and values of the other grand narrative – the narrative on the ascendant – that of Islamism, which of course incorporates both Iranian political and philosophical thinking.

A critique within the western sphere is of little value in terms of Foucault's insight, of course, unless accompanied by a positive vision too. The Islamist insistence on putting the human being back at the centre of society, and as the reference from which social values are derived, such as justice, equity and respect, seems a good place to start. These ideas have resonance among secular westerners who may not be drawn to Islam per se, and also are consistent with the original aspirations of the European Enlightenment.

It is important that Foucault's purpose is understood not as criticising the West for criticism's sake, but as a reminder that a critique can open new political space. It is also important to recall that some time in the early 1140s two scholars, a Christian and a Muslim, sat together in the former Mosque at Toledo in Spain, recently seized from Muslims as a part of the 'reconquista' of the land known to Islam as al-Andalus. In the course of the next half-century, these two scholars translated into Spanish and Latin no fewer than eighty-eight Arabic works of astronomy, mathematics, medicine, philosophy and logic, the very branches of learning that underpinned the great revival of scholarship in Europe referred to as the twelfth-century Renaissance.[22]

What *Resistance* Is About

The objective of this book – and therefore the reason it is shaped as it is – is to try to explain further the essence of the Islamist revolution. To go to the heart of it; to convey some sense of the power of the ideas as they have evolved; the excitement and the power of events and movements that are able to mobilise and energise millions. It is not intended as an empirical academic book. It does not attempt an overview of all Islamist movements, and nor does it make any claims to be a history of Islam.

Instead it tries to illustrate the essence of the recent renaissance of one of the grand narratives of history – one that directly challenges the western vision; and to speculate on the implications of the European vision becoming a minority view – following 200 years of its unquestioned supremacy. Were this to become the case, policy-makers will have to rethink the Euro-American project very fundamentally.

This book is about searching for the essence of Islamism and its message. Inevitably, this means that the book offers a personal view. To try to offer a 'balanced' perspective in the face of a torrent of scepticism and hostility towards Islamism – which seeks to brand it as nothing more than a violent, reactionary and transitory kick against the inevitable advance of modernity – by rehearsing all the old complaints against Islam and Islamists and attempting to refute them would, in my view, risk capsizing a lone and fragile craft with the deadweight of refutations and apologia.

It would in any case lend a pseudo-empirical air to this work – a dubious 'balance' that does little more than mask the fact that 'balance' is demanded in the case of Islamism more often than not in order to control and select discourse. Such balance is intended imperceptibly to constrain a positive and assertive political statement and to ensure – by insisting on refutation of all the usual charges against Islam – that defensiveness and a whiff of victimhood are the overall tenor conveyed.

This same argument underlines the relative paucity of current affairs and foreign policy analysis in the manuscript. It reflects the premise underlying the book that many of the localised crises that we face in the West's relations with Islam are symptomatic; and that if we wish to understand why these crises exist, we need to delve much deeper into the underlying causes of these tensions.

It reflects the argument that the West keeps misreading events in the region because the West interprets Islamism as a simple struggle over power and sovereignty. It is not. It is a distinct view of human behaviour that posits an alternative method of thinking about the human being; his and her place in the natural order; his and her conduct towards others; his or her place in society; the ordering of his and her material needs, and the management of politics.

It is this clash of two views of the human being: one view – the western one – privileges 'individuality', and defines this 'individuality' as the appropriate organising principle around which society should be shaped. The other view – the Islamist vision – sees the human to be integral to a wider existence; intractably linked, and not separated, as 'an individual', from others and the world that surrounds him or her; which sees the human as a multi-dimensional creature – larger than the sum of his or her desires and appetites, whose ability to access innate moral values, as the basis of his or her responsibility to the community, becomes the organisational principle for economics, society and politics.

This may sound simple, but the divergence of view regarding what constitutes the essence of the human being, coupled with the distinct mindset of a religious community as opposed to a secular mindset, has huge consequences. It is this deeper schism that represents the essence of the miscommunication and misreading of each other – rather than it being a matter of the foreign policy issues stemming from a series of subordinate and localised conflicts, which should be more appropriately viewed as the symptoms rather than the cause of the trauma.

In the same vein, this is not a book about Israel and Islamism, because Israel is viewed by the latter as no more than a sub-set of the western political and philosophic Weltanschauung. As this is a book about the Islamist resistance and the West, Israel occupies only a walk-on role in this narrative. This is not intended to imply that the Israeli–Palestinian conflict is unimportant. It is hugely important; but the aim of this work has been confined to the Islamist revolution in ideas; and how these ideas might intersect with western re-thinking. There is of course reciprocity between ideas and events, and there is no intention here to artificially de-link them, but rather to put the emphasis on the essential divergence in thinking in contrast to the plethora of works dealing with the details of these conflicts.

Similarly, this work does not deal with gender issues as a separate and distinct component of the Islamist revolution. It will therefore be open to criticism on this score. I expect that. Whenever Islamism is discussed, it is a key theme for criticism of Islamism.

The issue of gender is not included in the manuscript for two reasons: the first is that the approach to gender implied in these criticisms of the Islamists is often loaded with Euro-centric values – why, for example, is it okay to write about Israeli society and

Judaism without touching on the severe restrictions imposed on orthodox Jewish women, and about women's rights in orthodox Jewish society; but when dealing with Islamism, such omission is taken somehow to signal 'appeasement' of Islamists?

I have not dealt with women's issues partly on principle: because the Islamist revolution is not – at this stage – an issue that divides women from men in ideological terms and because their conceptualisation of a community of resistance is constructed around a corporate mobilisation; but more practically, because the separate issue of the social relations between man and woman in Islam is a hugely complex subject.

It is complex because the revelations in the Qu'ran on this subject both underpinned a genuine revolution for women (establishing equality and rights for women that pre-date those in the West by several centuries), and pointed to the complete severance with the then prevailing modes of social behaviour; but at the same time, other revelations seem to entrench male supremacy. The reconciliation of these different revelations is heavily dependent on the precise circumstances in which the Prophet sought a particular revelation (the specific context in which He posed a question to God that had been raised by one of his followers).

Interpretation of the revelation also had to be placed into the context of the politics of Medina, which at times hovered close to civil war. And the tensions of Medina were often reflected onto the conduct of the Prophet with His own wives: this frequently became the battlefront on which those in Medina who opposed Him, chose to wage their conflict.

This difficulty is compounded by several others. First, that the Qur'an is an edited version of the Prophet's revelations and its ordering is not chronological, but like-verses are grouped with like-verses. This subsequent editing makes setting a particular passage in its appropriate chronological and political setting and context a matter for the expert historian.

Sadly, some of the experts validated some of the Hadith (sayings by the Prophet relayed in an extended chain of repetition until finally noted and collected in works and commentaries) whose authenticity is almost certainly questionable. Some of those in doubt bear directly on the position of women; but despite the question mark hanging over the credibility of the Prophet having uttered the phrases, some have entered so widely and deeply into popular culture that to correct them has become almost impossible.

Also, as in Christianity, texts were subsequently amended and the male elite fought a vigorous campaign to undo some of the Prophet's revolutionary changes affecting women by claiming – after his death – that his changes referred to the public sphere only and that the private domain of the family should follow the old ways (of male supremacy). In short, the male elite succeeded over the ensuing years in undoing a number of key changes and in restoring some of the ancient social customs of the tribes of Arabia.[23]

I explain this to underline that the social relations between men and women are – as always – not something that can be quickly dealt with; but a topic that would require a separate book to illustrate. It is not easy to separate the original Qur'anic message from the separate strands of the Prophet's political needs to accommodate traditional rights of his soldiers; the uneasy balance of forces in Medina after his defeat at the battle of Uhud, and the amending efforts of the Second Caliph and the scribes who collected his sayings – often many years after his death. I believe that to try to include an analysis of all these disparate strands and their impact on contemporary Islamism in a book on resistance and revolution would only detract from the main theme, and little of substance would be added through a treatment of these complex social issues. But it is a fascinating area: feminism flourishes within Islamism; but not in the way usually understood in the West.

The emphasis on Islamist revolution and resistance in the text does not imply that there are not activists and movements within the West, or in other geographical regions such as South America, who may share some or all of the same objectives as Islamists; and indeed who are and have been moving in parallel directions to those outlined in this book. The evidence suggests that certainly they do; and the omission is not intended in any way to disrespect or belittle their huge achievements. However, the focus here is limited to the Islamist revolution and its implications. Others may be better placed to reflect on the South American resistance and to note any common elements.

In using such general labels as 'Islamist' or the 'West', any work can be held to be guilty of Edward Said's objections that there are no such categories – pointing to his own situation as a Christian Palestinian who uses a language of politics – Arabic – that is inseparable from Islam, despite being a Christian. Said noted that the language of politics for Arabs (and Persians) is 'Islamicate': there is no un-Islamicate idiom of politics available to Muslims.

Said was clearly neither external to the West nor to the Muslim world, but was a part of both, and although the text has tried to stand on the same principles that compartments such as the 'West' have never been – and are becoming ever less – immutable, it is hard to write broad-brush without taking some liberties with generalisations. These short-cuts are acknowledged in advance; and any damage to meaning inflicted by their use, is regretted.

It is quite right to acknowledge that, just as the Iranian cleric who has figured prominently in this introduction cannot speak for 'Islamism' as a whole, so there is no one Islam or Islamism – there are many. There is a problem with language on Islamism that compounds these difficulties. Islamism as a term has acquired adverse connotations in the West that inhibit effective communication – so too common terms like Shari'a (Islamic law); Salafi (those who model themselves on the early followers of the Prophet); Jihad (literally 'striving'), 'fundamentalism' and many more including 'resistance' have acquired a 'baggage' that impedes their use.

But what alternative is there? It is more accurate to state that there is no one Shari'a, and to distinguish all its variants; but if we do this on each occasion, and with each term, the ability to convey a message clearly and simply is impeded. Our objective here is to focus down to the essence of the Islamist revolution in order to convey the broader significance of what it portends to non-Muslims as well as Muslims. I therefore have continued to use these general terms, and ask the reader to understand that they do represent only generalisations.

Expectations: What is it All About?

Resistance is in four parts. In Part I, we look at what caused Muslims to come to the conclusion that they had to form a resistance. We ask what it was about events, occurring at a particular moment, which propelled a people in this direction; and ask why these events happened in the first place.

Part II looks at the ideology of resistance and revolution as it began to emerge. This is the theme of Chapter 2: it looks at the tradition of fighting on behalf of the faith from the early Muslim communities, and explores how the first forays into modern resistance ideology may have laid the basis for its subsequent separation into various distinct strands of resistance. We ask the question about the relationship of these various strands with the early traditions of Islam.

Chapter 3 follows the mainstream ideological ingredients through their stirring in Iraq – in its very different political context and with added ingredients provided by a chef from a different culinary tradition – to Iran where the dish evolved into the main course of one of the major historical events of this era. We ask what it was that made this dish so palatable to ordinary Iranians, and ask what it was that was so important that took place in Iran.

Chapter 4 in the same section looks at social revolution and asks why it is that its meaning for Islamists seems so different to what westerners have in mind when they use this cliché. It explores the myths and misunderstandings that are responsible for being at cross-purposes about something as apparently straightforward as social policy.

In the last part to this section, Chapter 5, we ask what the concept 'nation-state' means to an Islamist, and query why they see it as they do. The chapter explores the significance of this Islamist understanding for the future political order in the Middle East.

Part III looks at how two mainstream Islamist movements view armed resistance in practice. In Chapter 6, we look at Hesballah, a Shi'i movement's approach to resistance; and in the following chapter, explore how a Sunni movement, Hamas, sees the principles and objectives underlying its resistance. It asks whether these coincide with popular western perception.

In Part IV, Chapter 8 examines the roots of western language use with respect to Islamism, and with respect to violence in particular. It poses the question of what is the defining quality to Islamist violence; and then asks the same about the nature of western violence. It seeks an answer to why do both sides use the language they do.

Chapter 9 follows from the issues of language raised in the previous chapter to look at the ideological motives of the United States and its allies in this conflict. We ask whether the language used reflects true sentiments, or whether there are bigger objectives at play.

The last chapter, the concluding Chapter 10, harks back to the assertions quoted from the Iranian cleric about the steps that might help lead the two parties into conversation – and looks at how his comments appear in the light of the intervening argument. It looks too at where it is that we have arrived on this circuit; and tries to draw out some meanings from it all, with a tentative glance into the future.

Part I

1

IN THE SERVICE OF GOD AND THE INTERESTS OF THE PEOPLE

On 17 September 1656, Oliver Cromwell, a Protestant puritan who had fought a civil war in England, deposed and executed the King, and addressed the English Parliament as its new 'Protector'.

He began by asking his Protestant revolutionary Parliamentarians: 'Who are our enemies; and why do they hate us?'[1] There was, he said, an axis of evil abroad in the world:

> ... they hate us because they hate God and all that is good ... they hate us from that very enmity that is in them against whatsoever should serve the glory of God and the interests of the people; which they see to be eminently, yea most eminently patronised and professed in this nation – we will speak it not with vanity – above all the nations in the world.[2]

This axis, this axis of evil, had a leader, he told them: a great power – Catholic Spain – and explained that this 'hate' which his countrymen faced was, at its root, a problem of the Spaniard having placed himself in the service of 'evil'. This 'evil' was the evil of a religion – Catholicism – that 'refused the Englishman's desire for simple liberties ... that put men under restraint ... under which there was no freedom ... and [under which] there could be 'no liberty of individual consciousness'.[3]

Since Cromwell's day, the mainly English-speaking world has come to regard their enemies as 'haters of liberty and God' who possess no morality, and will do anything to win. English 'hawks', however – often Puritans and merchants – wanted an aggressive anti-Spanish policy that would weaken and undermine the Pope for more political ends too – principally in order to open new markets to burgeoning English trade.[4]

The problem with Catholicism, Cromwell hinted, was not religion per se, but its 'restraint' – the imposition of moral and communal norms and the 'lack of liberty' imposed by Spain on English traders and commerce: in short, at its crux, was the Puritans' objection to the moral values of a religiously inspired community that would not commit to embracing individual enterprise and free trade.

They saw in Catholicism an ethos that acted rather to preserve social continuities, and insisted on a timeless moral code of social responsibility to others – in short, one that was not welcoming to the restructuring of community around individualism, to personal pursuit of trade and profit, and to free markets. This was not an ethos in which the nascent capitalism of the time could thrive: this was the evil that the Anglo-Saxon world defined then – and condemns as vehemently today in Islam.

Cromwell's words symbolised the Protestant ethic that has taken the West to unrivalled power, and which has so shaped the European political project over the last 300 years. It gave western politics many of its key characteristics – and also one of its key instruments of power: the nineteenth-century concept of the nation-state as a community of individuals whose collective will manifested a new secular 'sovereignty' in the place of God.

Power was to be wielded by a tight and immensely powerful central elite enjoying a monopoly of violence – both internal and external. This elite enjoyed the additional ability imperceptibly to constrain and control peoples' behaviour and speech in many ways: a web of pressures, social conventions and norms set by institutions and economic interests both controlled behaviour and insisted on a top-down homogeneous unitary national 'family' that legitimised strong central government.

These power relationships, together with the press, provided the 'unitary, disciplinary power of modernity'[5] – insidious tools that enabled a collective of ostensibly 'free' and 'individual' citizens to be mobilised collectively and hegemonically as the sovereign 'will' of the nation-state. It was an instrument of immense power.

It was to this conceptualisation that our Iranian cleric referred at our meeting in Qom: just as Cromwell had complained of

Spanish and English Catholics who were opposed to those 'who served the Glory of God and the interests of the People', the Hojat al-Islam pointed out it was Muslims today who were perceived to be frustrating the 'will of God' by clinging to the failings of a static and backward religious ethos.

Max Weber, in his 1905 essay on the Protestant ethic and the spirit of capitalism, had identified a widespread belief in his day, dating back to puritan Calvinism, that market economies and social change manifest the 'will of God': to live in communion with God and to experience the hope of salvation meant, Weber suggested, furthering the waves of social change that capitalism unleashed – increasingly religion not only had to tolerate change, it had to advance it.

> Although they speak of 'democracy', democracy only possesses meaning for [western leaders] if it embodies their concept of the human being. In this context, their concept of the nation-state is no more than an instrument to achieve their goals. When a [Muslim] nation pursues any different path – inevitably it meets resistance from the western world.[6]

The West, the cleric implied, had lost the sense of what these ideas and the consequent huge project of nineteenth- and twentieth-century nation-state building – as a recipe for 'peace and freedom' – had wrought in Muslim societies. 'Only from such introspection can we begin to address what went wrong,' he argued.

It is from this point – the last 200 years of nation-state building – that this book starts its story of the emergence of the Islamist revolution. It would be possible to place the starting point at other staging-posts on the path of Islam; but the purpose of this account, as indicated in the introduction, is to try to convey the essence and the spirit behind the rising resistance to the West – rather than to attempt a historical survey.

The Protestant Ethic and the Demonisation of the Ottomans

The dynamic Protestant ethic that Cromwell had contrasted so unfavourably with static Catholicism drew on puritan Calvinism's emphasis on each individual's duty to use his or her talents as a call from God. This gave new significance and meaning to economic endeavour and to secular work: to serve the world in expanding the means of production was to serve God – and to prosper materially in this way, in trade or commerce, was a sure sign of God's grace. Salvation was achieved by work, and in such an environment social esteem and wealth would follow, Calvinists believed.

Above all, Protestants in Europe and in America came to believe that Abraham, the common ancestor of all religions, symbolised this new insight. Abraham's readiness to leave his home, sever his family ties and even to sacrifice his son Isaac, all exemplified a supreme readiness to 'embrace change'. It also exemplified 'faith'. Abraham was obedient to the call from God: Abraham had abandoned past beliefs; had quitted the familiar worlds and ideas of the past, and had journeyed toward a new 'promised land'. Embracing change – justified by faith alone, rather than reasoning – became a kind of sacrament.[7] The new mission was 'like that of the Jews in Canaan, "to subdue the land and possess it"'.[8]

In mid-nineteenth-century Britain, Richard Cobden and Jean Baptiste Say articulated the vision of how this ethos would usher in a millennial age of peace: free trade would promote peace between nations based on common interests and increasing prosperity. Jean Say wrote that 'the theory of markets will necessarily scatter the seeds of concord and peace', and Cobden believed that the spread of market principles and free trade would create a peaceful order of free countries in Europe.[9] This has remained the enduring western vision of utopia, despite it failing, over and over, to reflect reality of the tragedies to which it has given birth.

While both Protestantism and Catholicism have recently lost much of their influence on the European population, these principles represent ideas of Protestant origin that have moved well beyond the bounds of religion. This ethic has fused to the 'dynamic' of capitalistic change. The most important pieces of this construct also underlie modern secularism.

Modern secularists adhere to moral values that they believe are universally valid, and should be established and implanted

– by force if necessary – around the world until history as a linear continuum converges on its victorious utopian close. And like their Christian counterparts, who stress the personal and individual in their relationship with God, modern secularists prize above all else personal choice: Americans, secular and Christian, are all Abrahamic now – above all, their journey in life is about confronting 'personal choice' that will shape their destinies.

While many of the nineteenth-century thinkers were not particularly religious, their belief that 'order' arises spontaneously, as if by the workings of an 'invisible hand' from the free play of market forces within a powerful and centralised nation-state, is a way of restating some of the most powerful spiritual convictions of the English-speaking world, and subsequently of the western world. It makes those who hold these unrecognised spiritual convictions both individualistic and optimistic.

In the United States changes in society – the decline of the old East coast elites, the ascendancy of the South and the mass mobilisation of evangelical Christians over the last 30 years – have enhanced the power of the Protestant vision. President George Bush, who has embodied beliefs that resonate closely with Cromwell's speech of 1656, has promoted a tone of belligerent optimism, which links him with a powerful utopian current of Christianity in believing that evil can be defeated. At the same time he draws on both the early Christian apocalyptic theme that expects imminent catastrophe, as well as on secular hopes for continuing 'progress'.[10]

The impact of these ideas, and of the anthill of western constructions of nation-states in their societies, has been for Muslims an absolute disaster – more than a disaster. The nineteenth- and twentieth-century obsessive pursuit of the centralised nation-state has been a tragedy that created millions of victims – as it did also in Europe and the US. But it also, in one of those unintended quirks of history, facilitated the emergence of a revived Islamism that today is directly challenging the western vision.

Powerful, centralised western Great Powers began in the eighteenth century their mission to 'subdue the land and possess it' – with the optimistic intention that, by opening free markets, they would give rise to a more prosperous and peaceful order.

But it was in the subsequent century that the Ottoman Empire, which was the institutional structure embracing the majority of Muslims, came under massive and sustained attack – particularly in its western provinces. The Great Powers' competitive drive towards new markets of course could draw on the militarism of the era and its new technologies; but it was the Great Powers' focus on the leveraging of ethnicity and confessionalism – particularly among Christian communities within the western Ottoman Empire, with the aim of fostering and creating new Christian states emerging from out of the parts of the Ottoman Empire – that unleashed the bitterest clashes, genocide, massacres and deportations.

The relationship between the Christian Great Powers and inter-communal strife in these Ottoman societies dates back to 1569, when France was granted 'capitulations'. These subsequently were gifted to other European powers and made permanent. Christian powers vied to be named 'protectors' of Christian minorities under these aptly named 'capitulations', with the object of creating wedges to hammer into the edifice of Ottoman politics. Exhorted, encouraged and often armed by western powers, the Ottoman Christian minorities rose to fight for independence.

The most bitter wars were fought in what today is Greece and in the Balkans. Both were Christian semi-autonomous communities in the Ottoman western provinces. According to historian Justin McCarthy's *Death and Exile: The Ethnic Cleansing of Ottoman Muslims, 1821–1922*, approximately 5 million European Muslims were driven from their homes between 1821 and 1922.[11] This forced deportation represented the worst example of ethnic cleansing in Europe until the removal of Germans from Poland and Czechoslovakia following the Second European War.

A century of ethnic cleansing and murder converted the former western territories of the Ottoman Empire from having an absolute majority of Muslims to a region with a Christian majority. Between 1912 and 1920 alone, an estimated 62 per cent of the Muslim population of south-eastern Europe (excluding Albania) disappeared, fled, or was killed or driven into exile.

Competing identities and affiliations were perceived by Europeans to dilute and threaten the homogeneity necessary to empower a strong central government to emerge, and when these competing identities occurred, western powers – such as Germany, which was the Ottoman Empire's chief ally during this period – encouraged 'reformists' and emergent states to sweep them aside, ruthlessly and bloodily.

This ruthlessness was justified by almost every one of the German officials posted to the Ottoman territories in the late Ottoman period through the expressions of the disdain that they felt for one or other of the ethnic groups with whom they came into contact. These feelings were clearly predicated on a sense of European cultural superiority and the idea of a hierarchy of races in which nature dictated that the weakest racial groups were predestined to disappear from history.[12]

Military pressure on the Ottoman Empire was accompanied by relentless western demands for 'reform'. The 1856 reform package effectively was drafted by Lord Stratford, the British ambassador, and imposed on the Ottomans; and, as historian Donald Bloxham has noted,[13] the one consistent British demand in all their calls for reform was for liberalised markets. However, as Bloxham subsequently notes, the British and French 'reform' of seizing control of Ottoman fiscal policy – to ensure repayment of defaulted loans owed to the western powers – 'actually inhibited the ability of the Ottoman state to develop the economy'.[14]

This persistent pressure on the Ottoman leaders for reform sprang from a far-reaching experiment in social engineering conducted in England with the objective of freeing economic life from social and political control. This was done by constructing a new institution, the free market – and by demanding the weakening of social institutions and the breaking up of the more socially rooted markets that had existed in England. The rupture in economic life produced by the creation of the free market has been called the 'Great Transformation'.

Its effect was to sever cultural and institutional continuities in England, and its pursuit resulted in economic dislocation, social chaos and political instability in hugely different countries throughout the world.[15] The economies of the West did not emerge through a series of incremental 'reforms' as proposed by Lord Stafford to the Ottomans – they came about through the massive use of state power to impose the disruptive social change that free markets required. This was a power that the Ottoman state in any case did not possess, as it was organised on the basis of the devolution of authority rather than on its centralisation.

It is a myth to believe that free markets emerged 'naturally' once 'artificial' restraints were eliminated; and, as John Gray has noted, it is doubtful whether the free market would ever have been engineered in England if a popular voice had been able to articulate its protests at the miseries which this social engineering had brought to them.[16] Whatever the intended purpose of the European insistence on 'reform', it was not about spreading democracy or popular consent.

Much of the demonisation of the Ottoman Empire as the 'sick man' of the region, and the consequent pressure on it to 'reform', it has been argued,[17] has been shown by recent historical research to be largely a Euro-centric construct. Emphasising that the Ottoman Empire did not share in Europe's semblance of coherence and common purpose, and consequently was held in European thinking to be 'decayed', threw into relief the western narrative of the inevitability of the 'rise of the West'.

Homogenising Identity

Eventually, in 1908, 'reformers' did take over the Ottoman state. The ruling faction in the government, known as the 'Young Turks', took control. The Young Turk leaders:

> ... were explicitly atheistic, schooled in western secular thought whence they imbibed the anti-religious positivism of thinkers such as Auguste Comte and embraced the social Darwinism popular amongst nationalists across Europe at the turn of the century. These ideas would not only provide the ideological justification for removing Christians, but by freeing their proponents from notions of religious confraternity they also meant that

[the Young Turk] leaders could begin to think about the destruction of ethnic Kurdishness.[18]

In pursuit of the drive towards the hegemonic European state model of ethnic-national homogeneity, during the months from autumn 1914 to summer 1915, the Young Turk leadership made a series of decisions resulting in the decimation of its Armenian Christian population. This act prepared the ground for Mustafa Kemal's (Ataturk) secular Turkish republic, and his subsequent destruction of Islam as a major source of identity and of legitimacy.

Ataturk went on to complete the Young Turks' explicitly atheistic agenda to eliminate the idea of religious confraternity by discrediting Islam and by abolishing the Caliphate. The Caliphate was the institutional structure that bound together Muslim believers into a single transnational community, and it also symbolised the succession of authority transferred over the generations from the Prophet Mohammad to the Caliph of the day.

During the First European War, approximately 1 million Ottoman Armenians were massacred out of a total Ottoman population of 2 million, and a world-wide population of 4 million Armenians. A figure of 1 million or more dead for Armenians is equal to or greater than the entire losses inflicted on the British Empire during that war – and proportionally much greater, given their total population of 4 million. Most were either killed in situ, the fate of many of the men and youth; or deported to the deserts of today's Iraq or Syria in the south. Along the deportation routes they were subject to massive and repeated depredations – rape, kidnap, mutilation, outright killing and death from exposure, starvation and thirst.

Many of those who made it to the desert concentration centres were massacred in 1916.[19] Groups of starving deportees were tied together and thrown from the hillside into rivers where they drowned, and others were asphyxiated by fires lit in the mouth of cave that suffocated up to 5000 persons huddled in the cave's main body.

Bloxham is clear that the 'quintessentially western ideology of nationalism was the import that drove the genocide, the impulse "to streamline, make homogenous, organise people to be uniform in some sense ... to compete, survive and develop. It was also shaped by and in reaction to the ethno-nationalist movements in the Balkans"'.[20]

Although the Armenian massacre stands because of its size and the systematic nature of the decimation, other ethnic groups also were earmarked for ethnic cleansing by the Young Turk leadership: one quarter of a million Assyrians were also cleansed, as well as Greeks and Kurds in an essentially Darwinian struggle to survive and avoid becoming one of those 'backward' races destined by evolution to vanish.

It would be left to Kemal (Ataturk) to continue the homogenisation process by removing the remaining Armenian population, then the Anatolian Greeks and finally the Kurds – before turning on Islam to complete the transformation to a 'modern' unitary identity of Turkishness.

Ethnic Nationalism, Fabricated Identities

In a different context of identity-building, Edward Said, the celebrated Palestinian writer and thinker, in a lecture in London[21] in 2001 on 'Freud and the non-European', wistfully underscored how this might have turned out so differently – if western fundamentalism had taken a different turn: it did not have to be like this.

Edward Said pointed to Sigmund Freud's focus during the last years of his life, in his tract 'Moses and Monotheism', on the meaning of 'Jewishness'. Freud, Said argued, had been struggling, as a Jew, with a paradox: why had it been so impossibly difficult for Jews to acknowledge that Moses had not been a Jew, but was Egyptian – or to acknowledge that Moses' ideas about a single God were not his at all, but were derived from a non-Jew, the Egyptian Pharaoh, Akhenaton. Why did this apparently straightforward piece of information prove so difficult to acknowledge, and why was it kept under the table?

Said argued that Freud had in fact been attempting to open out Jewish identity by underlining the Egyptian-ness of Moses, which made him different from the Jewish people who had adopted him as their leader. Freud's reference to the non-Jewish origin of monotheism – both the central pillar of Judaism and its claim to uniqueness – served the same purpose of opening Judaism to acknowledge its non-Jewish contributions.

The 'non-European' in the role of Moses and Akhenaton suggested that Judaism did not begin with itself, but rather with other ethnicities and identities; and therefore, Said argues, would have provided considerable room to accommodate Judaism's non-Jewish antecedents as well as its contemporaries in the land of Palestine. In other words, Golda Meir, the Israeli Prime Minister, need not have erased Palestinian identity with her statement in 1969 that there were no such people as Palestinians. She had the flexibility and option to embrace all the historical diversity that had preceded the founding of the Jewish state; but she chose not to do so and instead swung the pendulum in the opposite direction.

An Archaeological War of Identity

This potential for the opening out of Jewish identity pointed up by Freud is compared by Said with the reality of the narrowing down of Jewish identity in the years that followed Freud's speculations in the 1930s. But the Zionists had before them the Young Turks' narrowing down of the Ottoman state to its new Turkish 'race' as a model of a 'great transformation' of a society towards 'modernity' – which was generally admired in the West, to the point of adulation, as an act of forceful leadership.

The Turkish massacres and deportations of Armenians, Assyrians, Greeks and Kurds nonetheless:

> ... represented a clear logic of ethnic nationalism when carried to its absolute extreme in multinational societies. It remains a seminal moment in modern history ... that foretold the massacres and break-up of Yugoslavia

after the Cold War, not to mention the innumerable episodes in between
... [including] the Israeli expulsion of Arabs in 1948.[22]

Said noted that 'the establishment of Israel in a non-European
territory consolidated a Jewish identity politically in a state that
took very specific legal and political positions to seal off that
identity from anything that was non-Jewish'.[23]

When the Prime Minister of Israel declared that Palestinians
did not exist, and as the Israeli state began harnessing cultural
and archaeological tools in order to fabricate a 'narrowed down'
and 'sealed off' identity, Israel was simply following the western
practice of fabricating a myth of a unitary homogeneous national
'family' – with its 'rediscovered' Jewish roots and 'Israeli' identity,
whose 'sovereignty' could then legitimise the acts and militarism
of a powerful centralised and militarised state.

The English had done the same from the time of their Civil
War in the seventeenth century. In order to legitimise their
struggle against monarchical 'restraints' and to give private
commercial entrepreneurship the latitude it sought, the revolutionaries looked back to the laws and institutions of the Germanic
tribes as described by the Roman historian, Tacitus, and from
this archaeology assembled a narrative that the Anglo-Saxons
in the seventh and eighth centuries were a free people, and that
those liberties to which Cromwell had referred in his address to
Parliament were to be found in these ancient traditions.[24]

The identification of the Anglo-Saxons with race, a genetic
rather than a cultural identity, came later; as the 'scientific racism'
of the nineteenth century drew support from Darwinism it gave
rise to the idea of the 'true-born Englishman'. This was a fabricated
myth that Daniel Defoe bitingly mocked in a 1701 poem in
which he suggested that England was a nation of immigrants – a
'scoundrel race' rather than an 'English race'. Defoe, like Freud
after him, was advocating the opening of English identity to reflect
'community' rather than the racial nationalistic definition that
was later to prove such a massively destructive concept in the
nineteenth and twentieth centuries.

Edward Said, in his lecture, pointed to the lengths to which this consolidation of a national identity could be taken: he noted the Israeli use of the 'science' of archaeology to build a narrative around which this unitary Jewish identity could be constructed – in contrast to Freud's own 'archaeology' of historical knowledge used to build Moses' Egyptian and non-Jewish other identity.

Using archaeology in an attempt to paint an overarching Jewish identity, Edward Said noted, had not succeeded without a struggle; it had provoked a resistance, whose purpose was to counter-attack and to preserve the sedimented layers of Palestinian identity – a form of archaeological 'resistance movement' had emerged.

The West too had had the flexibility and the option to embrace all the historical diversity of the Ottoman Empire; but it chose, like the Zionists, not to do so. Western powers had intentionally internationalised and exacerbated the issue of the Armenian Christians as a significant minority within the Empire; but western espousal of Christian 'rights' vanished when these clashed with western interests.

Silence and subsequent denial greeted the Armenian massacres. Adolf Hitler is reputed to have asked the question in 1939 of his generals – in reference to the Poles: 'Who after all is today speaking of the destruction of the Armenians?'[25] The Israelis, together with most of the international community, have difficulty even admitting that these massacres took place. It is plain that suffering on this scale, and the indifference and silence of the outside world, coloured Ataturk's subsequent actions. His 'muscular modernisation' programme seemed to provide to European eyes the 'solution' to 'population problems' affecting the creation of new westernised states.

We know also that pre-war Zionist committees were influenced by the Young Turks – Ze'ev Jabotinsky, the leader of the revisionist wing of Zionism, had edited a magazine for the Young Turk organisation called *Jeune Turque*. We also know that the 'territorial solutions' to population 'problems' used in territory of the former Ottoman Empire after 1918, with their debt to the Armenian genocide, were considered as a model by David

Ben Gurion, in 1941, concerning the future ethnic organisation of Israel.[26]

Those committees contemplated the transfer – ethnic cleansing – of Palestine's Arabs to, among other locations, the very deserts around Deir es-Zour and Aleppo in today's Syria in which the Armenian deportees had ended their miserable existence 20 years earlier.[27] When the Zionist movement anticipated the creation of a Jewish state in Palestine, it invoked the religious 'redemption' of an ancient homeland as their means to this state. But as Israeli historian Ilan Pappé has noted:

> ... this was the official narrative, and no doubt it expressed genuinely the motivation of most of the Zionist leadership's members; but the more critical view today sees the Zionist drive to settle in Palestine, instead of other possible locations, as closely interwoven with nineteenth-century Christian millenarianism and European colonialism. The various Protestant missionary societies and the governments in the European concert competed among themselves over the future of a 'Christian' Palestine that they wanted to pry away from the Ottoman Empire. The more religious among the aspirants in the West saw the return of the Jews as a chapter in the divine scheme.[28]

The paradox, as Pappé notes, is that Eretz Israel, the name for Palestine in the Jewish religion, had been revered throughout the centuries by generations of Jews as a place for holy pilgrimage, but never as a secular state. 'In other words, Zionism secularised and nationalised Judaism.'[29] It is not the Jewishness that is the problem, therefore, but rather the secular and aggressive nationalism that drives Zionism – and that aspect, secular nationalism, we have argued, is a direct import from the Christian puritan tradition.

The shocking massacres and ethnic cleansings of the last two centuries sent a strong signal to the Muslim world: do not expect the injustices of what has occurred to your peoples to be acknowledged in the West. They will be erased from memory. The justice of a cause is not enough to elicit support: no western state acted effectively in support of the Armenians, the Assyrians or the Kurds, or the earlier 5 million Muslims ethnically cleansed from Europe.

The Europeans were too heavily invested in their redemptive vision of social transformation, modernisation and liberal free markets to do more than occasionally wring their hands at the human suffering. The pro-western newly emerging Turkish state was strategically too important to their interests: the lesson of Armenia for Muslims was that there will be no one to help you – beyond you yourselves. Your victims will be overlooked or ignored. It also posed the question about western thinking: what was it that had allowed it to become so destructive, while yet believing that the West acted in the best interests of human welfare.

The answer, Islamists began to ponder, lay in the way westerners thought about thinking – in other words, in their instrumental reasoning. A rationality that, during the potato famine in Ireland in 1846–52, in which it is estimated that about 1 million starved to death, could believe that the priorities for the British authorities were to maintain free markets in food produce and to clear the starving from their land.

By the time the new state of Turkey was founded, one of its Generals, Kiazim Kavabekir, could claim, like Golda Meir in respect to the Palestinians, 'in Turkey there has been neither an Armenia nor territory inhabited by Armenians. Those Armenians living in Turkey committed murder and massacres, and have escaped to Iran, America and Europe'. [30]

Drawn from the same toolbox of western unitary identity fabrication, despite the 3000-year existence of the Armenians in parts of what is now Turkey, no archaeological site in Turkey is today permitted to be designated as belonging to the Armenian civilisation. The 'archaeological war of identity', that Edward Said noted as having been engaged in by Israel in the Palestinian context had been already deployed in Turkey.

The project of 'Turkification' was clearly racist: the massive expulsion of more than 1 million Greek Orthodox Anatolians to Greece in 1923 in exchange for 380,000 Greek Muslims, the continuous harassment of the Armenians and Assyrians, and the complete denial of the Kurdish identity all express a 'vibrantly exclusionary nationalism'. [31]

From 1923 on, Ataturk's repression of Kurdish nationalism and identity was savage and predatory. He filled the Kurdish South East with Turkish Administrators, settled Turkish war veterans on Kurdish lands, forbade the use of Kurdish language in court; and, most importantly, banned the native tongue in schools – effectively denying formal education to Kurdish children.[32]

These measures spurred an uprising that erupted in 1925: it was quashed with overwhelming force. Many were hanged; villages were destroyed and massacres were reported.

The motive of the uprising was the determination to fight for Kurdish identity. The Turkish state, from 1923, simply refused to acknowledge that the Kurds even existed – they were known, until the 1990s as 'Mountain Turks' – much as Palestinians initially were labelled using the generic term 'Arabs' by Israeli leaders who refused to call them Palestinians.

The Young Turks followed the European pattern in assembling a new Turkish identity: By harking back to the distant past, the Young Turks portrayed their race as the founder of one the great Asian civilisations – a narrative that neatly excluded the Kurds. Scholarly work on Kurdish history was outlawed; Kurdish village names were replaced with their Turkish equivalent – as later was to befall Palestinian villages, whose names were replaced by Hebrew ones. It was made illegal for parents to give their children Kurdish names, and Kurdish songs were outlawed.[33]

In some respects, however, the deportations, ethnic cleansing and killings of the minorities by Ataturk were less central to his project of creating a secular Turkish republic than they had been for his predecessor Young Turks. Ataturk's real focus, between 1920 and 1923, was to remove the ethos of Muslim confraternity in Turkey, which he and his fellow Young Turks saw as a competing affiliation to 'Turkishness' and an obstacle and restraint to their militant 'fundamentalist' project of western 'modernisation'.

Turkey's founder, Ataturk, is portrayed in the West as an enlightened 'Muslim' leader who mirrored the western synthesis in believing that the break-up of religious, social and community restraints to liberal markets, through the creation of a powerful centralised secular state within the Muslim world, was a model for all Muslim societies to follow.

This western endorsement is hardly surprising as Ataturk's project corresponded so exactly with the West's utopian vision for the future; this western assessment also showed very little understanding that Islamists, and most Muslims, see the enforced secularisation in Turkey, and the end of the Caliphate, in a totally different light.

Secular Modernism and the Emergence of an Ideology of Resistance

It was this aspect, the enforced secularisation of Turkey, more than any other event, however, that paradoxically was to facilitate the conditions in which a Sunni ideology of resistance could emerge; and which, coupled with the challenge of secular Marxist materialism, could prompt some of the Shi'i hierarchy to accept a sweeping reinterpretation of Shi'ism as a revolutionary ideology that would depose another secularising and modernising autocrat – the Shah of Persia.

When, in the aftermath of the First European War, Mustafa Kemal (Ataturk) repeatedly and inflammatorily described Islam as 'the symbol of obscurantism', as 'a putrefied corpse which poisons our lives', and as 'the enemy of civilisation and science'[34] he shocked and stunned Muslims everywhere. But, in the language he used, he could well have been Cromwell describing the 'evil' of Catholic Spain or the Pope.

Turkey then was the seat of the Ottoman Empire. It was also the seat of the Caliph, who was viewed by Sunni Muslims as the successor to the Prophet Mohammad himself. It was as if a vitriolic attack on Christianity had been launched from within the Vatican enclave.

Kemal's acid scorn and contempt for Islam delivered from the very heart of the Sunni Muslim world was an intentional slap at Muslims and at the Muslim confraternity as expressed by the transnational character of the Caliphate and its claims to authority over Sunni Muslims everywhere (Shi'i Muslims looked to the succession of Imams for their authority and leadership).

Ataturk, the hero of the West, the man who created modern Turkey, was a dictator. He was a military man; a military man's man – except to his superiors who found him to be quarrelsome and arrogant. Prussian military officers had virtually monopolised the training at the Turkish military staff college since the late nineteenth century. These were not just military trainers: they were elite officers who reflected the ideals of Prussian militarism, and of technical warfare, to their charges, as well as their convictions of European cultural superiority.

Turkish officers, such as Mustafa Kemal (Ataturk), who were exposed to this German military ethos at the peak of its self-confidence and swagger, were imbued with a militarism that came to view the military and its associated military ethos as symbolising the necessary leadership psyche appropriate to any modernising society.

Mustafa Kemal was a man whose colossal arrogance and callousness, contempt for women and Muslims, heavy-drinking and quarrelsomeness, led in later years to his becoming remote from his people – living isolated and moody in the former residence of the Sultan until his death from cirrhosis of the liver in 1938.[35]

The Turkish state created by Ataturk from 1920 to 1923 relied on military power and the military ethos. It also bore a troubling resemblance to fascism. It was, until many years later, a dictatorship that employed terror and propaganda at will, utilising a one-party state, and the army to proselytise coercively.

Having earlier dismissed the Caliphate as 'an embarrassment to the civilised world', which 'could only have been a laughing stock in the eyes of the civilised world, enjoying the blessings of science',[36] Kemal used the militarised powers of a dictatorship simply to erase public expression of Islamic culture. Islamic clothing, music and education were all outlawed and replaced by western models. A programme of mosque closures was initiated – many were locked and left to decay, and others were turned into warehouses or schools.

Traditional music was suppressed and replaced by a newly created 'opera'. Islamic symbols were removed wherever possible. Traditional clothing and headwear were banned. Even the written language was 'modernised' by using Latin script written in the western left-to-right style, rather than right-to-left in its traditional Arabic form.

It was not that the western model was to become an inspiration. It was to be duplicated slavishly – becoming often a parody of Europe – with the Turkish army encased in Russian uniforms, carrying Belgian rifles, English swords, riding Hungarian saddles and practising French military drill.[37] All aspects of westernisation were enforced rigorously in all spheres of life.

To be modern, civilised and prosperous meant projecting Islam as the insurmountable obstacle to progress, and meant aping western customs, institutions and culture unashamedly. Kemal's slurs on Islam have had remarkable longevity: they echo today throughout western discourse, as those who use them neglect the consequences of the purpose for which they were coined.

The act of terminating the Caliphate which had existed since the death of the Prophet Mohammad was an act of destruction that was traumatic to Sunni Muslims everywhere. The end of the Caliphate was perceived as signalling the weakness of Islam and evidence of the decline of Islamicate culture – that fabric of cultures, thinking and history associated with Islam.

The abolition of the Caliphate had repercussions across the globe. There was agitation and an uprising in India; and King Fuad of Egypt and the Hashemites made attempts to claim the Caliphate – but these efforts proved futile.

For a few Muslim intellectuals, however, the ending of the Caliphate, although a humiliation for Islamicate political and religious aspirations, provided an opportunity: an opportunity to redefine and reframe the Umma. For such thinkers, at a conference in Cairo in 1926, the disestablishment of Islam, the severance of ties to dynastic politics and to the murky realpolitik of state leaders, while symbolically a trauma, paradoxically also freed Islam to become a strong new identity.

As these ideas evolved, it was seen that the Umma could be reformulated as a modern internet-era virtual community with an ethical aspiration for a just, equitable and compassionate global order, and for a new community-centric vision of politics and personal behaviour. It was the opportunity to reformulate what Muslims meant by community. 'Community' – the Umma – was to be the converse of the thinking underlying the western nation-state. It was to represent the choice declined by the West: it was to be an opening out of identity to reflect the diversity of the communities from which it was drawn, rather than to follow the narrowing down of identity and leveraging of ethnicity associated with the racial nationalist nation-state in western thinking.

This in turn would underpin a networked, horizontally structured identity of a powerful transnational Muslim community bestriding Muslim societies and Muslims living in westernised secular nation-states. The concept of a networked community, bound by few formal structures, also provided better protection and safety for Muslims in an era of western depredations and domination – both from pressures exerted by western nation-states or their client rulers in Muslim societies. It was to become, too, the source of legitimacy for an increasingly determined resistance to the imposition of western thought. It would open the debate on the future of the nation-state and the meaning of politics.

Missionaries of Modernity and the Revival of Islamist Thinking

The historian of Islam, Karen Armstrong, summarised the essence of the Prophet Mohammad's vision of the future to be in the building of a just community in which all its members, even the most weak and vulnerable, were treated with absolute respect. The experience of building it, and living in it, would be a reminder of truths that everyone knew, and would give its members intimations of the divine – because they would be living in the way God intended for human beings.[38]

The essence of Islam, therefore, is the striving (jihad) to live in the way God intended. For Muslims, social justice in politics was the essential virtue of Islam: state affairs were not a distraction from spirituality, but the stuff of religion itself. It was this experience of building and living in a truly Islamic community, the conduct of its affairs (politics) and its success in attaining a just society, that would provide for Muslims their path to God. For Muslims, it was through the day-to-day experience of justice, equity and compassion, rather than through Pauline 'faith', that they would approach the divine. It followed from this that the well-being of the Muslim community, the Umma, was a matter of supreme importance.[39]

It was to this cornerstone that Kemal had taken a sledgehammer in a concerted and deliberate destruction of Muslim confraternity – the community of believers that had been established by the Prophet as the access path to the divine. This was an attack on perhaps the key insight offered to the world by the Prophet.

It is hardly surprising that Muslims understood this to be an assault on Islam: it was. It is also clear why western Christians and secular modernists cannot see this, and disagree with any suggestion that Ataturk's secularisation was anti-Islamic.

From Cromwell's time, but more particularly during the nineteenth century, the European objective was – through an act of massive social engineering – to free economic life from social and political control in order to release the dynamic energies of individualism, by making the individual responsible solely for his own welfare, rather than expecting it to devolve out of the community.

For western Christians with their puritan heritage, to engage in the struggle for change and reform was not, and is not, seen to stand in opposition to the religious instinct, but rather to give it its fullest expression. It represents Abraham's faithful response to change, and the Calvinistic call of God to make use of the individual talents that God has given each person. The prosperity and material benefits arising out of individualistic enterprise signalled God's grace for the individual who prospered. And the power that it gave to western societies seemed, in terms of their Protestant legacy, evidence that their societies were 'elected' by God to become missionaries of modernity to others.

These themes have persisted in the West even as the doctrines on which they were based fell into disuse or were synthesised into secular modernism. The idea that every Christian should personally experience God's call – as symbolised by Abraham – has for more than three centuries been strengthening its hold on western life. This has given Christians an increasingly individual relationship with God and shaped an inherently dynamic religion committed to the radical changes demanded by free market economics.

Islam, by contrast, represented the converse. The Qur'an's demand is behavioural: that human beings should behave towards one another with justice, equity and compassion. It therefore subordinated human drives and instincts and economic activity as a whole to this overriding demand. Politics was, therefore, what Christians would call a sacrament; and was dedicated to the striving towards these key values.

Day-to-day political and social intercourse was the arena in which Muslims could be opened up to a growing understanding of God. Growing closer to God and to reality came through experiencing these key values – as they acted upon, and modified, human behaviour. This, in turn, opened the possibility for the divine to function more effectively in human affairs.

The Islamic vision is not static but perceives progress primarily in terms of community well-being rather than individual self-development. Individual achievement as well as economic activity was also a call from God – but one that was to be performed in the service of all and not to be sequestered to the benefit of one or other individual. The political situation of the community of believers – defined in terms of the establishment of these key values – was the litmus of the human condition, and of the state of God's grace.

These represented two clashing visions; and Ataturk's enforced secularisation and abolition of the Caliphate marked for Muslims an assault on the essence of Islam. The story of the emerging Islamist revolution is largely one of an Islamic response to western thinking based around individualism and a personal relationship with the divine, in juxtaposition to Islam's insistence that the individual's wants and appetites must be managed within a system that gives primacy to a just and equitable community emerging – through which medium individuals might experience the divine. This was Mohammad's insight and contribution: individuals reach closer to God through experiencing values lived communally – and not through faith alone.

The events in Turkey became the catalyst to unleash and energise an Islamist mobilisation. This was based on a revival of Islamist thinking centred on human beings, community and behaving. Islamists believe that Islam will become the vision and 'grand narrative' of the future, juxtaposed to an unravelling western narrative in the postmodern world.

In the next chapter we explore the initial calls for Islamist armed resistance and the accompanying ideology, and try to separate out broadly the various strands that comprised it. The subsequent chapter looks at how this evolving Islamist ideology was shaped and extended further by the Iranian Revolution and with the input from specifically Shi'i thinking. It also highlights the emerging influence of what I have called 'political Shi'ism'. Finally, in this section of the book, we look at how these influences have impacted on two resistance movements, Hesballah and Hamas.

The use of Hesballah and Hamas as examples is not in any way intended to downplay or ignore other Islamist movements; but these two significant groups, one Sunni and one Shi'i, are intended to illustrate how some of these themes of resistance have emerged in practice in two movements with very different roots.

Part II

2

THE AWAKENING OF RESISTANCE

On the face of it an unlikely figure – here was a middle-class intellectual Egyptian from a traditional village background of waning family fortunes propelled into modern urban life. He was an intellectual – in London, he might have aspired to joining the Bloomsbury set – a writer of poetry and a rising literary critic; a man of sensibilities, a little priggish, even a touch prudish; a man who yearned for romantic love, but whose one love affair turned out to be a painful disaster. How did this lonely, prickly figure transform into the inspiration for a generation of revolutionaries, and himself end – defiant – on the gallows in Cairo in August 1966?

Sayyid Qutb's death at the hands of the Egyptian authorities outraged Muslims everywhere. His many books and pamphlets, and particularly his celebrated Milestones on the Road[1] booklet propounding his revolutionary thought, influenced a generation of revolutionaries, both Sunni and Shi'i.

The period 1919 to 1952 comprised the formative period of Sayyid Qutb's thought. The westernisation process, which had begun early in the nineteenth century, in the later years of his life was fully evident in all aspects of life in Egypt. A secular educational structure dominated, widening the gulf between those with secular and those with religious education.

Here was a man caught between his roots of a traditional religious education centred around village life and the secular urban modernism to which he subsequently migrated. His crisis, and his response to it, reflects compellingly the political and cultural dislocations of his time. Colonialism, the growing westernisation of Muslim societies unleashed by Mustafa Kemal's ending of the Caliphate, and the forced cultural suppression and demonisation of Islam in Turkey, had their impact. Closer at hand, disenchantment with the conduct and racialism of British soldiers during the Second European War, traced the path of a man returning to the values of his youth and to the Qur'an in the face of his alienation from the society around him.

Qutb's experience of western influence had already provoked in him a stern moralist response, even before his relatively mundane criticism of Egyptian corruption and policy irked the palace severely. He was 'exiled' in 1948 – albeit on scholarship – to the United States, where his experience hardened further his sense that western secular liberalism had created a de-humanised hollow society which soon would implode: 'The civilisation of the white man has already exhausted its restricted usefulness.'[2] The impulse toward radical change in his own society was given a hard edge by this western experience as this somewhat priggish man facing anger and resentment at home – rather than general admiration – for his forensic criticism of his own Egyptian society, which was enthralled by western materialism and mired in social injustice.

His frustration at the imperviousness of the Egyptian elite and of society as a whole to his admonitions, and their wilful closed-mindedness – as he saw it – to the societal and moral consequences of westernisation led him into direct involvement with the Free Officers movement and the Muslim Brotherhood. This was an involvement that was ultimately to carry him to nearly a decade of imprisonment from November 1954 until May 1964.

It is not too difficult to imagine the psychological impact of a decade in gaol for a man like Qutb. A man of neat, almost stiff appearance – a 1950 photo shows him moustachioed and immaculately attired in jacket and tie, smiling self-assuredly; a participant in literary circles, a poet and a bachelor – this fastidious man faced the horrors of the mistreatment and torture that was common in Egyptian prisons.

We are told of but one incident in 1957 when 21 Muslim Brothers were arbitrarily killed for refusing to report for their daily hard labour of rock-breaking. Qutb, we are told, was horrified by the barbarism of the gaolers towards other human beings. We can imagine how this incident and the routine of torture impacted on a man of sensibilities. He was sickened and revolted by this violent mindless assault on ideas – it is no wonder that he decided that intellectual suasion had no place in the horror of an Egyptian system that crushed dissent and which erased all humanity. Qutb decided to pull down the 'temple pillars'. He became a revolutionary.

Qutb was radicalised by his experience in prison. He was convinced that humanity was heading for 'the deep, awful precipice of destruction'[3] unless a determined Muslim vanguard was to take up the struggle. Jihad meant in his context a striving by each Muslim individual to spread the belief in Islam through tongue, heart, hand or sword against the modern version of that narrow-mindedness, that rigid mindset originally termed 'jahiliyya' which, during the early years of the first Muslim community, clung so tenaciously to narrow, tribal interest and closed its ears to the Prophet's revelation.

To convey his ideas more forcefully, Qutb adapted the original meaning of a term 'jahiliyya' to describe also its modern equivalent in Muslim societies. Qutb meant by his recovery of the term 'jahiliyya' to refer to contemporary features of materialist, self-absorbed western society that displaced God's sovereignty over man. This disastrous modern jahiliyya called for the defence of Islam, according to Qutb.

The Narrative of Jihad

The concept of the defence of Islam has its roots in the Qu'ran. Some elements, as Muslims know them today, came into existence during the lifetime of the Prophet Mohammad (around CE 570–632), but jihad as a fully fledged doctrine did not come into existence until considerably later, towards the end of the eighth century. From this time, until Qutb's intervention and subsequently, when a small minority of Islamists elaborated on the thinking of a thirteenth-century scholar Ibn Taymiyya, the concept of defence in Islam and jihad had very clear and precise meaning.

This earlier meaning is the one still espoused by the vast majority of Islamists today, including armed movements such as Hamas, Hesballah and most of the Islamic Jihad groups. In the West, however, the concept of jihad in media parlance is generally given a meaning inextricably linked to, and based on, the bomb attacks on civilians by those who adhere to the thinking associated with al-Qae'da. To impute this specific meaning of the word 'jihad' to all Islamists who take up arms in defence of Islam is to misunderstand both the tradition of Islam and the doctrine of defence of Islam.

Islam arose in an environment where warfare – or at least armed violence with some degree of organisation and planning – was a characteristic of everyday life: its threat was never far away, particularly in those regions of the Arabian peninsula that shared frontiers with the great empires of the time. Its presence as a major component of life is reflected in pre-Islamic poetry and songs of praise, some of which were devoted entirely to the joys and travails of fighting. Martial valour topped the list of values, followed closely by acts of generosity in these early works. It is not surprising, therefore, that we also find references to warfare and to fighting in the Holy Qu'ran; but there is much misunderstanding in the West about how this is treated in the Qu'ran.

The Qu'ran remains the source of inspiration for the doctrine and practice of jihad, but it is not the only authority. The Qu'ran does not attempt to be a comprehensive instruction manual covering every conceivable circumstance in life. The passages which deal with warfare and jihad are not numerous, and some of its themes are scattered in various places in the book. The passages may be vivid and memorable, but they do not comprise a doctrine. Furthermore some of the passages appear to be contradictory, and not easily reconciled.

There are verses that appear to endorse violence against non-Muslims (the often quoted 'sword verses'), but equally there are other passages that clearly and specifically argue against warfare with non-Muslims – unless the enemy is the first to use violence. But even when attacked, Muslims are required to display self-restraint, and the Qu'ran calls for reconciliation and peacemaking with 'People of the Book' (Christians and Jews).

The Qur'an, being the most complete, direct and final message to humans from God, is the primary source of divine law. At the same time, the historical Qur'an, as it is today, is the product of a complex process of editing that took place between CE 644 and 656, whose principles are largely obscure to modern scholars. Verses – often in rhyming prose, rarely in poetry – are arranged in chapters; but the order of chapters and the placement of verses within a chapter do not possess an easily comprehended logic. What seems certain is that the verses as they are read now do not appear in the order in which they are thought to have been revealed to Mohammad.[4]

Islamic jurists tried to cope with these apparently irreconcilable elements – as Christian scholars did with the Christian narrative – by editing the passages chronologically and then trying to situate the passages in the context of the narrative and events arising from the life of the Prophet. The doctrine of 'defence of Islam' evolved later, taking its final shape in the eighth century.

Islam had transformed the consciousness of its early adherents through its spiritual and moral message; but also transformed them through the activity of fighting on behalf of that message. The Arabic word 'jihad' does not mean 'holy war' or 'just war'. It literally means 'striving'. When followed by 'fi sabil Allah' which is often unspoken but implicitly assumed, it literally means 'fighting for the sake of God'. The urgency and the passionate message of generosity, charity and care for the unfortunate in the Qu'ran was matched by a motivation to fight for justice and against abuse of power.

Jihad was more than just a legal doctrine – the comprehensive manuals of classical law usually include a section called 'Book of Jihad' that covered all aspects of warfare. Jihad was also a potent system for popular mobilisation. Early Arabic poems express a heroic ideal, where the courage and endurance of a few individuals illuminate a dark violent world. Many of these narratives place emphasis on the fighter's pure intentions, his piety and his 'striving' (jihad) for the sake of God – and his volunteering for a life of sacrifice and asceticism.

In early Islam, on the frontiers with the Byzantine Empire, this took concrete form in the emergence of 'fighting scholars': scholars of Islam and philosophers who had volunteered to take up the sword to defend Islam during the day, but at night became pious teachers to the faithful. It was a life of discipline and hardship –as well as of study. In early Islam, these 'fighting scholars' were all unpaid. Emphasis was laid on the quality of being a volunteer: a volunteer in the service of fighting for God.

As Islam became established over a wide geographic area these societies acquired characteristics in common. One of these was the phenomenon of men of religious learning taking it upon themselves to perform jihad in person: one of them, an Iranian, Abdallah ibn al-Mubarak (died CE 797) attempted to recreate the early community of Medina, then and there, by the internalisation of the norms of behaviour reflected in the first Muslim community; and by then relating these norms to the feats of his companions. His account is the narrative of the martyrdom of heroes in the early wars of Islam. Many of these narratives also place much emphasis on the fighter's 'intention' in jihad. Thus al-Mubarak's own band of individuals takes form as a 'just' community through reflecting the norms of 'striving' and of 'volunteering' in the cause of service to the community and to God.[5] It is possible to see its modern counterpart today in Hesballah's 'culture of resistance' and the values it seeks to emulate and promote.

This vocation of fighting scholar echoed the Qur'an's emphasis on generosity and reciprocity: God's gift to humans can never be reciprocated; indeed, it is impossible to contemplate that the gift from God can ever in the least part be reciprocated. However, in the arena of human exchange, God's practice can also be followed: acts of service or generosity should not look for any recompense directly from the recipient, but should be done in the expectation of receiving none. In an Islamic community the service or gift offered is returned indirectly by the 'bestowal' of the aggregate of individual acts of generosity that ultimately do return to the donor.

It is clear from this brief account that the Islamic tradition of jihad was different from the Christian conception of 'Holy War'. The Christian theological struggle to reconcile 'love' with warfare was absent. The Christian narrative of passivity and non-violence was replaced in Islam by mobilisation and activism. Instead of Christian metaphorical soldiers of God, we have fighters who literally volunteer to take up arms and use them. The Muslim texts of tradition and law repeatedly affirm that the martyrs are those who die while fighting for their faith. And martyrs are to be rewarded by forgiveness of sins and a direct passage to paradise.

Europeans have often struggled to understand how Islam, which arose in one of the poorest regions of the world, could have become such a transforming factor in history. How could a people who had lived on the margins of the world for so long rise suddenly to defeat the two superpowers of the day, Rome and Persia? How were armies assembled? How was the world so energised and mobilised by these events?

Whereas Muslims attributed their motivation to Islam and to God, medieval Christians and Byzantines subsumed into the Islamic world naturally looked for other reasons for this 'catastrophe' for Christianity that had befallen them. Generally they explained the Islamic early success as the will of a vengeful God angered at Christian failings, but they also focussed on vilifying cruelly the Prophet as the cause of their misfortune. Crucially, they highlighted, by way of explanation, the Muslims' 'love of violence'. Here was the beginning of a misunderstanding that has survived until today.

Critics of Islam today continue to argue that the concept of jihad provides proof of the essential 'violence' of Islam; but this is to misconstrue its place in Islam. Islam – and particularly Shi'i Islam – does have a tradition of 'resistance' and rebellion against oppression that is not shared by Christianity; but it would be a distortion to single out the taking up of arms for censure without understanding the key litmus of 'pure intent', the struggle against tyranny and the tradition of those 'few individuals whose courage and endurance illuminate a dark, violent world'.[6] Of course, not all who claim to practise jihad in current times have a deep knowledge of Islam or pure motives; but this is a minority who are widely condemned – by mainstream Islamists more than anyone.

'The Freedom of Man from Servitude to Other Men'

Sayyid Qutb's solution to the contemporary situation of Muslims was to establish a vanguard whose role would be to fight a present-day jahiliyya of materialism and self-centredness; to carry the message of Islam as a system for modern life that is complete and balanced, that embraces modern technology for its own ends, but which is situated in real human needs. Qutb adds that there 'are many practical obstacles in establishing God's rule on earth, such as the power of the state, the social system and tradition and, in general, the whole human environment'.[7]

It is clear that Qutb saw this as a revolutionary struggle to change the nature of society and of its government too. But his innovation – one that would influence a small but crucial minority of revolutionaries – was his criticism of Islamic authorities who tried to restrict Muslims to 'defensive war' only. This he branded as 'defeatist'.[8] The place of 'Jihad through the sword' is 'to clear the way for striving through preaching'. Islam is not a 'defensive movement', but a 'universal proclamation of the freedom of man from servitude to other men ... and the end of man's arrogance and selfishness.'[9]

It is this latter aspect that is really radical. By asserting the impossibility of living in corrupt Arab societies irretrievably overtaken by materialism and westernisation, Qutb metaphorically took a sledge hammer to a 1400-year-old Sunni social compact. After the murder of the fourth Caliph Ali, the Prophet's son-in-law and cousin, in CE 661, Sunni Muslims acquiesced to the seizure of the Caliphate by the then Governor of Damascus. This was the beginning of the very worldly Umayyad dynasty – kings and conquerors rather than guardians of the Prophet's revelations.

In accommodating the hereditary Umayyad dynasty, the Sunni made their historic compromise with power – a compact rejected and shunned by the Shi'i. In acquiescing to the Umayyad leadership in Damascus, Sunni Islam had acquiesced to a worldly 'Caesar' as Caliph – pragmatically ignoring any un-Islamic conduct by the family dynasty – providing only that this leader maintained order, protected the Islamic territories and left theology to the Ulama (the learned scholars).

For Qutb, the advent of secularising westernised Muslim leaders, such as Ataturk, the Shah of Iran and King Faruq of Egypt, was more serious than the problem of a worldly corrupt Caliph or King: secular modernism posed an existential threat to Islam.

He saw that the adoption of secular modernism vacated Islam of any substance. The political end of striving for a just and equitable society as the purpose of life for Muslims was impossible as long as liberal economics demanded the suppression of all political and social restraint to free markets; he understood that the western principle of individualism, and of personal relationships with the divine, undercut the possibility of recreating the only route by which a Muslim can reach God – through the experience of living in a society that reflected the way God intended that they should live.

Qutb saw that secular modernism was incompatible with all the Islamic principles of politics, social justice and economics, and, as a scholar widely read in Islamic culture, and as poet and a literary critic, he could not help but hate this westernising influence, which 'tricks by its lustre, noise, and sensual enjoyment; in which the soul suffocates; and the conscience dies down, while instincts and senses become intoxicated, quarrelsome and excited'.[10] Culture too was being emptied and de-politicised by the search for 'good time, fun' and the desire for geniality and having 'a good time'.[11] In short, culture was being de-politicised and degraded.

Qutb defined this outcome in Egypt and other Muslim societies as jahiliyya – and called for God's rule rather than rule by some worldly 'Caesar'. It moved Sunni Islam closer to the Shi'i demand for social justice; and placed just (i.e. Islamic) governance onto the Islamist agenda.

The armed vanguard, Qutb accepted, may need to use the sword to achieve the end of jahiliyya. To complete his pulling down of the 'temple pillars', just as Martin Luther denied the role of the priest as mediator between man and God, so Qutb consigned the Sunni clerical hierarchy and the superstructure of Islam to the dustbin, insisting that the Qur'an must be accessible to all. There was no need for the intervention of a learned scholar to interpret or mediate it; nor should it be read only through the dry prism of traditional commentary.

In proposing these revolutionary changes, Qutb again – albeit posthumously – is in the dock, on this occasion facing the charge of having laid the foundations for radical jihadists to emerge through his espousal of an offensive jihad against jahiliyya. Adnan Musallam, in his biography of Qutb,[12] concludes that Qutb's execution in 1966 pre-empted any final judgement on this issue as his intentions could not be clarified effectively. Admirers have argued that the jihadists have distorted his concept of jahiliyya by justifying war on those fellow Muslims whom they choose to label as 'unbelievers'.

Musallam's analysis suggests that Qutb may not have intended this elaboration of jihadism, although it is easy to see that the step might have seemed logical in the face of the ruthless repression and cruelty inflicted on the early Qutbists, who would have asked themselves how Muslims could inflict such repression and ill-treatment on fellow Muslims seeking to free man from selfishness and materialism.

However the legacy that Qutb gave should not be centred on this dispute, important though it may be. Qutb – through his prolific output that has been devoured by Islamists everywhere – may finally have left his most important legacy to mainstream Islamism in the form of direct activism. His message has been taken up in the context of confronting not just jahiliyya, but the imposition of secular 'modernity' as the template assumed to be appropriate to the evolving world order. It is not enough to be passive; it will require a more assertive struggle to shape a just world order. Almost all Islamists would agree with Qutb on this. In this aspect, he is the father of revolution.

While it is his ideas on resistance that have attracted most attention, Sayyid Qutb also provided the outlines of an Islamist ideology. He wrote on social justice – placing the emphasis on the Islamic concept that an individual is not solely responsible for his own welfare; instead he argued that an individual must undertake responsibility for others in a community, just as that community owes a duty of care to him or her. He also outlined the principles of a political system based on the concept of an impartial and just leadership, and described an economic system that was subordinated to the objectives of equity and free from the subordination of any individual to the domination and exploitation by another.

It was largely for his tract Milestones that Sayyid Qutb ultimately was hanged. And it was his account of the importance of the Umma – following up on the ideas of the earlier Islamists, who in 1926 had posited the idea of a de-territorialised community, on which he had elaborated to define it as a community of resistance – that was so damagingly quoted by the prosecutor at his trial in Egypt in 1966.

Qutb defined the Umma thus:

The homeland of the Muslim, in which he lives and which he defends, is not a piece of land; the nationality of the Muslim, by which he is identified, is not the nationality determined by a government; the family of a Muslim in which he finds solace and which he defends is not blood relationships; the flag of the Muslim, which he honours and under which he is martyred is not the flag of a country; and the victory of the Muslim, which he celebrates, and for which he is thankful to God, is not a military victory.[13]

His critics complained that Qutb's writings were the stuff of imaginings, and that his ideas lacked rationality. In the period 1939–47, as he became isolated and under increasing attack, he did evolve a stern moralist tone; but this was not the whole story. Although he stated that his writing had been drawn exclusively from the Qur'an and the Traditions of the Prophet, and had not been influenced by philosophers such as Ibn Sina (Avicenna) or Ibn Rusd (Averroes) or any other Islamic philosopher, and that he regarded their works as no more than shadows of the Greek philosophers, he was – perhaps surprisingly – drawn to the strong Islamic tradition of mysticism. His works on social justice reflect

his powerful call for compassion which echoes strongly the poetry
and thinking of Ibn Arabi, who died in 1240.

The Dissident Voices of Salafism

Qutb was certainly not mainstream. The movement to which
he nominally adhered was the venerable Muslim Brotherhood
of Egypt which had been founded at the end of the nineteenth
century. The Muslim Brotherhood, however, was, and still is,
mainstream. In contrast to the groups that subsequently claimed
inspiration from Qutb, it represented a very 'un-militant'
Islamism. Although currents of Egyptian thinking would take
armed vanguardism to the point of assassinating President Sadat
in 1981, the Brotherhood – which was, and is, the major Islamist
movement around the world – was, and is, essentially a social
and educational movement, that believes that change can only
be brought about incrementally, by a slow process of educating
people in Islam and through community support programmes.
This predominant current has not sought political confrontation
nor has it generally resorted to violence.

After Qutb's death, and even before it, the Islamist revolution
essentially diverged into a number of different strands: the
Brotherhood continued in its patient policies of good works and
preaching the call of Islam; armed vanguardism in Egypt had a brief
flowering before its suppression by Sadat's successor, President
Mubarak; and two key ideologues, in what was eventually to
become al-Qae'da – Dr Abdallah Azzam and Ayman al-Zawahiri
– acknowledged their intellectual debt to Qutb.

While the Brotherhood remains, to date, largely non-confron-
tational and non-violent, a more politically activist approach
evolved in Iraq in the late 1950s associated with Mohammad
Baqir Sadr, which is explored further in Chapter 3. This group
also initially drew on Qutb's Sunni thinking but took it down a
different Shi'i course; this strand subsequently became a nexus
of key Islamists and a conduit of ideas to Iran, contributing to
the revolution, and to Lebanon, contributing to the ideology of
Hesballah. This key evolution is the subject of the next chapter.

The Sunni Palestinian Islamist movements, Hamas and Palestinian Islamic Jihad were both post-Iranian Revolution offshoots of the Muslim Brotherhood. These two movements also adopted an activist and more confrontational posture than that of the Brotherhood. But none of these movements followed Qutb's ambiguous rejection of the classic doctrine of 'defence of Islam', or the line of thinking that would lead to armed offensive jihad against the West, and rulers of Muslim societies or Muslims who did not subscribe to the idea of offensive jihad.

All of these movements, whether armed or non-violent, adhere to the classic concept of 'defence of Islam': they do not see themselves 'at war with the West'; and nor do they approve of attacks on it. Iran, Hesballah and Hamas were among the first to condemn the 9/11 attacks on the World Trade Center.

However, a small splinter group of Salafi thinkers began to dwell heavily on the West's hostility to the Islamist 'awakening' and on its occupation of Muslim lands. This movement was influenced by a particular variety of 'puritan' Islam – the Wahhabbi orientation within Salafism – and by the thirteenth-century scholar Ibn Taymiyya, whom we encountered earlier as the one early dissident voice to the doctrine of 'defence of Islam'.

Ibn Taymiyya's dissidence had its roots in the Sunni revival that had paralleled the so-called 'counter Crusades', and had combined jihad with an intense intolerance towards any forms of unorthodoxy. A Syrian scholar who died in 1328, Ibn Taymiyya had developed a particular hatred for the Mongol rulers who, after sacking Baghdad in 1258, killing the Caliph and taking his title, had attempted repeated incursions into Syria and Egypt, which had also borne the brunt of the fight against the Crusaders.

Ibn Taymiyya was an embattled scholar in every sense. The Syrian–Egyptian armies had fought off the Mongols repeatedly. He had preached jihad in a variety of writings, but for Taymiyya jihad largely was about the suppression of heretics, by which generally he meant the Shi'i, the curtailing of unorthodox practices such as visiting tombs and keeping non-Muslims firmly in their place. His dissidence, however, lay in his view that the Mongol rulers who had converted to Islam on seizing Baghdad were Muslim in appearance only. They remained the heathens they always were, and their rule amounted to jahiliyya.[14]

It is not difficult to see how the parallel between Taymiyya's stern conservatism and hatred for foreign invaders and the Shi'i might resonate with today's Salafis, again facing foreign western incursions into their lands – and which, in the case of the occupation of Iraq, has resulted in Sunni neighbours falling under Shi'i dominance.

Taymiyya's thinking and his prejudice against the Shi'i had been revived and transmitted by Abd-al Wahhab (died 1792) who founded Wahhibism, the dominant form of Islamism in Saudi Arabia which constitutes a particular – and some would say ultra conservative – orientation within Salafism. Salafism is a school of thought that seeks to purify Islam from its later 'impure' accretions that have accumulated since the early Muslim community. Salaf translates as 'pious ancestor'. Salafists, therefore, are those who model themselves after their pious ancestors (of the early community).

This tiny and generally reviled group within Salafism concluded that the West would never permit an Islamist government – whether duly elected by the people or not – ever to take office. This meant that a true Islamic community or state was an impossibility. They concluded – in the face of western obstruction, overwhelming power and domination of the international order – that the structure of power relationships controlled by the West had to be destroyed and the 'system' burned. The colonial enterprise had to be ended completely and only when this was accomplished would an Islamic phoenix, a true Islamic society, purified from its subsequent impurities, emerge from the ashes.

A Salafi described it thus:

> You must understand that, at core, this way of thinking is eschatological ... it is about the world moving towards its conclusion ... its end.
>
> The language and writings have become long, obscure corridors of theological debate reflecting something like the religiosity of Christians when Thomas Aquinas and other Christian theologians haggled over the implications of the question of how many angels could dance on the head of a pin ... Because of these debates there are many schisms.

But they are very, very angry. They are angry at what the West is doing in Iraq. I am angered too: What it has started in Iraq ... it will be years ... even if America departs now ... before the consequences of their acts there finally work themselves out ... so many will die; it will be very bloody. I was so angry when I heard that 300 Afghan civilians had died in Western bombing of their villages: this is barely noticed in the West – 300 lives ... a footnote, a tiny paragraph in the press. Three thousand Americans died and the hullabaloo ... 300 Afghan innocents? Who cares?

These Salafis, in their anger, have begun to see this as 'evil' ... that the West is evil ... That the West is an evil for all Muslims, to be sure ... many see that; but more than this ... that this thing ... the Western thinking ... is seen now by these Salafis as threatening not just Muslims, but the whole of mankind. It is an evil that must be destroyed completely. It is an eschatological matter ... unchecked, this will destroy all humans whatever their beliefs.

This is the belief of many Salafis. They see it as an imperative of the historical moment to fight this evil of Western beliefs. They have no thought for the future after the struggle ... their responsibility is to the historical moment now ... the afterwards ... whether it is a Muslim Caliphate of all nations ... this is God's responsibility to bring about ... the Salafi has no part in that ... his duty ends with the historical moment in which he is engaged.[15]

The array of Salafi cells and groups spun off by western military interventions in various Muslim societies, and influenced by al-Qa'eda thinking – but not sharing its philosophy – shares some characteristics in common apart from deep anger. They represent a harsh Sunni reaction against Shi'ism, and any Shi'i claim to Muslim leadership, which echoes the train of thought of Taymiyya.

They are also implacably hostile towards Sunni movements such as Hamas, whom they perceive as compromising with this 'evil' of the West, by participating in elections and by their willingness to entertain relationships with western states which these Salafis view as collaboration. Their numbers, although small, are growing rapidly, as Saudi interests direct substantial resources toward radical Sunni groups that they hope will form the nucleus around which a new Sunni revival will occur. The objective of this Saudi largesse, as in the earlier post-Gulf War period, is to empower the proxies who will contain Iranian and Shi'i power. The Iraq conflict has become a renewed catalyst for this proxy war; but as with the earlier Saudi attempts to contain Iran by empowering Wahhabism with its anti-Shi'i colouring, the Saudis are likely to find that these radical Sunnis harbour little love for the Saudi rulers either.

These smaller Salafi groups, as the Salafi speaker noted, are fragmented and divided by theological disputes equivalent to the earlier 'angels on the head of a needle' disputes in Christianity. Most of these centre on the argument about the justice of killing innocent Muslims for a higher ideal; but they also revolve around the circumstances and finality of the present war: has the final struggle that signals the end of the world fully begun, or are we witnessing only the preliminary skirmishes, they ask themselves.

'Who Are Our Enemies and Why Do They Hate Us?'

It is clear that the growth of eschatological speculation represents an 'end to politics' for this minority. It is the final culminating struggle between 'good and evil' and there is no 'politics' to follow. It is here that they differ from al-Qae'da. The latter want to implode the western system – as the USSR imploded; to crash it so completely that all the legacies from the colonial era, including the corrupt rulers of Muslim societies, are swept away. But this is a form of revolutionary thought that is familiar to Europeans: it is a cleansing by violence and by complete rupture with the past that launches the creative cycle. Creation begins with destruction – it is the theme of the French Jacobin revolutionaries. And, like the Jacobins – and unlike their eschatological Salafi colleagues – al-Qae'da does foresee politics in the sequel to the conflict.

The approach of Salafis and al-Qa'eda could not be more different from that of mainstream Muslims. Mainstream Islamists are horrified by this type of thinking: they believe that just as the French revolutionaries ended by consuming their own revolution, so too al-Qae'da risks plumbing the darkest depths of human nature by unleashing overwhelming feelings of anger, hatred and desire for revenge. The consequences of loosing an uncontrollable torrent of anarchic violence will lead to nothing good. This can never be the route to a just Islamic society, the mainstream Islamist majority believes. For movements such as Hesballah, revolution must never be allowed to overreach itself, or become detached from popular support.

Mainstream Islamists – possibly 95 per cent of all Islamists – have disowned and rejected any amendment to the classic 'doctrine of defence of Islam' or the propagation of any new doctrine that calls Muslims to an all-out offensive war. The eschatological and al-Qaeda-type radical movements have retaliated by placing such groups as Hesballah and Hamas, as well as the Shi'i, on their 'death lists'.

The focus in the West on a struggle with 'extremist Islam' and its preoccupation with violence has largely obscured this crucial divide between resistance and 'shock and outrage'-motivated violence. The conflation between, on the one hand, mainstream Islamists who adhere to the idea of resistance in 'defence of Islam', and on the other hand, those who hope to provoke 'Armageddon', far from having contained Islamism, has served only to strengthen those who want 'to burn down the system'.

When the Soviet Union invaded Afghanistan in 1979, Muslims everywhere were affronted by the occupation, by the brutal suppression of civilians as well as by tales of atrocities committed. Muslims rallied to the support of their co-religionists from all societies and from all shades of Islam to volunteer to help defend Islam and the Afghans. There was no dissent: here was an open-and-shut case – a Muslim society attacked and occupied by an atheist western state. All Muslims could see their obligation to volunteer in 'defence of Islam'.

In the early 1980s, before the Taliban as a movement existed, Afghanistan and the neighbouring areas of Pakistan became a cauldron of new ideas and thinking about Islam. Here was the front line both in defending Islam, as well as in evolving new thinking about an Islamist society. It became the forum for debate and all strands of Islam were represented – from Sufi mystics to Ayatollahs in exile from Iran. It was an exciting moment, as well as being intellectually stimulating. It was into this heady mix that a small Saudi Arab contingent began arriving – among whom was Usama bin Laden.

In parallel to this influx of Islamic movements and leaders into the Pakistani region adjoining Afghanistan, the President of Pakistan, General Zia al-Haq, had already embarked on his own major project of Islamisation of the Pakistani army and of society. The Soviet invasion and the gathering of so many Islamist currents gave Zia al-Haq's project a major boost of manpower, of ideas and of cash. For, in the wake of the Soviet invasion, the CIA and the US began pouring millions of dollars into Pakistan and – via the Pakistani authorities – into the Islamist movements based on the frontier with Soviet-occupied Afghanistan.

Not only were the US and other western states funding Islamist movements either directly or indirectly, but the cause of defending Afghanistan had mobilised donors from Saudi Arabia, the Gulf and further afield. *Madrassas* (technically meaning nothing more than a high school, but which in the context of President Zia al-Haq's Islamic project tended to have a conservative Deobandi curriculum, or a Saudi Wahhabi influence) sprang up in the border areas and flourished.

What today in the West are termed the 'terror training camps' in Afghanistan were set up in the early 1980s at the instigation of Pakistan with tacit support from the US and Saudi Arabia. They were established to train the Afghan mujahedeen (jihadis) in military skills. This was the closing era of the Cold War and the US was intent on imposing a military defeat on the Soviet Union.

The huge western programme to force the Soviet withdrawal from Afghanistan came to fruition in 1987. With this foreign policy success – arguably brought about more by the political implosion that was under way in Moscow, than by a military defeat dealt by mujahedeen – the US and Britain disengaged from Afghanistan. It was in the wake of the Soviet withdrawal from Afghanistan, and western disengagement, that the idea 'to implode the system' of the small, perhaps 250–300 strong group associated with bin Laden began to evolve.

It was intended as a rival contender to the project of mass popular mobilisation espoused by mainstream Islamists: al-Qae'da sought to provoke seismic change at the global level directly – ignoring the need to mobilise popular support – by short-cutting the revolutionary process and adopting the tactics of 'shock and outrage'.

It constitutes an extreme form of vanguardism that promotes violence in a nihilistic fashion – that has no direct specific strategic purpose beyond the indirect aim of provoking a breakdown of the existing relationships between people in society, and between peoples and their government, by creating feelings of overwhelming anger, hatred and fear.

It is a 'big bang' approach to creating a new society: it sees violent incidents – a 'shock and outrage' approach – as both a cleansing agent, a sentiment shared with the Jacobins in the French Revolution, and as an agent of revolution. It was intended precisely as a 'Jacobin' orgy of violence and turmoil that would unleash unrestrainable forces of unreason and anger, and of the dark side of human passion that would destroy the Arab regimes and their collaborators.

Its leaders, like Ayman Zawahiri, assert that an Islamic state will simply arise in consequence. Unlike mainstream Islamists who present an ideology and a platform for a new Islamic society, and are actively engaged in its construction, al-Qa'eda in common with apocalyptic Salafi groups assumes that the dynamic of destruction is the historic necessity at this time – and that no preparation beyond the need for creating a trigger to this dynamic is required. The subsequent course of events lies beyond their personal responsibility: it is the responsibility of God.

Usama bin Laden's purpose is not to defeat the West militarily (he lacks the power to achieve this); but to poke at it – in order to cause the West, like the Soviet Union, to implode from its internal contradictions.

Although it is questionable whether al-Qae'da now draws direct loyalty of any substantive size, polls show that many – perhaps 30 per cent according to some polls – applaud their confrontation with the US. Al-Qae'da's setting out of an alternative Muslim historical narrative that repeatedly and insistently chips away at the western historical narratives appeals more widely among a broad Muslim audience – even if they condemn their actions more generally.

The Deconstruction and Re-assembly of Islam

The historical narrative woven in bin Laden's speeches and on websites has thrown open to Muslims in the West novel ways of conceiving a future Islam. Bin Laden largely achieved this by breaking down the old-fashioned narratives of clerical, mystical and even fundamentalist authority, along with their respective forms of organisation, but also by recombining these dispersed elements in fresh conceptions.

Young Muslims living in the West, like their counterparts in Muslim societies, have been afflicted by what has occurred over the last 200 years; but, in parallel, they have been energised and uplifted by this 'dispersal' of new ideas and thinking that accompanied the Islamist revival. At the core of this revival has been the attempt to step past the constraints and failures of the recent past by revisiting the roots of Islam in terms of seeking that essence which originally energised and transformed the world in the wake of the Message relayed by the Prophet Mohammad.

It might have been more accurate to begin this account of the emergence of an Islamist resistance in the late nineteenth century, when Islamist thinkers first began to consider how to maintain Islamic identity as a minority group in Hindu India; but, as indicated in the introduction, this book does not seek to be a history of Islamism. The point that I have sought to bring out in setting its beginnings with Sayyid Qutb in Egypt and Mohammad Baqir Sadr's al-Da'wa 'nexus' in Najaf, was that it took the 'modernisation' of Turkey, followed by the secular modernisation of other Muslim societies, to facilitate the transformation from what had been a somewhat apologetic genre of nineteenth- and early twentieth-century writing into a resistance idiom.

Paradoxically, therefore, it was the Kemalists and Turkey's transformation, which westerners so admire that, inadvertently – in driving Islam down to the level of popular street and mosque culture, and severing the links to its superstructure that had provided stability for 1400 years – created the conditions in which Islamism could transmute and evolve into a revolutionary movement. It was this, plus the brutality of the repression suffered by Islamists, that did so much to set the frame for wider resistance.

The Kemalists effectively had cut the guy ropes tying Islam as practised by ordinary Muslims to that superstructure of learned Islam, its commentaries, its schools of law, its esoteric language that needed 25 years of prior study in order to interpret the holy texts – all these ligaments that had been holding the body and doctrine of Islam whole, and largely constant, for over 1000 years, were dismantled, marginalised or co-opted into the dead hand of the civil service.

This breaking up of the corpus and of the structures inadvertently gave space to new thinkers such as Qutb, and Shi'i thinkers and leaders – Sayyed Baqir Sadr and Imam Khomeini, among others – to challenge the orthodoxy as fundamentally as did Martin Luther in the Christian context. It also, of course, permitted bin Laden's dispersal of – and subsequent reassembling of – the various components of Islam. Bin Laden, by acting as his own entrepreneur of identity and tradition in this way, has also succeeded in fragmenting authority in Sunni Islam so severely that it is probably, for the time being, irretrievable. One unintended consequence of this is to leave the collegiate Shi'i leadership as the only body remaining institutionally intact.

These various Islamist ideologues of differing hue have all welcomed this as a period of renewal and relative fluidity in which to build an ideology of revolutionary Islamism. The Holy Qur'an has been made available to the ordinary man, as his or her blueprint and system for life without the need for the mediation of a scholar. This may signal as important a change as was the dissemination in the vernacular of the Bible for Europeans in the fifteenth century, and which, in its time, sparked upheavals throughout Christianity.

3

POLITICAL SHI'ISM

When the youth of Tehran, the vanguard of the coming Islamic Revolution, poured into the streets in the tumultuous winter of 1978, they engulfed the streets of the capital chanting the name of one man: it was not that of a cleric; it was not that of Imam Khomeini, but that of a melancholic teacher and university lecturer, Dr Ali Shariati. This was the man of whom Jean-Paul Sartre once said, 'I have no religion, but if I were to choose one, it would be that of Shariati.' It was this melancholic man who furnished the revolution with its ideology of mass mobilisation and for whom the youth took to the streets.

The repression of Islam and the destruction of the Caliphate initiated by Mustafa Kemal that had led Sayyid Qutb to preach revolutionary vanguardism until his execution in 1966, had shaken and reverberated around the Sunni world, but also had its impact on the Shi'i. Qutb's writings from 1948, but more particularly his *Social Justice in Islam*,[1] coincided with mass protests throughout the Muslim world at the partition of Palestine which gave his words particular resonance.

Qutb's writings of the early 1950s had laid the groundwork for a revolutionary ideology with huge potential to bring about change. But it was events in Iraq and the confrontation between Najaf, the seat of Shi'i religious learning, and Baghdad, the seat of state power, that helped shape the next stage of its evolution. More significant, however, was the nexus of key Islamist personalities who visited or stayed in Najaf during this period. This chance confluence became the centrifuge that spun off the key framework of ideas to the revolutionary movements that were to emerge in Iraq, Iran and Lebanon.

The seeds of 'political Shi'ism' were established by this nexus. But one event more than any other – the execution by Saddam Hussein of one of the most prominent Islamist thinkers, and the leader of the Najaf activist element – became the focal point for renewed struggle: the murder of the Shi'i cleric, Mohammad Baqir Sadr, and his sister in 1980 extended the Islamist struggle to the whole Middle Eastern stage and tinged it with Shi'i thinking.[2]

By the early 1950s, the Sunni Muslim Brotherhood of which Sayyid Qutb was a leading light was entrenched across the major cities of Iraq. Its members were drawn from the ranks of high school and university students, lawyers, engineers, doctors and lower and mid-level bureaucrats. This well-educated and activist membership was attracted to the Brotherhood by the movement's ideology and internationalist outlook. The ideology naturally was based almost exclusively on Sunni Islamist intellectuals and ideologues – principally Qutb and Hassan al-Banna, the leader of the Muslim Brotherhood in Egypt.

The Brotherhood membership in Iraq was predominantly Sunni, but it had attracted a small but significant number of Shi'i activists too. Although its Shi'i membership was small in comparison to its Sunni complement, the Brotherhood exerted an influence on the Shi'i, beyond its size, by virtue of its standing and uniqueness. The Shi'i at that stage lacked any ideological-political resources of their own. The intellectual renaissance that took place among certain Shi'i intellectuals and clerics in Najaf, and epitomised by Sayyed Baqir Sadr, between 1950 and 1980, therefore was strongly influenced at its outset by Sunni ideologues,[3] foremost among whom was Sayyid Qutb.

The relative paucity of Shi'i political thinking at this time was the result of an earlier authoritarian crackdown: the last time that the Shi'i clerics had exercised any real political opposition was in 1923–4. This opposition had ended badly for the clerics, with their most famous leaders from Najaf being exiled abroad by the British authorities.

This bitter experience had led to a Shi'i political mutism and 'quietism' that lasted three decades until the late 1950s. By this time, the overt hostility radiating towards Najaf from Saddam

Hussein, and the threat of complete Shi'i marginalisation because of the inroads that the communists were making among young increasingly secular Shi'i, threatened the seminaries of Najaf with oblivion. The stimulus of Qutb's and other Brotherhood thinkers' revolutionary Sunni ideology seemed then, against this dispiriting backdrop, to offer to some younger clerics the opportunity of reform and revival.

Our Philosophy

Despite caution and some scepticism on the part of some senior clerics, Sadr and the Najaf 'nexus' responded with verve. Baqir Sadr founded in 1957 the first revolutionary Shi'i movement – a clandestine organisation, which adopted a cellular structure for security reasons – Hesb al-Da'wa.[4] Baqir al-Sadr published his book *Our Philosophy* [5] in 1959, which dissected the western philosophical roots leading to Marxism, and compared and contrasted it with the Islamic tradition of philosophy. This was followed by *Our Economics*, which did the same for economics.[6] He was subsequently commissioned by the government of Kuwait to assess how that country's oil wealth could be managed in keeping with Islamic principles. This led to major work on Islamic banking that still forms the basis for modern Islamic banks. These works propelled Sadr to become the foremost theoretician of the Islamic renaissance. A third work, *Our Islamic Society*, was never published, although elements of his thinking on this topic appeared in articles published at the time.

Sadr rejected the notion of the primacy of private property being sufficiently justified from the notion of individual 'rights'. He argued instead that both private and public property are equally justified, but that the rights and obligations of both private individuals and rulers should be subordinated to God's demand that human society should be conducted with justice, compassion and equity. He explicitly rejects the conclusion that this made Islamic economics indistinguishable from social democracy, arguing that capitalism and socialism each come about as the natural conclusion of the western ideological legacy, whereas

Islamic economics flows from its privileging of the ethical and behavioural requirements of Islamic society; and therefore is justified entirely independently of other systems of economics.

Our Philosophy offered a better understanding and a closer look at Marxism. Sadr's book represented a detailed critique of the most sophisticated expression of materialist philosophy then available in the Arab world – but which in today's post-Marxist world might seem a bit dated. As Chibli Mallat has noted, an appendix to the first edition reveals Sadr's Marxist sources. For a Shi'i scholar and jurist, the effort is remarkable.[7] His pioneering initiative contributed to the Iranian post-revolutionary decision by universities to embrace both western and Islamic philosophy.

The clandestine al-Da'wa organisation was conceived as a Shi'i response to the events of the time, and particularly to the then prevalent attraction to Marxism among young Shi'i. Much of Sadr's principal works therefore is comprised of a reasoned critique of Marxism and socialism as well as an attempt to develop a full Islamic system of thought.

The Shi'i members of al-Da'wa however did not all withdraw from the Sunni Brotherhood or from Hesb al-Tahrir;[8] and some al-Da'wa members remained profoundly influenced by Qutb into the 1960s[9] espousing key radical components of his thought.

The fact that a key Shi'i cleric such as Sadr was stepping into political ideology at that time was, in itself, revolutionary. Predictably this was met with wariness and opposition among the older generation of clerics such as Ayatollah al-Khoei, the mentor of the fellow quietist Ayatollah Sistani who subsequently was the head of the Shi'i seminaries during the US and British occupation of Iraq in 2003.

Baqir Sadr was the outstanding Shi'i cleric of his age – having completed his instruction at the seminaries of Najaf at 25 years of age – an unprecedented feat. Many good students took most of their life to complete their studies. Clearly he had inherited the intelligence for which his family was reputed.

The Sadr was a celebrated family. Originally of Lebanese origin, they traced their lineage back to the Prophet – hence the title Sayyed. Many prominent scholars figure in his family: his father was an Ayatollah and his grandfather a Grand Ayatollah. It was a family of immense influence and prestige in Iraq and beyond: an older cousin had led the rebellion against the British in 1920. He was the father-in-law of Muqtada Sadr, the present leader of the 'Mahdi Army' in Iraq, and cousin of Grand Ayatollah Mohammad Sadeq Sadr, who together with his two sons, were murdered by Saddam Hussein in 1999. He was also cousin to Imam Musa Sadr, who was the seminal influence in the Shi'i mobilisation in Lebanon that led to the forming of Hesballah.

Although the older generation of clerics were to an extent grateful for the success in countering communist influence, they still recoiled from political activism, recalling the consequences of the 1920 rebellion. As the conflict between Najaf and Baghdad escalated from 1968, when the Ba'ath party came to power, some senior clerics attempted to constrain the activities of the Najaf nexus.

Output by the nexus during the 1960s was substantial and touched on political mobilisation and on taking stands against injustice and wrongdoing. These works were authored from within this nexus by activists who were to become the leaders of the next stages of the Shi'i political revolution.

Mohammad Baqir Sadr's political philosophy, known as 'governance of the people' set out his view of a modern-day Islamic state. Using his mastery of the Qu'ran and his innovative subject-based approach to Qur'anic exegesis, Sadr demonstrated that governance is 'a right given to the whole of humanity' and explained it to be an obligation given from God to the human race to 'tend the globe and administer human affairs'.

This was a major advancement of Islamic political theory. Sadr stated that the legitimacy of a government in an Islamic state comes from the people, and not from the clerics. Sadr explained that throughout history there have been two roles: man, who inherits the earth and stands as its trustee; and the Prophet, who acts as a guardian for man's trusteeship of this legacy:

> Lastly, I demand, in the name of all of you and in the name of the values you uphold, to allow the people the opportunity truly to exercise their right in

running the affairs of the country by holding elections in which a council representing the Umma [the people] could truly emerge.[10]

This innovation and thinking helped underpin the popular mobilisation of the Iranian Revolution and his last work, written in 1979, foreshadows plainly the Iranian constitution that came into being in late 1979. Sadr elaborated his earlier concept of trusteeship to propose a direct popular electoral process in order to elect both a parliament and a president, while the guardianship of the whole project would be overseen by Islamic scholars expert in their learning of law. In this concept, the guardianship role could be seen as a homologue to, for example, the role of the US Supreme Court as guardian of the values of the US Constitution and legal arbiter on social issues.

In the Wake of the Intellectual Renaissance of Najaf

From 1970 onwards, as a result of the growing Islamist following and his writings, Sadr was arrested several times by the Ba'athists and subjected to torture, but continued his work after his release. In 1977 he was sentenced to life imprisonment following uprisings in Najaf, but was released two years later due to his personal popularity. In the last such instance, in June 1979, as he was preparing to go to Tehran to greet Khomeini he was detained and held under house arrest until his removal to Baghdad in April 1980. Najaf lore has it that Sadr only escaped this fate at the time of his original detention in June thanks to his sister's rallying of the crowds with cry of 'Your Imam is being kidnapped'. But when further troubles occurred in early April, the government secured the silence of his sister by removing her from Najaf together with her brother.

His sister, Amina Sadr bint al-Huda, was also imprisoned, tortured and executed. It has been alleged that Sadr was killed by having an iron nail hammered into his head[11] and then being set on fire. In the March 1991 Iraqi *Intifada* (uprising), some eleven years later, pictures of Sadr were paraded in the cities of southern Iraq until the revolt was brutally quelled by Saddam Hussein.

Some years later, during the execution of Saddam Hussein, chants of 'Long live Mohammad Baqir Sadr!' were heard from some of the Shi'i guards.[12]

The execution and martyrdom of Baqir Sadr in 1980 by Saddam Hussein effectively ostensibly returned the seminaries of Najaf to their former apolitical and quietist stance; but the intellectual renaissance in Najaf and the manner of its ending – Baqir's execution – effectively diffused the Shi'i awakening to key areas of the Middle East and further afield – to Iran, Lebanon, Kuwait, Pakistan, India and Sudan during the following decade. A glance at the most prominent figures of the Islamic movement in the late 1970s and 1980s will show that, without exception, they had studied in, resided in or visited Najaf.

The cultural and political renaissance in Najaf and the shaping of what was to become political Shi'ism had one further element – and the town housed one further resident – without which Shi'i Islamism might not have acquired its universal character in the challenge that it presents to the West today.

In 1964, Ruhollah Khomeini arrived in exile in Najaf. Initially he retained a low profile and did not openly side with the nexus members. From 1964, and until the death of his main protector, Ayatollah Muhsin al-Hakim in 1970, Khomeini enjoyed some immunity, but from 1968 with the accession of the Ba'ath to power and their conflict with Najaf, Khomeini was obliged to be extremely circumspect with respect to Iraqi politics. Nevertheless, in 1970 he shocked his fellow scholars when he delivered in Najaf his celebrated lectures on *wilayat al-fiqih* (rule by a supreme jurist) and on Islamic government.

Khomeini's somewhat imprecise and rhetorical definition of *wilayat al-fiqih*, however, lacked the outlines of a constitution to complete the picture – the component that was so urgently needed from 1978 by the revolutionaries in Iran. It was Baqir Sadr, writing a few weeks before Khomeini returned to Iran to lead the revolution, who therefore foreshadowed the key elements of the Iranian Constitution of 1979. A few months later Baqir al-Sadr was dead; and all history relating to his life that the regime in

Baghdad could reach, was erased; but his death, like that of Sayyid Qutb, energised Islamists throughout the Middle East.

Changing the Meaning of Language

The Najaf renaissance, as Chibli Mallat has noted,[13] was an intellectual phenomenon involving primarily jurists and its literary output essentially was legalistic texts. It might have been highly significant in Shi'i clerical circles, but it was elitist and inaccessible to the public. If the ideology was to reach out beyond its small circle of adherents, the public needed to be mobilised. The formulation of this ideology of mobilisation represented Ali Shariati's particular genius and contribution to the Iranian Revolution.

Shariati was convinced that Islam constituted the most effective medium of communication with his Iranian compatriots. But the central intellectual issue which he had to settle for himself was whether Islam was a truly revolutionary ideology smothered and obscured throughout the centuries by conservative clerics and the self-interest of the authorities; or whether it was primarily a belief system, the social and economic aspects of which were negligible and at best outmoded.[14]

During his time in Paris in the 1960s Shariati read voraciously from all the contemporary western schools of thought, and he began to come to the paradoxical conclusion that Islam could be rediscovered through the ideas of western intellectuals whose radical and progressive message was ostensibly anti-Islamic, but was, in fact, no more than the mirror image of the original Islam – the authentic Islam – before it had become smothered and clouded over the ages.

Shariati concluded from his reading not that Islam was outmoded – but that Shi'i Islam already possessed the quintessence of all western progressive schools of thought: 'All that Pascal, Marx and Sartre contributed in Europe could be found in Shi'ism under the name of Ali.'[15] It was Sartre who later returned the compliment when he said of religion that were he to choose one, it would be that of Shariati.

Shariati began a research project in France with Abolhassan Bani-Sadr in 1963 to determine, by recourse to original sources, whether Islam as practised by the clergy was the authentic Islam, or whether its liberating and progressive message had been obscured by them as Shariati suspected. If this proved to be the case, they agreed to attempt to revive the authentic Islamist ideology.[16]

If Shi'i Islam was shown to be an earlier version of liberating and progressive western thought embedded into a different paradigm, Shi'ism had a further advantage the pair believed: Shariati argued that the leftists always talked about the people and the masses, but were they to go the villages of the poor and try to rally the people to revolution in the name of Marx, they would be laughed out of town. But, Shariati argued, call on them to unite and to avenge the murder of Hussein, the Prophet's grandson, and they would rise up immediately.

The conclusion to Shariati and Bani-Sadr's joint research was that the Islam of the clergy was incompatible with the authentic, revolutionary and progressive Islam. Shariati proceeded to research and formulate the ideology and Bani-Sadr went on to become the first president of post-revolutionary Iran.

Among his western intellectual mentors, Shariati was most excited by the writing of Frantz Fanon, whose *The Wretched of the Earth* so touched him and his friends that that they translated it from French into Persian. It was from Shariati and his friends' translation of the title of this book as *Mostazafin-e-Zamin* that Khomeini borrowed his rallying cry in support of the oppressed and dispossessed.[17]

From Fanon, with whom Shariati was in direct correspondence over the role of Islam, he was reinforced in his belief that the colonised or semi-colonised Third World person had to return to himself, search for the appropriate cultural elements and then create 'a new man' based on a 'new idea' and 'a new history'. From Sartre, he drew inspiration from existentialism about the concept of individual freedom of choice and of the individual's right to rebel.[18]

Jacques Berque showed Shariati how to observe the world through a sociological perspective; Berque also taught him how the real meaning of words could be changed in order to transform redundant and passive concepts into energising instruments of change. This was a key idea. It was this idea that was borrowed, and used by Khomeini, Musa al-Sadr and Fadlallah; and it this idea that is so well understood by Sayyed Hassan Nasrallah and Hesballah.

Berque suggested that although words had a unique and eternal meaning, their intent could be transformed over time by framing their context in a different way: 'Words could thus be transformed from passive means for idle chatter and tools of stupefaction into instruments for socio-political change.'[19] Shariati took each commonly used term in the vocabulary of every Muslim and reinterpreted it. Words and concepts resonating with resignation, fatalism and self-pity were transformed into forceful and dynamic concepts for action.

Shariati is usually brushed aside in western commentaries as an activist who used the secular Marxist concept of class struggle and Marxist language in order to mobilise the youth of Tehran. This Eurocentric optic implies, condescendingly, that Shariati was forced to prop up the weak appeal of Islam by inappropriately borrowing secular western Marxist language.

In fact Shariati was engaged in a strategic project to re-position Shi'i Islam as a revolutionary movement; but this had to be done surreptitiously, under the noses of a hostile conservative clergy who were antagonistic to his ideas – even as they tried to draw comfort from his success in repulsing Marxist inroads among young Iranians.

Shariati had no standing to challenge Shi'i theology – he was no jurist. He was forced therefore to walk the tightrope between a hostile clergy on the one hand, and a suspicious SAVAK, the Shah's secret police, on the other hand, who wondered whether Shariati really was challenging the Marxists; or whether he was intent on fomenting revolution. The SAVAK vacillated uneasily between these two conclusions.

Shariati could not challenge the clerical establishment of Iran directly and therefore reinterpreted words to give Islam's intent a strategic shift to become an instrument of mobilisation and change instead of being what Musa al-Sadr later described as the 'ritual' concocted by the 'deviant' men of religion who had turned Islam from 'movement, vitality and work ... into what it is today. It now stands for lethargy and abdication.'[20]

In attempting to create an ideology of social justice and revolution Shariati was not engaged in what might be described in the West as some 'make-over' of Shi'i Islam. The origins and ethos of Shi'i Islam were exactly those of radical activism, fighting against tyranny and a struggle for social justice.

The Revolutionary Legacy of Shi'ism

Shi'ism is by virtue of its history a more revolutionary sect than Sunni Islam. Shi'ism and Sunnism not only understand Islamic history, theology and law differently, but each possesses a distinct ethos that nurtures a particular approach to what it means to be a Muslim. This difference in temperament and philosophy derives directly from the succession crisis that followed the Prophet's death in CE 632.

Most of the Prophet Mohammad's small community of followers in the aftermath of his death – for which there was no prepared response – fell back to the default option of tribal tradition, according to which a council of elders would choose the most senior and respected elder to lead the community or tribe.

This group were the forebears of the Sunni (followers of tradition). Some of his followers found justification in the Prophet's saying that 'my community will never agree in error'. This group were not seeking any special qualities beyond seniority and respect – a 'safe pair of hands' to lead the community ably and virtuously.

Another group, a minority who would become the forebears of the Shi'i, believed that the successor to the Prophet (the meaning of Caliph) had to embody special qualities that go beyond tribal convention and consensus. They argued that humans needed more than a 'safe pair of hands' to continue to lead them; they needed the divinely imparted and innate qualities of leadership, without which the true meaning and intent of Islam could be obscured

– and that this was more likely to derive from the bloodline of the Prophet than emerge from election by consensus. This group favoured Ali, the son-in-law and cousin of the Prophet. The name Shi'a means 'partisans of Ali'.

In the end, consensus prevailed, and Ali was passed over in the elections to lead the community. Indeed Ali was passed over three times until finally elected in CE 656. In the interim, until Ali finally succeeded, the period was far from tranquil. The second Caliph was murdered by a prisoner of war; but, more notably, Ali's immediate predecessor, the third Caliph, was murdered by mutinous Muslim soldiers.

The community was shocked. Ali finally succeeded to the Caliphate; but his tenure was plagued by the consequences of his predecessor's murder. Mutinies proliferated and Ali was pressed severely by the family of his murdered predecessor to avenge this assassination. The tribal demand for justice eventually erupted into a power struggle between the new Caliph and the Governor of Damascus who led the tribe of his murdered predecessor.

A civil war ensued between Ali and the Governor of Damascus which only ended when Ali was assassinated by angry extremists who blamed both him and the Governor for the crisis.

Unlike Ali, the Governor survived the extremists' wrath and managed to seize the Caliphate. Sunnis agreed to acquiesce to this improper – there was no election or any direct blood link with the Prophet – seizure of the Caliphate by a Governor who lacked any religious legitimacy. This was the beginning of the very worldly Umayyad dynasty – kings and conquerors, rather than keepers of the Prophet's revelations – to which Qutb had drawn adverse attention.

This episode was momentous. By accommodating the hereditary Umayyad dynasty, the Sunnis made their historic compromise with power – a compact rejected and shunned by the Shi'i. Sunni Islam embraced what was to become their traditional pragmatic stance and ethos of accepting a worldly ruler – providing only that he maintained order, protected the Islamic territories and left theology to the scholars.

The Shi'i after Ali's death refused this tawdry compromise with pragmatism and refused the authority of the Caliphs. The Shi'i argued that the special qualities of leadership needed for Islam would not emerge from some communal effort at consensus compromise. The Prophet's leadership had been metaphysical and of a different order to that of some banal tribal elder. As his leadership possessed elements of the divine and of the metaphysical; it could persist only in the bloodline of his family – through Hussein, Ali's son and Mohammad's grandson by his daughter Fatima, the Shi'i believed.

When the Governor's son, Yazid, had Hussein, the direct descendant of the Prophet, and his companions massacred at Kerbala in CE 680, this crystallised Hussein as the epitome of martyrdom – and as a manifest victim of an outrageous abuse of power against all Shi'i. This murder was all the more obnoxious to the Shi'i for having been committed by a man who had succeeded to the Caliphate by virtue of hereditary succession rather than from any spiritual qualities or election: Yazid was the son of the man who had hounded Ali, whom the Shi'i viewed as the true successor to the Prophet, and had seized his title.

Hussein's refusal to acknowledge and accept Yazid's illegitimate power, his refusal to accept the hopelessness of his rebellion against military imposition – his tiny band were massively outnumbered – and yet still to persist with it, and his refusal to tolerate this injustice – all this cast Shi'ism in the mould of a moral and religious resistance against abusive power and oppression, and elevated the concept of 'true' Islamic leadership being the just and legitimate 'other' in counterpoint to the shabbiness of worldly pragmatic political power.

A leader of Hesballah and a learned Shi'i said to the author in this context that he believed that had Hussein not been murdered at Kerbala, the history of Islam would have emerged very differently: he believed that the bloody conquests and the imperial expansion of Islam would never have occurred under Shi'i leadership.

The Sunnis, having made their historic compromise with kings and with worldly power, assumed the character of a natural majority and with it a lasting sense of their right to rule.

Sunnis customarily have placed more emphasis on the personal performance of outward aspects of Islam and a pragmatic approach to the world.

The Shi'a by contrast – frequently a persecuted minority – have leaned to the study of philosophy and a search for the inner metaphysical meaning of the Qur'an rather than to literal inter-pretation; they have held that the Prophet's message was about principles, not pragmatism, and represented a clarion call to all men and women to struggle against social injustice and tyranny of all types.

Social Mobilisation and an Ideology of Balance

This radical legacy of activism represented for Shariati the authentic Shi'i Islam that he sought to revitalise – to brush away the dust and the accumulation of over-painting accreted over the years. He aimed to re-order the original components of the Shi'i Islamic tradition in harmony with other parts of the Persian philosophical and Sufi legacies. The object was to forge an ideology of balance that could answer people's daily welfare and social needs in equilibrium with their ethical, philosophical, aesthetic and metaphysical requirements – and one which could mobilise a society.

It was not just new vocabulary – an Islamic 'new speak'. He believed that the ideology had also to be relevant to modern living. In short, he argued that healthy and harmonious modern societies had to be concerned as much with material well-being as with wider social and metaphysical needs. This he had learned from the Marxists and socialists: an ideology of Islam had to provide for the material well-being and social needs of people as well as offering a compassionate compass in life.

Shi'i Islam had slipped, in the years since the killing of Hussein, into a defensive mentality of victimhood. It was not an outlook that lacked just cause, however: the Shi'i had been history's persecuted minority too often. But being history's victims had also induced passivity and an attitude of enduring resignation – awaiting alleviation from being a marginalised and dispossessed minority only with the eventual coming of the Redeemer, the Mahdi.

The object of ideologising Islam, Shariati asserted, was to raise the consciousness of the people in order to 'enter into action'; to grab the collar and shake it into a liberation movement and to give birth to an energised and determined entity. What made Islam appealing to those who embraced it was not just the Qur'an and the concept of resurrection, he argued, but its deep commitment to social justice and to revolutionary leadership. Shariati sought to exorcise the prevalent monarcho-clerical Islam by effecting a social revolution that would unleash a miraculous 'spurt of energy'.

He argued that a conscious and alert individual was the building block of mobilisation. The individual needed to be strengthened by emphasising the primacy of willpower and volition as the motor of social revolution; and by adopting the virtues of selflessness and of scientific and rational reasoning. The ideal human being is armed with ideology, a sense of justice and with 'iron' representing military might. Without weapons, Shariati declared, consciousness and faith alone were incapable of attaining an ideal society.

Leadership, in his perspective, was to be both revolutionary and democratic; and in emphasising its temporal and socio-political aspects he identified it as egalitarian. 'Yesterday has to be understood as belonging to the past, while today has to be understood with a modern perception.'[21]

The substance of Shariati's 'Islamology' bore little resemblance to the prevailing clerical, middle class Shi'ism of the more conservative clerics; but the youth loved it and flocked to his lectures in their thousands – spilling into the neighbouring streets and bringing a part of Tehran to paralysis.

His popularity and his increasingly radical interpretations of Islam brought on him the wrath of the conservative Shi'i seminaries. They sought to have his books banned, but when they approached Ayatollah Ruhollah Khomeini to add his support, the latter surprised his fellow clerics by saying that, having read them, he found nothing to contradict Islam in them. They retreated, silenced.

Khomeini never openly endorsed Shariati, although he borrowed many of his slogans and formulations; but his unstated support was there; so too was the almost unanimous but quiet endorsement of the Imam's circle.

Shariati was not unique in some of his ideas; in a more legalistic medium the Najaf nexus had already prepared the ground, and Shi'i scholars are quick to confine the credit owed to Shariati to the field of mobilisation – pointing out that it was due to Khomeini and others such as Shariati's colleague Morteza Motahhari that the institutions of an Islamic state were formed.

It was Imam Khomeini however who established the concept of Islamist revolution as a basically non-violent popular upheaval based on mass mobilisation and popular legitimacy. And it was a friend of Shariati, Musa al-Sadr, the cousin of Mohammad Baqir Sadr, who took these ideas of political mobilisation and awakening to Lebanon, and who, with the former Najaf nexus member, Sayyed Fadlallah, shaped the future Hesballah movement.

Transcending Political Revolution

Imam Khomeini did not follow Shariati in looking to western thought as a catalyst for evolving his ideas on revolution and its leadership, despite his close acquaintance with Shariati's writings. He followed Baqir Sadr in drawing on the Qur'an directly as the underpinning to his ideas; but he was also deeply influenced by the ideas of Mulla Sadra (1571–1640) and also by Ibn al-Arabi (1160–1240).

Contrasting with the austere and authoritarian image of Khomeini in the West, these key sources of influence reflect a side to the Imam little known in the West. Christian Bonaud has highlighted how, in the immediate aftermath of the revolution, Khomeini chose to deliver an address on the Qur'an that had substantial recourse to gnosis or transcendent wisdom. The idea that a leader who has just successfully mobilised a people, mounted a revolution and overthrown the Shah should, in its immediate aftermath, decide to give lectures on self-purification and the path of the soul, was, as Bonaud notes, quite a revelation for him.[22]

The reference to Mulla Sadra was no chance event: Khomeini was profoundly influenced by his ideas. Sadra was a thinker whose writings have had a major influence over Persian philosophy for the last 300 years. Khomeini's analysis of Sadra's *The Fourfold Journey*,[23] however, was not presented as an obtuse academic speculation, but was intended to highlight Sadra's ideas as directly relevant to the revolution and to Khomeini's leadership of it.

Sadra had founded a school of transcendent wisdom in Isfahan which articulated the unity of three tools of analysis and thinking. The first was the methodology of purely theoretical, discursive and analytical thinking; the second was intuitively or metaphysically derived knowledge; and the third was revealed knowledge in the form of the Qur'anic teachings. It was, in short, an integration of three distinct categories of thinking.

Sadra brought a new philosophical insight in dealing with the nature of reality through an existentialist approach that preceded Jean-Paul Sartre by several centuries. This unity of creation which he deduced was especially crucial to the Islamic perspective of the purpose of existence, and it coordinated philosophic reasoning, as inherited from the Greeks, with the teachings of Islam. It offered, Khomeini was suggesting, an answer to the prevailing western 'modernist' current that was unable to see beyond the narrow limits of empirical 'scientific' methodology.

Mulla Sadra's concept of 'substantial motion' was also highly relevant to the revolution. Basing his argument on the premise that all of existence undergoes continuous transformation and change, Sadra maintained that political reform was inseparable from spirituality. Existence was dynamic and not static: politics and spirituality both had to embrace change too. Sadra firmly held that truth could not be imposed: he was therefore sharply critical of the intolerance of Islamic clerics whom he accused of perverting spirituality. Khomeini shared this conclusion, frequently clashing with his austere colleagues for their tendency, as he saw it, to stay in the Middle Ages.

In the *Fourfold Journey*, to which Khomeini provided a fully elaborated commentary, he described the mystical training that a leader must undergo before he could start to transform the banal world. He must undertake the necessary disciplines: a leader should divest himself of ego. Pride and attachment should be broken, and he should open himself to esoteric intuition.

It was a training that could bring a leader a similar kind of spiritual insight or revelation to that of the Imams. It was this type of leadership which made Islam the dynamic and changing entity that had mobilised and transformed the world in the seventh and later centuries. In his final address to the Iranian people, in 1989, he begged them to continue the study of the field of knowledge known as *'irfan'* (theoretical gnosis) since there could be no truly Islamic Revolution unless there was also a spiritual reformation.[24]

In the light of Khomeini's commentaries it is clear that his conception of Islamic leadership is far removed from the western stereotype that presents his *wilayat al-fiqih* concept (the leadership of a jurist) as a legalistic and backward-looking constraint on change and popular aspirations.

It is clear that his concept of leadership, derived from Sadra, was the opposite: it was dynamic, reformist and forward-looking. The reality which many in the West find difficult to accept is that Khomeini was a charismatic and highly complex character who valued and understood the importance of popular participation: he echoed Mohammad Baqir Sadr's justification of popular elections: 'the affairs of the country must be administered on the basis of public opinion expressed by means of election'.[25] Indeed, according to his son, Ahmad, 'what made him [his father] the "Imam" and led to the historic and victorious Islamic movement was the fact that he fought the backward, stupid, pretentious, reactionary clergy'.[26] Perhaps it is because Khomeini's ideas on the nature of leadership are so removed from western concepts of a political leader that they have proved so difficult to comprehend.

In Khomeini's concept, mass popular mobilisation and uprising would require strong, active, and intuitively imaginative revolutionary leadership. Such leadership and guidance was necessary to transform an entrenched mass mindset. This is a legacy that can be observed in Hesballah today. Sayyed Hassan Nasrallah's addresses to the people are notable for their lack of ego, pretension or dogmatism. These concepts have taken Islamism far from the initial ideas that surfaced in Egypt after the last European War, of an Islamist revolution to be achieved by a small clandestine armed vanguard.

Revolution and the Closing of the Intellectual Divide

It is not our purpose here to offer an analysis of why events in Iran subsequently took the course they did. That is a complex matter, and one for historians. Our purpose here has been to outline the broad sweep of thinking from the first stage of the revolution that seems likely to impact on Iranian approaches to the subsequent stages of their revolution, and on Islamism more generally. The important social aspects of popular mass mobilisation are dealt with more fully in the Chapter 4.

Whatever might be the assessment of the Iranian Revolution in the West, its significance has been clear to Islamists, according to Ayatollah Fadlallah, an original participant in the Najaf 'nexus', and an Islamist who enjoys personal authority and legitimacy in Lebanon, Iraq and Pakistan. Its overriding significance in Fadlallah's eyes lay in the dispelling of 'the popular perception of indigenous inferiority in relation to western superiority' and in its bringing about 'the deliverance of the human will from a state of submission to iniquitous, aggressive, or infidel power; and the transformation of that liberated willpower into a practical, positive programme dictated by a comprehensive reading of the Islamic Shari'ah, in its economic, political and social dimensions'.[27]

It was in this transformation that Michel Foucault, walking the streets of Tehran in the early stages of the revolution, sought answers to the question the experts of Europe were endlessly repeating: 'We know what they don't want, but we still do not know what they want.'[28]

Foucault asked all strata of society this same question: 'What do you want?' 'During my entire stay in Iran, I did not hear, even once, the word "revolution", but four out of five times, someone would answer: an Islamic government.'

Foucault concluded that this 'ideal' expressed through the wish for Islamic government was not to be seen as a demand for the creation of a narrow, theocratic state. Foucault argues that escape from clerical legalism and the structures of passivity is precisely that for which 'Shariati who addressed a public that was his, and that could be counted in the thousands; and who died like a Martyr, hunted, and with his books banned' had given his life. Indeed, Shariati saw his work as an attempt to reconcile freedom of action with binding Islamic precepts.

For Iranians in the throes of revolution, Foucault suggested, the phrase 'Islamic government' placed the emphasis on the spiritual existence of the people. By returning to a spiritual existence, he implied, 'Iranians could not only change the political order in Iran, they could change themselves, their way of being, their relationship with others, with things, with eternity, with God.'[29]

The liberating experience of a return to that exciting and vital period, at the time of the Prophet, when religious experience took precedent over mere obedience to a code, suggested that Shari'a was not viewed by Iranians as a narrowing, constricting legacy: 'Islamic government held out the promise of breaking with the structures of personal identity, of economy, of society and of politics that constituted for them "the stubbornness of their destiny".'[30] Shi'i Islam held out this possibility of a continuous and active creation of a political order because of its openness to the updating of law by reason; but also, more importantly, from the prospect of radical renewal and fresh revelation via the Imamate.

The Iranian Revolution had given clearer focus to the Islamist vision – ideas that had been translated from Egypt, via Mohammad Baqir Sadr's and Ali Shariati's contributions, to the Iranian revolutionaries. The elements were the primacy of establishing the just, equitable and compassionate community, both as the experience through which humans could 'taste' the divine, and in fulfilment of God's demand that humans behave in this way with each other.

This community should be free to elect its leaders and to manage its affairs, but the project of bringing about a truly just society would also require guardianship and strong, revelatory and dynamic leadership. Social and economic aspects of life were to be free, but remained contingent upon the need to act with justice and respect towards others. It would be a mobilised and cohesive society exemplified by interpersonal responsibilities to one another, in which the link between the giving of a service to others and the expectation of direct return was broken.

Not surprisingly the original trail of ideas originating in Sunni thinking and writing, which had been taken up and tinged with a Shi'i colouring by Baqir Sadr and his 'nexus', had completed the circle, in the wake of the revolution, by returning to influence Sunnis. The essence of the divide in Islam between the 'partisans of Ali', the Shi'i and their Sunni 'followers of tradition' counterparts, historically had centred on the Shi'a assertion that Islam demanded 'justice' and that it was not possible to have a just society without just governance directed by Qur'anic revelation.

But in 1923 the Caliphate had been abolished, and the Sunni community of believers, or Umma, became de-territorialised. It lost its geographic designation, it lost its symbolic head, the Caliph, and it lost its institutions. And the Sunni traditional underlying presumption of the 'right to rule' was emptied of meaning. The Umma became a de-territorialised and structure-less entity. A form of involuntary globalisation was forced upon it by an unsympathetic ruler, Mustafa Kemal, set on destroying the symbol of pan-Muslim identity.

The shock of the demise of the Caliphate undercut Sunni Islam's customary posture of accommodating power. The Caliphate may have been flawed and weak; but it had retained its vestiges of legitimacy. The new secular Westernised rulers had none – in Islamic terms. The space for Sunni pragmatism and accommodation shrank accordingly.

It was Sayyid Qutb who initially took the sledgehammer to that 1400-year Sunni social compact with worldly 'Caesars'. In a decisive and momentous rupture with the past, Qutb effectively defined that pragmatic historic compromise with power as 'jahiliyya' – ignorance – and called for God's rule to be re-established in Muslim societies, rather than rule by some worldly westernised 'Caesar'.

His message broke the mould of Sunni 'quietism'. He argued for the need to confront – not just jahiliyya but injustice, corrupt rulers and the secular modernising mindset. It was not enough simply to preach and to be passive. It required a more assertive 'revolutionary' striving by Muslims to shape an Islamist vision. The threat from secular modernist thinking threatened Islam. Almost all Islamists now would agree with Qutb on this.

However, this key shift in direction by Sunni Islamists – an identity formulated around resisting western hegemony and framed in terms of the fight for social justice – inevitably has taken Sunnis several ideological steps closer to the modern Shi'a vision of Islam.

Both the Sunnah and Shi'i now have common ground – whatever their historical differences – in two highly significant areas: the refusal to continue to accommodate and to compromise with 'iniquitous, aggressive or infidel power' as Fadlallah termed it; and the requirement for a revolutionary struggle for reform and social justice.

It is not surprising, then, that we have seen Iran and Hesballah at the vanguard of this revolution; and that Sunni Muslim movements, such as Hamas, are seen as being close to Iran and Hesballah, as the two sects – Shi'i and Sunnah – find common ground, despite the many differences and antagonisms that persist.

When Hamas uses a new Muslim identity that is focused on the struggle for just and effective governance and on a set of ethics to underpin social change, Hamas is moving closer to a Shi'i perspective that Islam is a revolutionary movement based on the struggle for justice. This does not imply that Hamas has become Shi'i – as its secular detractors taunt it. It has not; it retains its clear identity as a Sunni Palestinian national movement.

But this drawing closer of intellectual positions between movements such as (Sunni) Hamas with (Shi'i) Hesballah is very significant, despite the overshadowing effect of sectarian conflict generated by the occupation of Iraq. The sectarian rift obscures the way in which the new revolutionary 'activism' of a movement such as Hamas has distanced it from its Muslim Brotherhood roots and moved it intellectually towards Shi'i thinking.

The direction of influence – under the impact of US and European hostility towards Islamist movements – between the principal Sunni movements has reversed. It is now more likely that Hamas will be the future model for the Muslim Brotherhood than the Brotherhood being a model and source of influence for Hamas, although the foundations of Brotherhood thinking remain the touchstone of legitimacy for the large majority of Sunni Islamists.

For the Shi'i, their revolution in 1979 in Iran represented a definitive rupture from the earlier Shi'a posture of victimhood and a 'quietist' disengagement from active political life as they awaited the eventual return of the Mahdi to set matters straight. And for the Sunnis, the new 'activist' Islamism also represents something of a change in direction, from the apologetic defence of Islam of nineteenth-century modernists such as Jamal al-din al-Afghani (1838–97), who were prodding Islam along, reading into scripture new needs and changes, and smuggling change into an old tradition that had fallen behind the West. The new Islamist purpose, in the words of Musa Sadr, was to remove from Islam the 'dust of ages'.[31]

The Essence of Political Shi'ism

This is the essence of 'political Shi'ism'. It does not represent a formal process; it is not about conversion from one sect to another; and it is not a process linked directly to the Iranian government or managed or directed by it.

Political Shi'ism, loosely, is the concept of mobilisation and of activist revolutionary ideology mooted by Sayyid Qutb; taken up and adapted by the Najaf nexus; translated into popular mobilisation by Shariati; and taken to a revolutionary conclusion by Khomeini. It has then evolved under the direction of Sayyed Hassan Nasrallah into a more incrementalist form of mobilisation that respects the limits of the capacity for popular mobilisation.

Hamas has evolved from this activist impulse its own programme of mobilisation, using symbols and icons that resonate with its Sunni constituency. Hamas ideology has its own distinctive character reflecting its Muslim Brotherhood roots, but its social vision is probably more adventurous and experimental than that of other Islamist movements – reflecting the diverse nature of the Palestinian electorate.

The ideas are still evolving in response to both events and the bad experience suffered by Islamist movements in attempting to achieve reform through the electoral process. The electoral experience of Hamas in Palestine, and the continuing repression of the Brotherhood in Egypt and Jordan and elsewhere have had their impact.

With their constituencies increasingly questioning the value of pursuing the electoral route, moderate Islamist movements may have difficulty in managing the radicalisation of their constituencies. Much will depend on the intellectual response of Iranian thinkers and the leaderships of Hamas and Hesballah. It is likely, however, that we shall not see any return to militarised vanguardism divorced from popular legitimacy, but rather an evolution of the ideology of mass popular mobilisation.

For those living in the West who are concerned at the enervated and flagging response to concerns about injustice and social fragmentation in their own societies, the experience of Islamists in finding their energy to respond in the ideas of Sartre, Berque and above all Fanon, opens the question whether the circle may complete itself with western activists, in turn, finding in some Islamist ideas the energy to revitalise their own activism.

4

SOCIAL REVOLUTION

Thomas Macaulay in his celebrated History of England describes the two key forces at work propelling history to move in the right direction for building a better world. The implicit corollary to Macaulay's analysis was that it is both our duty and our interest to cooperate with this thrust of history. He begins with:

> ... how, from the auspicious union of order and prosperity of which the annals of human affairs had furnished no [equivalent] example ... [in which] a gigantic commerce gave birth to a maritime power compared with which, every other maritime power, ancient or modern, sinks into insignificance.[1]

Macaulay's narrative is cheerful. It tells of a better world – intellectually, socially and economically – emerging naturally out of the disparate elements of past struggles. It was, Macaulay suggested, a tale of general improvement in all areas of life that 'unless I greatly deceive myself, will ... excite thankfulness in all religious minds, and hope in the breasts of patriots'.[2]

This narrative of optimism had, and still retains, one striking component: that this general improvement, this emergence of a new force for good, had come about not by human design but through the inscrutable and gradual working of Providence. This Protestant and secular-modern narrative of history has been, for the last 200 years, essentially 'a forensic study of the fingerprints of the 'invisible hand', and, just as the invisible hand retains an extraordinary power in Anglophone culture, so to many English-speakers the narrative still seems the obvious and unquestioned form that history should take.[3]

The incorporation of the principle of the working of the invisible hand into a general principle of history reflects, in religious and secular alike, their belief that order arises spontaneously from the unrestricted free play of natural and seemingly inchoate forces. The adoption of this conviction that the world is built in such a way that free play creates an ordered and higher form of society is found in all spheres of western thought, and is a way of restating some of the most powerful spiritual convictions of the puritan Protestant ethic.[4]

This one idea armed the rebels led by Cromwell in fighting the monarchy in England. It underpinned the Protestant struggle against the religious community of Roman Catholicism. It underpinned ideas of democracy; it lies at the root of the western concept of human and women's rights; and it still today is the buttress on which western hostility towards Islam rests.

It is a theory of history that sees the slow and gradual march of progress in a free society as the dominant force shaping English and American societies. In this view the same forces and potentials were latent in all societies – if only the dusty cobwebs of illiberalism and restraint could be removed.

Cromwell and his puritan followers in the seventeenth century did not see themselves as modernisers taking up a new revolutionary theory of history. They were not against tradition, rather they saw themselves as defending it. Their ideas had been assembled from an imagined past era of Anglo-Saxon history. But their rearward-looking rummage through the traces of seventh- and eighth-century history in Roman history books did provide them with a new narrative and identity. It was a recasting of the cultural and historical components of the past that was also to furnish the world with a utopian worldview for the future.

The new narrative represented a vision that was rooted in an imagined golden past, in which free yeomen (independent farmers) of England had fought for and achieved those institutions and laws that had arisen in the seventh and eighth centuries out of the turbulent jostling and clashing of the Germanic tribes – the forefathers of Anglo-Saxonism.

It was from this rough-and-tumble tribal clash that the institutions, customs and law of Anglo-Saxon society emerged. This had not occurred out of any deliberate design but had come about spontaneously, as if by the unseen working of the hand of Providence. It was this legacy, Cromwell believed, that made the Anglo-Saxons a free people with the spirit to fight and reject the feudalism imported with the Norman conquest. And it was this story of Anglo-Saxon 'traditions' of freedom that Cromwell recalled when he challenged the divine right of kings in England and mounted his rebellion against King Charles' 'modern' import of authoritarianism and absolutism.

These ideas were not confined to Englishmen. The imagined era of Saxon freedom and happiness as a natural order brought about by the invisible hand of Providence was of particular interest to Thomas Jefferson in America too. He was a life-long proponent of Anglo-Saxon studies, and from this he came to believe that the laws of the Anglo-Saxon era were based on natural rights. It was, he surmised, the 'evil' Norman conquest of England that had introduced kings, priests, feudalism and the whole apparatus of corruption and tyranny into this Anglo-Saxon idyll.[5]

According to John Adams, the great seal of the United States as proposed by Thomas Jefferson had two sides: one was

> ... the children of Israel in the wilderness, led by a cloud by day and a pillar of fire by night [towards the land promised to them by God]; and on the other side, Hengist and Horsa, the Saxon chiefs from whom we have the honour to be descended, and whose political principles and form of government we have assumed.[6]

From this imagined past has derived the sustained certainty that there really was a difference between the Anglo-Saxon heritage of free men, with their institutions and culture of 'freedom', and on the other hand the 'tyranny and illiberalism' of, first, the Normans with their kings, feudalism and priests, and then 'illiberal' Catholic Spain and Catholic France with their absolutism, Jacobin terror and Napoleonic megalomania. This view was to evolve into the idea of the 'open' society, with its personal freedom and free markets, versus the 'closed' societies of static religion and illiberalism.

The Protestant world, ever since Cromwell's casting of Catholic Spain as an evil empire, has subsequently labelled all its enemies as illiberal, absolutist or totalitarian and haters of freedom. The fact that England and America both won all conflicts with their illiberal enemies over the last 300 years, and emerged not merely the victors, but went on to become the world's superpowers, reinforced their certainty that Providence intended that men and women should conduct their behaviour according to the Anglo-Saxon model of free men who respected the principle of allowing the invisible hand to bring about, in its own fashion, the best interests of all men.

These sentiments prompted Abbot Lawrence to write in 1850, while serving as American Minister in London, that 'if the Anglo-Saxons of Great Britain and the United States are true to each other and to the cause of human freedom, they might not only give their language but their laws to the world, and defy the power of all despots on the face of the Globe'.[7]

It was not of course by accident that seventeenth-century Cromwellians should have looked back to an idyll of supposed freedom in the seventh century to support their rebellion against King Charles I of England. The impulse to adopt a narrative and new identity from this past era had sprung from another conflict: the religious struggle between Protestantism and Catholicism.

The Ethos of the 'Personal'

The key reference point for the transformation of values that emerged from this inter-Christian conflict was, as we saw earlier in Chapter 1, the reinterpretation of the significance of the story of the patriarch Abraham. As Ali Shariati had attempted to give a new significance and meaning to Imam Hussein's martyrdom as a symbol of supreme personal sacrifice for the principle of justice, so too Martin Luther, some 500 years earlier, had given new significance to the Abrahamic story.

Luther had described Abraham's faithful, initial response to God's call, rather than repentance for sin, as the basis for salvation. Justification by faith alone – the core tenet of Protestantism – was established by this reinterpretation of Abraham's story, Luther and his followers believed.

Abraham's act of faith in preparing to sacrifice his son symbolised the freedom to choose: to make a personal choice. It symbolised the individualistic and personal nature of faith in opposition to the concept of a community bound fast by religion; it symbolised the unconditional embrace of change; and it symbolised obedience to a call to journey, regardless of the social or personal consequences, towards an unknown future, in a new land.

Progress on this individual journey demanded that the faithful obey the call to use the personal talents given to him or her by God. This call gave new dignity and importance to economic tasks. It provided the basis for the synthesis of the Protestant ethos with nascent capitalism and linked it to the unfolding of God's will. To succeed in commerce signalled God's favour and grace.

As the Protestant ethos of work and saving was pursued, people generated the capital and the work habits that made capitalism grow. This created widespread belief that a free market economy represented a new call from God. This was a self-reinforcing circle of belief: as the community prospered, it signalled God's grace more strongly, and in signalling this way, drew more individuals towards capitalism.

The Protestant emphasis on a personal relationship with God, contingent on an act of individual choice and on pursuit of personal enterprise, meshed well with the imagined Anglo-Saxon era of freedom. It was this double meme that was mobilised by the Cromwellians as a grand narrative to justify hostility towards both the English monarch, Charles I, and the illiberal Catholic powers. It also sat well with the interests of a burgeoning class of English capitalist traders and merchants.

The Anglo-Saxon narrative of an order that had been inherent at the outset of their history was supported by the Protestant insight that order and institutions can emerge naturally and more or less spontaneously from change. In holding to this insight Protestants saw themselves as emulating Abraham's act of faith. They were reaching out, as Abraham had done, to a journey towards a more positive promised land. To trust in this instinct reflected the core of Protestantism: willing acquiescence to the changes to which Providence was leading and faith in this invisible process.

The belief in a natural order arising as if by the workings of an invisible hand has dominated the western imagination for many centuries. This faith has not been confined to Protestants or to those who are religious. Empiricism and science in the nineteenth century seemed to confirm that, behind the apparent disorder of the universe, rational order could be observed to be inherent in the nature of the physical universe, rather than the hand of Providence. Positivist philosophy, which denies any validity to deductive thinking or metaphysics, provided the bridge for an empirically deduced, but otherwise similar, confidence in natural order and progress to cross into secularism.

The task of leaders and law-makers in this vision, therefore, was to uncover this order that was already there by freeing it from restraint and, pointedly, the role of the political was not to impose any grand design on an unformed and chaotic society. Laws and institutions either evolved or were elucidated and discovered by careful scientific study – they were emphatically not shaped by grand and sweeping abstractions.[8]

The 'Invisible Hand'

Where science led, economics followed. Adam Smith, in his *Wealth of Nations*, published in 1776, posited the workings of the invisible hand again as the basis of economic theory. It was the same hand that brought order and fulfilled the best interests of humanity. It did this from out of the uncoordinated and self-interested actions of a multitude of buyers and sellers – by matching one to the other by the mechanism of the free market.

This idea became the inspiration behind the 'Great Transformation' in England. It elevated the free market to become the organisational principle of society, to which nation-state, politics, community structures and institutions were to be subordinated. It was the belief that the action of educated individual human beings, controlled only by their sense of personal welfare, would, when their unforced personal choices combined together, produce an orderly and harmonious society. It was this utopian vision that, from the nineteenth century onwards, was to be exported and imposed on Muslim societies.

The concept of the free market as the genesis of 'natural order' may be one of the most durable and deeply held doctrines in the history of man; but it is also a myth. It is a myth around which western political life has been shaped; but it is a myth nonetheless.

To be fair to Smith and the classical economists, they did believe in progress by stages of development, rather than Milton Friedman's later theories of shock and disorientation leading to a single destination – a commercial civilisation based on free market exchange. But they also had a clear idea of the flaws of market economics. Smith did at times refer to the market, or the 'system of natural liberty' as he often calls it, as being a utopia; but by that Smith meant that it was probably the best system available, not that it was without serious flaws. While he was impressed by the efficiency of markets, he feared their moral hazards.[9]

For example, workers would no longer require a good education to fulfil the simple repetitive tasks that industrial production required of them; Smith also foresaw the prospect of anonymous urban misery belts springing up around the factories, which would not encourage virtue. In the long run he felt this posed a risk to commercial civilisation itself. More modern economists have returned to the free market idea in an absolutist form, but despite it being advanced as deriving from scientific enquiry, it remains a doctrine rooted in religious faith.

It was always conceived of as God working through human sentiment – and reason played little if any role in this process. The market did not emerge because humans understood its advantages. It developed as a by-product of instincts that God had implanted in them. In the 1840s Richard Cobden waged a successful campaign against protectionist Corn Laws in Britain with the slogan 'Free Trade is the International Law of God'.[10]

This might have sounded good; but it was simply not true. The free market is an artefact of state power. If Adam Smith had shown that human welfare was optimised through the working of the free market, then it followed that markets had to be made as free as possible. To this end, nineteenth-century England saw the deliberate destruction of socially rooted markets that had existed for centuries, and the freeing of those markets from political and social restraint. The aim was to remove markets from the remotest possibility of political restraint.

Free markets came about in England through a conjunction of favourable historical circumstances: the recovery of the Anglo-Saxon narrative of freedom and Protestant individualism combined with the unchecked power of a Parliament in which most English people were unrepresented.

But the free market lasted in England for barely a generation. From the 1870s onwards it was gradually legislated out of existence. By the time of the First European War, however, the free market had virtually ceased to exist in its most extreme form. It had run aground on the rock of the enduring human need for economic security: free markets simply did not meet human needs – including the need for personal freedom. The free market was regarded as a doctrinaire excess or else an anachronism until it was revived by the New Right in the 1980s.[11]

The use of state power to engineer free markets and to break social continuities in order to promote labour mobility was no expression of 'individual unforced personal choices combining together to bring a harmonious society'. The invisible hand had proved to be a myth, and free markets were uncovered as the enemy of democracy, as a few modern politicians implicitly acknowledge in their explicit admission that curbs on democracy may be necessary for further liberalisation.

The damage done by the free market to other social institutions and to human well-being triggered political counter-movements in England and across Europe that caused it to be radically changed. The normal consequence of free market engineering was not stable democratic government, as claimed by its advocates, it was the politics of volatile insecurity. A spate of legislation, provoked by different aspects of the free market in action, re-regulated it, so that its impact on other social institutions and on human needs was tempered. 'It is not', as Professor John Gray notes, 'a vehicle of modernisation. It belongs to John Locke's world not ours.'[12]

John Gray goes further: in *Black Mass* he suggests that when the West lectures Muslims on the need to reform and modernise – to adopt the free market and the 'strong' centralised state necessary to bring it about – it seems that one aspect of it has been erased from the narrative. Seemingly westerners are so taken with this central meme that they overlook the fact that 'whenever an attempt has been made to impose a western model of development on non-western countries it has involved mass terror'.[13] Free market advocates have exhibited an unbelievable and criminal lack of sympathy for the casualties of their human experiments. This may seem to readers unduly harsh; but if the experience of Turkey and Iran is recalled, it is perhaps a just description.

Legacy of a Myth

In terms of Muslim societies the myth of the invisible hand has brought not just social dislocation and instability on a huge scale, it has, as we saw earlier in Turkey, brought about terror, massacres, ethnic cleansing and suffering. Pursuit of this myth also resulted in a campaign across the Middle East of enforced secularisation and repression of Islam in the name of nation-state building – itself a secular extrapolation of the idea of the invisible hand. Writing more than 200 years ago, Johann Herder attacked the consequences of European colonialism and trade around the world. 'Do not these lands more or less cry for revenge?', he asked, adding that we 'blasphemously pretend that through these acts of injury to the world is fulfilled the purpose of Providence'.[14]

John Gray concludes that while 'twentieth-century Europe was itself a site of unprecedented state murder; terror has been an integral part of the modern west'[15] – to which the ethnic cleansing and massacres that accompanied the emergence of the 'strong' nation-state in Europe bear testimony. It is hard not to see the religiously inspired utopianism of the nineteenth and twentieth centuries as primarily responsible for the complete erasure of any sense of remorse or sympathy with regard to the bloody consequences of this policy.

This history and its results represent the reality of western 'modernity' for Muslims. One of the consequences of the failure to grasp how the events of the last 200 years have looked to Muslims – and the degree to which they have perceived their tragedy in a way that is radically different from the western instinctive blocking out of this aspect – is a profound misunderstanding of the purpose and intent of their economic approach.

Islamists are effectively assembling their own Islamic narrative as a distinct and alternative antithesis to the meta-narrative of the invisible hand. As the Cromwellians assembled the cultural components of freedom from a distant era, so Islamists have assembled the cultural components of their vision from the Qur'an and the principles it reflects that, as the Qur'an insists, are no more than a simple 'reminder' of truths everybody knows.[16]

Islamist economics is not an attempt to compete with the western system in terms of offering more and faster growth; its purpose is, as the Qur'an demands, to return human beings back to some of these 'old truths' of which they have lost sight. The first of these truths, known to all, is that the invisible hand is a myth. There is no God-given nature implanted in human beings, whereby, controlled only by pursuit of their own personal welfare, their unforced personal choices would combine together to produce an orderly and harmonious society.

Islam begins with a very different view of the human 'essence' – which was the starting point of this book. In Islam, the human being is characterised by innate tendencies towards avariciousness and the domination of others. A just society has the responsibility to protect the vulnerable from the avariciousness and domination entrenched in the customs and practice of human collectives, just as society itself must be protected from dominant individuals with these characteristics.

This basic insight underlies the Islamist effort to haul human society away from a flawed western utopia with no purpose higher than achieving mere affluence, towards another 'old truth', which is that human happiness and harmoniousness depend more on struggling and sacrificing for ideals, rather than in accumulating material possessions.

Another old verity comes in the Qur'an's message about a human individual's relationship with God: it does not emerge instantaneously out of a single act of faith as St Paul suggests to Christians. It emerges slowly from the experience of the living God's demand that humans behave towards one another with justice, equity and compassion. The gradual understanding of God also comes from looking for Him in history, and from engaging the esoteric content of the Qur'an with reason, imagination and intuition – in order to better understand the reality of 'being'.

This truth essentially subordinates the 'personal aspect' on two levels: on the one hand, it is through behaving and experiencing others behaving similarly that understanding is advanced. This implies a community-centric, rather than personal path to a relationship with God. Second, the reflective introspection on 'being' that is the route to a comprehension of the oneness of man with man, man with nature, and man with the universe, implies the curbing of the personal. The understanding of 'connectedness' with other humans and with the surroundings diminishes the sense of individual 'self'.

This knowledge or 'relationship with God' is only to be achieved through restraining the ego or 'nafs', rather than privileging it as in the West, which has elevated individualism to become the basis around which politics, economics and society is organised. It is a very different view of 'faith' from that of the Christian, and throws open to question the western view of 'closed' societies acquiring their characteristic from the supposedly constraining nature of traditional 'faith' – an argument culled from the old struggle against 'static' Catholicism.

Essentially, whereas western economics sought to free market structures and to protect them from social and political intervention and restraint, Islamists have interpreted these 'old truths' to require the re-regulation of economic and social activity in order to achieve a behaviourally just and equitable society.

There is nothing inherently wrong with private property, markets or trading from the Islamist perspective – the Prophet himself was a trader – but Islamists insist that markets should be community-rooted and subordinated to the behavioural aspirations of an Islamic community. It is the opposite of nineteenth-century European thinking, which sought to break up and destroy socially rooted communities.

Another key theme in the Qur'an relates to generosity and giving. 'The righteous are those who give food – though it be dear to them – to the poor, the orphan and the prisoner.'[17] Alms are taken from individuals, 'though they be dear to them', as much to 'cleanse and purify them'[18] as to meet the immediate needs of the poor. In other words, sacrificing is a key component to human coping with material possessions. To avoid over-attachment to possessions, an individual must 'detach' from them by the sacrifice of part of them.

But the Qur'anic idea of giving is also associated with a distinctive view of the circulation of goods in society. It advocates giving to the less fortunate for a second and separate motive: 'lest it [goods and money] become something that circulates among the rich among you'.[19] In other words, bad circulation is one in which money increasingly circulates among the rich – passing between the rich among themselves, and good circulation one is in which it circulates between rich and poor. This notion of circulation of money is founded on acts of generosity and of service to the poor.[20]

The Qur'an takes the idea one stage further by suggesting that equity and justice demands the avoiding of great disparity of wealth. The Qur'an presents 'giving' as the redistributive mechanism to prevent excess disparity in wealth; as being conducive to a sense of 'detachment' from worldly possessions among the well-to-do; and for preventing accumulations of wealth leading to monopolies and the domination of others.

In this context, the Qur'an establishes the idea that acts of service and sacrifice to others in the community must be divorced from any expectation of linked or direct 'return'. A 'return' to the original donor, however, eventually will come about. In his act of giving he should not expect to be, and will not be, directly reciprocated; but a return will arise out of the complex pattern of criss-crossing of acts of generosity and selflessness of a community in which all follow a similar pattern of behaviour – according to their means. Ultimately the donor will receive some service or an act of help – a return that he cannot predict but that will come to him from an established culture of service to the community.

The Qur'an's purpose is not to offer an alternative concept of the 'invisible hand' at work in the community, but to implant the principle on selflessness and care for others into the economic arena – rather that the principle of maximising of one's selfish gain.

To ask whether Islamist economics would be as productively efficient as the western model is to try to compare oranges and apples: the western model offers an economic grand theorem – albeit one that has been unravelling since the 1870s. Islamists offer no comprehensive theorem however.

They propose only the principles and systems, drawn from Mohammad's restatement of 'truths that we all know', by which economic activity can be put in its proper place as an important sphere of human activity that must be regulated in order to prevent the twin monsters of human avariciousness and the desire to dominate others trampling on the delicate artefacts of a just and equitable community.

It suggests that a different question to that of which is the more technically efficient should be posed: the Islamist economic system is a response to what it sees to be the adverse consequences of the western economic system in terms of human welfare and true happiness. Its claims focus on redefining the meaning of 'best human interests'. Islamists ask for their system to be judged on which principles, western or Islamic, are the more likely to further justice and human welfare.

Western commentators dismiss the very concept of Islamist principles as little more than a technical effort to shape western financial instruments to be compliant with Shari'a (Islamic law). This view is reinforced perhaps by the fact that Muslim economists are often the employees of western banking and financial institutions with an interest in selling western financial products in Middle East markets. This image has reinforced the impression that Islamist economic principles lack substance and are largely a series of technical niggles connected with finding work-arounds for Shari'a compliance.

What is difficult to express in the West is that Islamists here are attempting to evolve a system of 'ethics' rather than a theorem that better explains the mechanisms of production and exchange. The Islamist aim is to radically change the ethical relationships between economic actors; to set a moral framework for those relationships; and – as a political objective – to tip the economic balance in favour of the individual and small-scale enterprises, and away from monopolies and large-scale economic concentrations of commercial power.

It pursues this latter aim not from any theorem that small-scale production is more efficient but rather from ethical objectives: to prevent concentration of economic power exerting domination over human beings. This forms part of a wider purpose: to demand that economic activity be viewed as but one component of the complex human dimension – a human condition that is linked, and is an integral part of a wider 'being' that encompasses the world in which we live. It is a component that should be guided by values – the need to maintain the cohesion and resilience of a community, and as a part of a balanced and multi-dimensional life.

It is, in short, an evolving attempt to reconfigure economics as a positive ethical dynamic to strengthen community, rather than letting it continue to act as a centrifugal force, spinning individuals apart in pursuit of their material self-interest, and separating out the rich 'cream' from the poor 'milk'.

Islamists have developed three principal strands to this reinterpretation of economics as a cohesive tool rather than a divergent centrifugal force. The issues surrounding Shari'a compliance of western financial instruments are not prominent among them.

The key to the Islamist parting of company with the West, as we saw earlier in this chapter, lies in the fundamentals – in their analysis of human motivation. In western economics, humans are held to act 'rationally' when they seek to maximise the sum of their personal and material welfare. In classical western economics, this individual pursuit of self-interest turns into a benign act, as we saw, through the action of the invisible hand.

'Our Islamist Economics'

Islamist economic principles start, as we saw, from a more pragmatic and jaundiced view of human nature. Baqir Sadr in *Our Economics* suggested that, at the economic plane, humans are dominated by their inner instinct of self-love; however 'rational' a person may be, humans have a disposition to become avaricious and domineering – and predatory and careless in their use of their environment.

To reflect the real nature of humans, the Islamist economic approach is to construct an ethical framework of regulation that sets limits to the actions of the individual and the state as economic agents. It seeks a distribution of income that does not permit disparities sufficient to cause social antagonism and division, and to define closely what constitutes public and what may constitute private property – and the duties and responsibilities of each type of ownership. For example, the natural resources of a nation belong to the public sphere and not to the private. Islamist principles also look to reform institutions – particularly financial institutions – in such a way as to reflect these ethics.

In terms of setting an ethical framework, Islamist economics is based on the moral suasion of God's demands for justice and respect – as well as on detailed regulation to back them up. Although the call to a culture of selflessness, respect for others and an ethos of generosity may seem excessively idealistic to modern western eyes, they reflect the ideas and the aspirations intended to mobilise human beings towards revolutionary change.

In Baqir Sadr's principles, the state occupies a role that is distinct from both the western model, with its insistence on its withdrawal from setting any grand objectives for society – preferring 'order' to emerge naturally, and from the Marxist view that the state should control all aspects of economic activity.

Unlike classical economics, which eschews any overriding project, the Islamist project revolves around setting 'grand objectives'. In *Our Economics* Sadr argues that the state should set the direction of economic activities, but unlike in Marxism should not attempt to micro-manage them: an Islamist government would act as the 'guardian' of the grand objectives, but would leave it to individuals' private enterprise to achieve them.

The government's role is to oversee and to regulate – but Sadr proposed that in the exercise of this function the government should enjoy a wide range of latitude in developing the regulatory system in the light of events and according to the circumstances of the state. In other words, there is no single model of an Islamist economy: any Islamist state would and should follow a pragmatic course of setting, and determining the mix of, public and private sector activities that best meet the needs of the moment. Sadr is clear, however, that it is the priority of the government to be activist in diligently growing the economy in such a way as to increase the welfare of all citizens.

As we saw in the last chapter, Mohammad Baqir Sadr, in his work on Islamic economics, viewed it as part of a wider project for a complete Islamic social system. The behaviour of the Islamic economic system, he argued, would not be able to be judged until after the creation of an Islamic state, when the whole realm of socioeconomic human behaviour would be determined according to Islam. Unless a solution emerged to regulate human self-love and to channel it into more socially beneficial processes, to mitigate the tension between the elite who controlled the resources and those who had access to none, the potential for human exploitation and for civil strife ultimately would lead to further disasters. Sadr believed that the western social order therefore rested on flawed foundations.

Sadr specified three components of the Islamic solution: an end to the various forms of oppression manifest in the unjust distribution of economic resources; the disciplining of the human instinct for personal accumulation; and the prudent use of the planet to satisfy the varying needs of all humanity.

As noted earlier, giving represented a central theme of the Qur'an and Islam has developed precise rules of charitable giving. The 'relinquishing' of a proportion of income to give to the less fortunate is required of all Muslims, and the khums – the giving of a fifth of personal income to charity required of Shi'a – are designed to protect the disadvantaged and as a deliberate redistributive act that is separate from taxation. It is intended as 'reminder' that humans are but the 'trustees' of the material world, that it is not their possession and that they should avoid becoming overly 'attached' to it.

Redistribution of income also reflects the Qur'anic injunction that money should circulate vertically in an economy, rather than horizontally in separated planes. Horizontal circulation of money among the rich risks the accumulation of resources among the commercial elite – to the detriment of all. It was similar thinking that prompted Lord Keynes, the dominant economist of the early twentieth century, to suggest something similar in terms of the causes of economic recession. He suggested that when the circulation of money slowed in an economy – owing to increased concentration of wealth in few hands – it would result in the failure of those who produced goods to be able to earn the income with which to purchase them. In Keynesian terms, there would be a failure of demand and recession would be the result.

Islam has complex and detailed laws covering personal inheritance of property that also seek to ensure that individuals do not accumulate wealth disproportionately. Islamists recognise that there will be inequalities of wealth, but insist that inequalities of wealth should be tolerated only to the extent that the disadvantaged, as a first priority, enjoy proper care in society. Again, community cohesion is the key, and progress is defined collectively, rather than as an aggregation of individual selfish needs.

Discerning the Flaws of the Financial System

The critique of the western financial system is more developed. In brief, Islamists criticise the West's facilitating of the creation of new money in the commercial banking system known in economic terms as M^3. This addition to a nation's money supply is separate to any printing of money or expansion of the total of the money available to a nation done by the central bank at a government's behest, and which is controlled by the central bank.

The ability to 'create' new money – to add to the nation's total of money holdings – came about as the result of the acceptance in the era after the Second European War of a fractional reserve banking system in place of the former gold standard.

The fractional banking system allowed commercial private sector banks to re-lend the 'same' money several times over, backed only by holding a small reserve that represented a fraction of the total of new loans extended. This ability to re-lend several times over the value of a single deposit allowed private sector banks effectively to inflate the money supply – to create new money. It was theoretically regulated by the central bank, but, as has now become all too apparent in the financial crisis of the West, it has resulted in an explosion of liquidity of unknown dimensions, and of personal and commercial debt. It also fuelled the trend towards concentration of economic power in the hands of a small elite.

Islamists have argued for some time that this huge injection of M^3 liquidity has fuelled the consumer boom, and has also created dangerous imbalances in the financial system that threaten its stability. Equally, Islamists have argued that a culture of liberal credit, again fuelled by the exponential creation of M^3, has led to massive indebtedness, which in turn leads to exploitation and to a form of modern bondage within the economic system.

It is undoubtedly true that the overhang of personal debt is now both threatening the stability of the system, as well as generating a new form of 'slavery'. Islamists would argue the merits of a return to a financial system based on some standard – such as the gold standard of the past – that limits the creation of money by central banks, and which prohibits fractional reserve banking.

Islamist condemnation of interest relates as much to the structural problems that fixed interest rates cause to an economic system as to the injunction against usury. Under a fixed interest rate financial structure any business that enjoys, say a 15 per cent rate of return on capital at a time when interest rates may be at, say, 7 per cent, would, Islamists argue, be better off borrowing millions, or billions, rather than some small sum.

This combination of massive liquidity and cheap fixed-interest credit was the fuel that powered the takeover bonanza that has led to fewer and fewer businesses accumulating in fewer and fewer hands.

The Islamist objection to these concentrations of commercial and financial power among a small and powerful economic elite relates first to the stifling of the smaller businesses and of individual initiative implied by loading the system in favour of large concentrations of power; and, second, to the damaging and exploitative impact on individuals of the power relationships that result.

The effect of fixed interest rates in a modern economy according to this analysis is to skew the financial system towards bulk lending and increasing indebtedness – at the expense of small businesses. The really big businesses are in a position to borrow more – on fixed terms – and the larger the loan, the easier and cheaper it is for the issuing banks. The incentive is for the already large firms to borrow hugely and to buy smaller firms. Lending small packets of money to start-up entrepreneurs is both risky and expensive to monitor, which makes the prospect relatively unattractive. Islamists would argue in favour of a lending system centred on micro-equity finance that would allow lenders a stake in the business, and correspondingly assume the risks of that business.

The concept is that small businesses generally do not have the capacity to pay interest at the outset, or when times are bad, and that financial lenders should assume the risks of the lean years – and of course the rewards in the better years. Payment of interest in this way works mainly to the benefit of capital accumulation, rather than to personal development and self-reliance.

Islamist economic principles offer a sharp critique of western financial, trade and development theories. Free markets have always represented for Muslims a construct of state power that was popular only so long as a booming economy masked their deeper impacts. These impacts were the growing subordination of the individual and his freedom to power relationships imposed by a small and increasingly dominant economic elite – a factor that also compounded the economic insecurity of the individual.

From the Static to the Dynamic

When, in 1972 in Tehran, Ali Shariati gave his first lectures on Islamology, he described the object of ideologising Islam as being to excite the intellectual and social energy that would awaken and mobilise people, and lead to the creation of a liberation movement. This process, he said, would give birth to a meaningful, goal-orientated and dynamic entity that used only those religious, philosophical and literary concepts which were of use to us today.[21] He was in effect insisting on a re-assembly of past cultural values to underpin an overturning of the existing order.

When Shariati lambasted the existing order he was not pointing at secularism alone: it was just as much an attack on 'false and institutionalised religions that vacated the authentic ideological content of their doctrine and replaced [it] with rituals and rites'.[22] This sentiment reflected Shariati's belief that the truly revolutionary nature of Shi'i Islam had been smothered and pacified over the years by clerics in search of an accommodation with power.

He, together with his following of activists, intended the liberation ideology of Islam to be not only a world outlook, but a philosophy of history, a sociological outlook, an ethical doctrine and, finally, a social mission. Shariati, in effect, was redefining the political: the social and behavioural 'grand objective' of demanding a just community redefined the social, not just as mere provision of better services but as a strident call to revolution.[23]

This ideology was to be based on, and inferred from, the body of knowledge that already existed in Islam, and its 'credal doctrine' was a world-outlook of 'a just society'. This, he argued, meant a reinterpretation of the individual, society and human life in all its aspects. It should provide an answer to the questions: 'What is the individual's state of being? What is to be done? And how should the individual be?'[24] In other words, the sphere of social behaviour was to be the vehicle for redefining the individual and connecting him to past cultural values that would serve his needs today. It was also a step in redefining democracy in terms of Clinias' city rather than Athens' port in Plato's dichotomy.

In his lecture on martyrdom, the first expressing his support for revolutionary theory, he argued that when authority, blind to real justice, subdued the people with coercion, money, fear and deception, it was only the conscious choice of martyrdom that could break the silence and put the regime to shame.[25]

Shariati and also Sadr therefore were radically reversing the ordering of social objectives from that pursued in the West. In western societies social policy was tied to moderating the impact of free markets on the more vulnerable in society. But despite its efforts at mitigation, social democratic western society remains centred around the idea that it is the unforced interaction of personal choice in a polity relatively unencumbered with restraint that brings a natural order, and fulfils the best interests of humanity. It does this economically by matching buyers and sellers through the mechanism of the free market. In other words, social democratic efforts to alleviate the worst effects of the market mechanism were well-intentioned but misguided: the issue of human conduct was left untouched.

Shariati and Sadr, from their different standpoints, were saying that it was not a question of a little better provision for the victims of the system. They were arguing that the social democratic attempt to reconcile social objectives with an economic system based on the 'rational actor' seeking to maximise his or her private situation – was simply false reconciliation. Islamic behavioural demands for justice and freedom from domination were not reconcilable with secular individualism and human susceptibility to greed.

The problem was not the market mechanism per se, but human nature. Trying to fine-tune the market mechanism was not the answer: unless a revolution could be effected that transposed ethical objectives into the place of market objectives, and subjected human acquisitiveness to moral control, injustice and domination would persist.

Shariati saw that the only answer was insurrection that would touch on the nervous system of the Iranian people, to awaken them with a socio-political process of the message and sword. Islamic freedom fighters would fight a 'social and ideological jihad and a scientific and rational "ijtehad"' By ijtehad – which formally means the Shi'i doctrine of the renewal and modernisation of law by critical reasoning – Shariati was here tying the revolution to a forward-looking posture, even though its rediscovered cultural identity was drawn from the Islamic past.

Many in the West, including Muslims, will see this approach as too combative and too dichotomous: they point to the mix of free market and social democratic policies that exist in western societies. Since the 1980s, Britain and the United States, under the influence of the New Right, may have adopted neo-liberal economic policies, they suggest, but other countries, such as the Scandinavian ones, have attempted to find a median between policies designed to promote free markets and social objectives.

Baqir Sadr's point is that such attempts represent a false reconciliation of two dynamics – politico-social objectives such as justice on the one hand, and equity and personal interests on the other – that in reality pull in opposite directions. It is not the market mechanism that is at the root of this tension: but human nature itself – the instinct of self-love that drives man to secure survival for himself only. Such an instinct is normal to survival. However, when left without moral control, economic accumulation eventually capsizes into various forms of political and economic power relationships that lead to exploitation and domination. There is no need to abolish ownership of private property or the market mechanism: the trick is to change the social values related to the possession of wealth and private property.

The only way to resolve this tension is to demand that humans behave to each other with justice, compassion and respect – not because they are compelled to do so, but because they genuinely believe that ultimately this is in the true interest of human beings. This is why Islam is an essential element, therefore, to resolving the inherent contradiction between the social and the private, Sadr argues.

Free Markets and Democracy: Lacking Natural Affinity

In Europe this problem of reconciliation is acknowledged. After its initial successes in the early years after the last European War, the

European project of reconciling market economics with democratic government has been in retreat. Social democracy continues to exist, but such governments lack the leverage over economic life that they were able to exercise during the post-war years.

Free markets and democracy are competitors rather than partners. And the rise of the New Right paradoxically eroded and inflicted huge damage on democracy – while claiming to be acting in its name. In Britain, Prime Minister Thatcher pursued policies that weakened social continuities and forms of self-governance in professional and other institutional structures. She introduced 'markets', or simulacra of markets, in all spheres of government as 'management tools', and contributed to dissolving the last remnants of the social order that had sustained community in the nineteenth century.[26]

The New Right propagated an individualist ethos and personal responsibility, but at the same time brought about types of late capitalist structure that were wholly dependent on liberalised money and credit being used extensively. In this neo-liberal world the original puritan virtues of Calvin, of saving and planning for the future, became not just redundant but were seen to be harmful to the drive for consumer growth. This has brought about a makeshift 'lifestyle' way of living that is better suited to the incessant mobility of career-hopping latter-day capitalism. It has also marked what has been called the post-political era. 'There is no such thing as society', Mrs Thatcher once remarked, 'only individuals' – adding, as an afterthought, 'and their families, of course.' It was 'lifestyle' politics: a world where everything is permitted so long as it is on offer as an individual pleasure, in a universe of freedom of choice.

This achieved a reconciliation, but it was a reconciliation between the increasingly rich and powerful elite and the people – by fabricating individuals smitten with a false sense of equity generated by the 'harmony' of private pleasures taken in a climate of self-pacified hedonism. It was not a reconciliation between the social and the private: that seems to have come to an end with competition between the market economy and democracy producing a clear victory for the market economy in this latest round.

Shariati's lectures to the youth of Tehran, and Sadr's speculations, plainly marked a fundamental rupture with the past, and with the prevalent Shi'i thinking of that era that separated 'this-worldly' and 'other-worldly' matters. Until this time, traditional Shi'ism was centred around gatherings that essentially were mourning sessions in which the lives of Imams were narrated by a member of the clergy or a preacher stirring sorrow and sympathy for the worldly sufferings they experienced, as a price for their eternal bliss in the hereafter.

The role of religion was to usher the faithful down the correct path to the hereafter, rather than do anything about the here-and-now. The suggestion that Islam had a social dimension of attending to the welfare needs of the faithful that might be a rallying cry for popular insurrection outraged many in the religious establishment, who were deeply opposed to any liberalising, democratising or socialising of their Islam.

The young students' and activists' aim, however, remained to shout the social significance of their revolution and to rouse the people behind it. The revitalisation of Islam was possible if people were convinced that solutions to their mundane day-to-day secular needs and tribulations could also be found in religion, Shariati believed. If this could be achieved, the activists hoped, Islam could be transformed into an idea capable of providing real solutions to the problems of living in the here-and-now world. This vision of a revolutionary social Islam has become a key tenet of 'political Shi'ism', and has had a pervasive, but often overlooked, influence, despite the Iranian experiment being bled by a war with Iraq and by internal reaction,.

Both Shariati, and his father, Mohammad-Taki before him, believed themselves to be locked in an epic struggle with Marxists. This sentiment was mirrored by Mohammad Baqir Sadr, who wrote his key works as direct rebuttals of Marxism. This required that they all became very familiar with Marxism. For Shariati, this familiarity had led him to an unexpected conclusion: far from Marxism representing the inexorable threat to Islam that many perceived, his own study of Marxism had convinced him that Islam already possessed the solutions to all the present-day social, political and economic problems faced by Muslims – if only they could be revealed beneath the layers of accumulated dust.

The Marxists, like the religious establishment, were outraged by Shariati's lectures – albeit for very different reasons. The Marxists saw the work of Islamist students and activists in the run-up to the overthrow of the Shah as an attempt to 'Islamise' their Marxism. Bitterness over the Islamist seizure of a revolutionary social discourse continues to poison the relationship between the secular left and Islamism today.

They understood, however, the revolutionary potential of what the Iranian activists were attempting: Islamists were taking up a sword to sever social policy as a tool for transforming relations within a society from the body of the nation-state.

Shariati and his colleagues intended to capture and redefine the social sphere as the arena of contention for Islam, rather than being about the provision of welfare services conceded by a 'caring' western-style nation-state. They hoped thereby to transform Islam into an internationalist idea, capable of providing solutions for all oppressed peoples in a balanced way; to provide for their material well-being as well as attend to their metaphysical needs.

The Iranian students' slogans challenged the traditional meaning of incidents and the narrative of certain events, and gave them new interpretations emphasising their social and political meaning. Their reading of events underlined their potential for political change: 'We must enter into action: preaching like Zaynab, and resisting injustice like Imam Hussein', Shariati instructed the students, while conversely condemning pacifying, depoliticising and ritual-based 'static' religion as hypocritical and deceptive.

Justice: Transcending Human Fallibility

One key element to achieving the objective of justice was to remove the law from being the plaything of human whimsical notions and interests, as the Islamists saw it, by reverting as closely as possible to God's original demands for human behaviour – that is, by reasserting Islamic law. Having anchored law as the basis of justice, Khomeini saw that once the people had secured their revolution, social justice and the survival of Islam would still require active intervention – affirmative action in today's terminology. Social justice, he asserted, should also dictate the character and nature of government: governance henceforth must become the servant of social justice, rather than being its master.

In making this claim on governance, Khomeini was effectively reinterpreting its role within the nation-state in a novel fashion: government was not to be the arm executing the interests of a powerful elite, operating on the fiction that their interests coincided with, and accurately represented, the collective will of sovereign individuals. It was to become the catalyst and tool for igniting and promoting massive behavioural change, in order to bring about a just community. It was conceived as an attempt to recover government for human interests.

The liberating experience for contemporary Iranians of the promise to recover the excitement and innovation of the era of the Prophet, when religious experience took precedence over mere obedience to a legal code, suggested that Shari'a was not viewed by Iranians as a narrowing, constricting legacy – as it is seen in the West: 'Islamic government held out the promise of breaking with the structures of personal identity, of economy, of society and of politics that constituted for them "the stubbornness of their destiny"'.[27]

Shi'i Islam held out this possibility of a continuous and active creation of a political order because of its openness to the updating of law by reasoning. But also, more importantly, from the prospect of radical renewal and fresh revelation via the Imamate. The willingness to look to intuitively derived solutions put to the test of deductive and syllogistic reasoning permitted Islamist leaders to escape from becoming captives of the past and of past precedents.

In short, the Imamate concept of leadership was an extremely dynamic and innovative approach. Shariati considered the appeal of Islam for the people to rest as much on the prospect of revolutionary Imamate leadership as on its claim to justice.[28]

Khomeini too, as we saw earlier, was concerned that the revolution would require a strong revolutionary leadership that could draw on the resources in terms of revelation that had made the Imamate so innovative. It is likely that his concern to protect the revolution and to progress it was an important factor in his advocacy of waliyat al-fiqih, in which role the people eventually honoured him as 'Imam'.

Although Iran, for complex reasons, lost some of its capability to be innovative, this latter characteristic can be clearly seen today exhibited in the creative and novel thinking by the leadership of Hesballah. The Iranian Revolution effectively had redefined Islam as a dynamic forward-looking entity embracing change, but Khomeini extended these attributes to government also: he intended it to be not a passive regulator, but an actor in the struggle to transform society.

By promoting resilience, and by energising a community, Khomeini suggested that the passive colonised brain could be superseded by 'an independent brain'; but that this would not come about if they remained fatalistic, if they were 'satisfied with saying God willing'. Instead he asserted: 'You should act!' The call for an 'independent' brain echoes critical theorists' view that social enlightenment could only be attained through rational human activity, and through critical thought. Only by cultivating this independent rational brain, the Frankfurt School believed, can a community locate the renewing and energising aspects of modern society, and differentiate them from the irrational and regressive ones.

Both Sunni and Shi'i have before them the example of the first Muslim community at Mecca. When the Prophet Mohammad decided in CE 622 to distance himself and his small community of believers from the harassment and persecution in Mecca by seeking refuge in Medina, he was followed by his adherents. They left behind all earthly possessions for their submission (Islam) to God and his messenger. They renounced their social status, tribal affiliation, home and property, and were greeted by Medina's newly converted Muslims, who offered the Meccans a share of all their belongings.

This is Islam's counterpoint to the Calvinist and Protestant emphasis on the iconic story of Abraham's embrace of change. As we have seen, it was this reinterpretation of Abraham's story, to which many westerners point as the turning point that transformed the West into a 'dynamic' and 'open' society – as opposed to the 'closed' society of static religion that holds its members fast to its precepts and traditions. Shariati and the young students used the metaphor of the Prophet's metamorphic journey from Mecca to Medina to signify the need for Muslims also to undertake change: to journey from a Mecca trapped in old-think to a Medina in which the first Islamic community was to flower and flourish.

Islamists regard Mohammad's emigration from Mecca as a transforming moment that signalled an unconditional embrace of change and submission to God. But, unlike the Christian story, this act of submission did not constitute salvation: this still had to be achieved by living and behaving as a community that broke with past patterns of behaviour – by living as God demanded.

We have argued here that western economics, which presents itself as secular and universal, is no such thing. The ideas that lie behind it reflect some of the deepest Christian instincts. We have also argued that these two visions are not strictly competitors in terms of economic 'theorems', but are irreconcilable in terms of their fundamentally opposing views of the 'essence of man'. These different approaches point to Islamists seeing the paradigm of the nation-state in a completely different fashion from the way it is seen in the West.

We have tried to demonstrate here Islam's departure from a 'static' and passive posture, to recover its earlier revolutionary ethos. In the previous chapter we explored the evolution of a political ideology. In this chapter we have attempted to show how that political ideology and, indeed, all the institutions of government and state, were to be defined by and harnessed as collaborators in the quest for social revolution. We have argued that this constituted a radical re-thinking of the social sphere. The next chapter looks at how these different perspectives have impacted on the way Islamists conceive the nation-state.

5

GOD IS A LIBERAL

The idea of the 'open' society, from which came the revived claims to 'freedom', and of the futility of opposition to the western meme, derived originally from a discussion about the organisational habits of bees, ants and otter colonies.

The man responsible, Henri Bergson, was an evolutionary philosopher who tried to understand how the requirements of species' evolution affected habits and instincts, and how these were modified by the intervention of species autonomy and independence. When *The Two Sources of Morality and Religion* was published in 1932, it posited the existence of two kinds of social organisation in nature.

One was the beehive or the anthill. This represented a community guided wholly by instinct: there is nothing voluntary in these societies. Each individual simply fulfils an allotted role. There are however, Bergson suggested, less extreme forms of instinctive society in the animal kingdom. Otters live in communities and mostly follow their instincts, but enjoy considerably more autonomy than ants and bees. Bergson supposed that humans must have lived more or less in this way, before the development of human consciousness. He calls this kind of intellectual society a 'closed' society.

Yet people are not ants: they possess individual will and that causes them to 'choose' – to behave in one way, or another. In Bergson's analysis, religion arises as a kind of mental habit that binds human intelligence to the instinctive drive for solidarity and continuity. It is, he suggests, the voice of instinct sounding in consciousness.[1] This kind of religion Bergson calls 'static' religion: it aims to keep people where they are.

There is another side to human nature, Bergson noted, that is open to learning and change, and change pulls human societies away from the closed world of tradition and pattern. Bergson defined the 'open' society as the type of society in which this human drive for change can be fulfilled. In an open society the traditional unities break down. Custom loses its coercive power over individual lives. Women can do things formerly reserved for men, workers no longer have to defer to feudal lords, and individuals are freed from the encumbrance of traditional roles and family ties.

Karl Popper leaned on Bergson's powerful metaphor when writing his hugely influential *The Open Society and its Enemies* published in 1945. This work of philosophy was unusual in that it had a huge impact, beyond the normal scope for a work of this nature. It has, to a large extent, defined the way that Americans and many Europeans saw and see their societies up to the present time – and, more significantly, it has come to shape how they see and think about other societies.

Bergson's animal kingdom imagery became the central element for Popper's philosophy of history. It was history understood as a series of attempts by the forces of reaction to smother an open society with the weapons of traditional religion and traditional values, by which he meant the cultural and social values of a society.

History, he suggested, in large part was the record of efforts, more often successful than not, of the advocates of closed society to shut down open societies. Popper condemns Plato's Athenian reaction to the elemental, anarchic and commercial 'bad smell' emanating from the Athenian port as but one of a series of reactionary responses, passing via the Hegelian backlash against the French Revolution, to the Marxism of his day – all seeking to extinguish the open society.

The message was clear. It was a secular reformulation of the Anglo-Saxon myth of freedom and its culture of constructive competitive jostling that gave England its free institutions. As Cromwell had struggled against reactionary kings and Catholic absolutism to preserve the 'open' Anglo-Saxon society, Popper sought to extend the old Saxon analogy into the scientific setting of evolutionary Darwinism, to protect the open society from secular Marxism.

Writing at the outset of the Cold War, Popper detected in Marxism doctrines of historical determinism, borrowed from Hegel, which he found profoundly inimical to the idea of human freedom. Marx and Russia were cast as the reactionary threat to the open society subsequently taken up by Reagan and reconnected to Christian apocalyptic and Manichaean tradition, touching a nerve in the US by casting the Soviet Union as an 'evil empire' seeking to destroy freedom.

It was an updating of a narrative that, in borrowing the science of species evolution, had masked its antecedents in the Protestant legacy of a natural order spontaneously arising from competitive market exchange. For many Americans, Popper's writing supported an understanding of the free market economy as both a product of, and a motor for, the open society. They also saw static religion as one of the forces threatening their society; and they understood from Popper that 'traditional' cultural values were part of that instinctive complex, holding humans back from embracing the dynamic society.

From this formulation came the secular-liberal dichotomy between those who are ruled and determined by their culture, and those – generally identified as living in an 'open' society – who are elevated above it and are free to choose it. This dichotomy has had profound implications for Muslims living in the West – as manifested in the insistence on the de-politicisation of Islamic culture as a collective force, and its reinterpretation as a personal choice to 'enjoy', or not.

Walter Russell Mead, in *God and Gold* summed up what most westerners felt, from Popper's analysis, to be the futility of opposition to free market economics:

> As an economic mechanism, the free market enriches and empowers societies that embrace it. Closed societies that try to swim against the tide are weakened, impoverished, and eventually overcome. With the development of capitalism, something new happened: history ceased to

be the record of openness followed by reaction and closure. It became instead the story of a continuing move west and a demolition of the restraining walls.[2]

Popper's other purpose in his book was to suggest that secular modernism alone was insufficient to guarantee the creation of the open society: Marx may have had aspirations to liberation and justice, but these could not mitigate the 'closed' aspects of a communist or totalitarian system. Only men's and women's unforced and rational choices, cumulatively intersecting through the mechanism of free exchange, could bring about 'a growing measure of humane and enlightened life' and the 'open' society. In short, freedom and democracy meant the adoption of this model exclusively.

The 'Open Society' Ideology

The concepts of the open society and the free market had become irretrievably harnessed together in the understanding of most Americans and Europeans. They would become the familiar themes underpinning an 'open society' project of human 'redemption' in the subsequent neo-liberal revival in Britain and America.

This, then, was the template of the principles underlying the nation-state that held the imagination of Americans in the era of the Cold War. It was one that exercised a hugely powerful hold over the western mind, but it was not one that held any appeal for Islamists, who could see clearly its roots in Christian thinking.

They identified in this model the same tension that, according to their analysis, existed in the western economic model, as noted in the previous chapter. The western principles all stemmed from the belief that the exercise of self-interest in an individualised society best met the needs of human beings. Put simply, Islamists disagreed profoundly.

The principles which Popper had identified, however, were already subsumed in the structure and institutions of the nation-state. The newly independent colonists of America had not had the benefit of reading Popper, of course, but their ideas reflected the continuum of thought stretching from the Protestant struggle against the concept of religious community through English puritanism to the puritans' descendants – the early colonists in America.

These roots in the struggle between Protestants and the great sacral community of Christianity are important, as in them lie the roots of the nationalist impulse that so disfigured the nineteenth and twentieth centuries – for the cultural processes that originally had led to conflict contained also the seeds of the destructive militant nationalism that overwhelmed Europe in succeeding centuries.

One of these processes was the need to invent the 'sovereignty of the individual' to substitute for that of God, which had been at the apex of the religious community, and which was no longer appropriate in the Protestant fight against the sacral community. It was this transformation, more than any other, that facilitated the emergence of a strong, centralised, purpose-led nation-state, centred on an ethnic identity and the use of the vernacular, as the Holy Roman Empire dissolved into secular nation-states with the Treaty of Westphalia.

Another of these processes was the enthusiastic embrace of capitalism and of capitalism's requirement to open new markets on the part of Protestants; and a third was the severance from a wider sacral community caused by the Protestant personalisation of the relationship with God and the embrace of robust individualism.

These processes helped shape the western nationalist impulse, and the connection of these impulses to nationalism has also helped form the Islamist response to the nation-state.

Thomas Jefferson, making his contributions to the draft for the American Declaration of Independence of 1776, followed the puritan idea that human nature had been constructed in such a way that good order would emerge naturally as a historical process of progress out of the free unforced choices of an educated majority. Human rights, Jefferson held, also emerge from this natural ordering of human affairs. This was to be a central theme shaping democracy and the persistent conviction of future

American generations that the American nation-state can provide a recipe for peace and freedom throughout the world.[3]

The system of checks and balances among the three branches of government, between the federal government and the states, and the representation of different classes of citizens and interests in the House of Representatives and Senate, represented an attempt to recreate in politics, and in the institutions of government, a simulacrum of the interplay and competitive jostling of the economic free market mechanism. Jefferson's conviction was that this inter-institutional competition would not lead to chaos and collision, but to harmony and order.

It was the rough and tumble and competition of the Germanic tribes of the pre-Anglo-Saxon era replicated in institutional form. It also represented a narrowing down and fixing of the concept of nationhood to a very limited meaning.

Christianity had injected the belief that history is a continuing process that has a pre-determined end, and it was from Christianity that the certainty sprang that, when this end was finally achieved, history would come to a close. Secular thinkers such as Marx and Francis Fukuyama inherited this teleology, which underpins their talk of 'the end of history'.

Standing behind this conception is the belief that history must be understood not in terms of the causes of events but in terms of its purpose, which is the salvation of humanity. This idea entered western thought only with Christianity, and has shaped it ever since.[4]

As Americans came to see their history through this lens, so the belief in manifest destiny that was formulated in the nineteenth century became a part of this process. The idea of a messianic saviour was transformed into a belief in America as a 'redeemer nation' – a redemption achieved through human will and action.[5]

These themes sustained a powerful form of faith that was secularised in the eighteenth century by positivist thinkers who believed that the growth of knowledge was the driving force of social and political progress, and who celebrated science and technology for its ability to expand human power.

Human intervention, harnessed to scientific thought, offered the promise of a transformative power that was equated to the apocalyptic event to which Christians looked as the instrument to metamorphose humans.

This new creed was accompanied by a vast expansion of instrumental reasoning. It seemed increasingly absurd to many ordinary men and women in Europe and America, as science and knowledge grew in importance and esteem, to trust management of the modern age to divine guidance, or to seek the help of scripture for piloting an aeroplane, for example.

These positivist theorists held that science, rather than religion would reveal the true ends of human action, and that scientific enquiry would eliminate vexing social problems, resolve the scarcity of resources and create a better world.

In some ways this was true. In many, it was the opposite: major contributions to the advancement of science were juxtaposed with others – like the concept of market reform and ethnic engineering in Muslim societies – which, as we saw in earlier chapters, led directly to genocide, massacre and ethnic cleansing.

Many of those who subscribed to the fashionable and prevalent European nineteenth-century view of racial inequality believed that social reform held some potential to compensate for the innate disadvantages of inferior breeds: ultimately all human beings could participate in the universal civilisation of the future – but only by giving up their own ways of life and adopting European ways.[6]

So, too, the positivist creed committed itself to developing a science of society; but they were insistent that such a science must be based on human physiology. Positivists believed that people's physiological characteristics could explain much of human behaviour. This was to lead to the nineteenth-century pseudo-science of phrenology, which claimed to be able to identify the mental and moral faculties of people, and their tendency to criminality, by studying the shape of their skulls. This was subsequently refined to assist courts in their deliberations about guilt and innocence.

Racial science, the Nazi experiments of the twentieth century, phrenology, Freudian psychology, planned industrial development, Marxist-Leninist policies, eugenics, and the sterilisation of the insane – each one of these ideas has at various times been enthusiastically pronounced to be scientifically true. The consequences have been both brutal and tragic.[7]

Capsized Rationality

In the introduction to this book, we quoted the Iranian cleric's noting, from the Islamic optic, the magnitude and seriousness of these brutal and tragic consequences, of which Muslims were often the victims. He said that in the tragedies which the West had brought upon the world – beyond comparison with any from the past – it had used science and knowledge, the most sacred things man has, to justify its actions. What had made these disasters all the worse, he said, was that they were the acts of politicians who were doing what they believed to be right. They had all been done in the name of democracy and in the name of human interest, he lamented.

The cleric pointed to the three elements that he considered were responsible for causing western thinking to capsize into committing – with the best of intentions – such huge acts of terror and brutality in the name of science, democracy and human progress. He said that they had occurred, first, because western empiricism had led to humans being treated as mere specimen-objects that have significance only if human subjects bestow it upon them.

It reduced them to specimen-objects for study, and to ever more narrowly focused and fragmented objects of enquiry. In doing this, the West was missing the wood for the trees: it had lost the understanding of man as a part of humanity, of man as a part of nature and of the universe. It had severed him or her as a 'being' from a wider knowledge. This had led him to treat nature in the same atomised way, as an object to be controlled and dominated too.

The second misstep, he said, had been for individuals sating their desires and appetites to have been taken – somehow – to represent 'real values'. This misrepresentation crucially had divorced the 'being' from his or her innate knowledge of the moral. Instead of man accessing his or her moral conscience, founded on concepts of justice, respect towards other humans and a sense of equity, he or she began to recreate his or her values around his or her own needs and wants.

It also separates him or her from collective culture which has a political significance. A just society is one that can create a collective culture of selflessness, but by turning culture into a privatised matter of choice as a way of life – a set of personal and private beliefs and practices – culture literally is transformed: the same set of beliefs and practices is no longer backed by the binding power of a collective and becomes an expression of personal and private idiosyncrasies. It is no longer the public network of norms and rules to which a community that is committed to collective ethical objectives can aspire.

The third and the most grave aspect to which the cleric pointed was the West's universal adoption of the instrumental thinking that the positivist school so dramatically represented – and to which the Young Turks had proved such ardent devotees.

Islamists believe that instrumental rationality – namely the calculation of the most efficient means for achieving a given desire – has overwhelmed western thinking in the last 300 years. Letting instrumental rationality become the dominant form of knowledge is a development that sharply separates western thought from the common origins of both western and Islamic philosophy in the Greek classical tradition.

While Islamists acknowledge the validity and merits of the western empirical approach, they argue that, when used as a unique category of reasoning, without recourse to other categories, it will lead to exactly the excesses that have stained western history over the last two centuries. This is particularly true when instrumental reasoning is partnered by militant nationalism. Islamists view these events and the social consequences that they have entailed as the actions of humans whose faculty of reason has atrophied to a mere calculus of the most efficient means to a given end.

The increasing scientific objectifying of nature has led to the demise of deductive and syllogistic methods of thinking; and, more importantly, it has separated humans from myth, legend, intuition, vision, poetry and awe, all of which come to us from beyond our tactile and visual perceptions, and offer us other forms of knowledge and different understandings of reality.

For Islamists the institutions and structures of the western nation-state reflect their free market and Christian antecedents, but they also see instrumental rationality increasingly shaping and manipulating individuals. Social patterns evolve into more institutionalised forms of instrumental rationality. These both imperceptibly constrain behaviour and also condition the way of thinking by which westerners view the world. This generates an empirical, calculating and functional mindset. A vicious circle ensues, in which instrumental rationality becomes exclusive and total.

As instrumental rationality becomes dominant, Muslims such as the Iranian cleric perceive that the early positivist celebration of science and technology for its ability to expand human power distorts into a will to dominate and control. Ironically the very processes of the Enlightenment that were supposed to liberate man from nature were warped, and have rebounded against him. As the western market economy took hold, human beings were being subjected to ever more pervasive networks of administrative discipline and control from increasingly powerful and centralised elites.

Islamists see these de-humanising, individualising and controlling aspects of instrumental rationality as a loss of freedom – and the prime route by which the domination of others has been validated. This analysis has profoundly shaped their view of what 'freedom' means and, consequently provoked a reconsideration of what democracy and the nation-state should signify.

If democracy has been defined by the West in terms of James Paine's institutionalisation of the invisible hand, with the nation-state as its political expression, then these are irreconcilable with Islam for the same reasons that free market mechanisms are irreconcilable – because they are unable to solve the tension between the private and collective objectives of humans.

What the Iranian Revolution demonstrated was the possibility for Iranians to escape the realm of obedience to secular norms and instrumental western ratiocination. They were free to draw on the long tradition of Persian philosophy and to reason anew. This is the feeling of liberation and freedom that so puzzles westerners, who view Islamism as inherently a curtailment of freedoms – an imposition of religious irrational faith. The revolution was seen by many Muslims as a break with the 'blackmail' of a western thought system that, as a matter of policy, excluded metaphysical and other categories of reasoning from its 'objective' secularised modernisation.

The 'Blackmail' of Empiricism

One Islamist writer and scholar has described the way in which western instrumentalism had constrained and depleted Muslim writing and thinking over the last 200 years – until recently. What was worse, from his perspective, was that it was Muslim scholars themselves, caught up in the drive to westernise, who had self-imposed this 'blackmail'.

Frantz Fanon, in his exploration of the psyche of the colonised Algerian in *Black Skin, White Masks*, describes the situation of Muslim writers in this period well:

> Every colonised people – in other words, every people in whose soul an inferiority complex has been created by the death and burial of its local cultural originality – finds itself face to face with the language of the mother country. The colonialised is elevated above his jungle status in proportion to his adoption of the mother country's cultural standards. He becomes 'whiter' as he renounces his 'blackness', his 'jungle'.[8]

Iranians escaped their role as cogs in a machine. They escaped 'this indifference, this automatic manner of classifying him, imprisoning him, primitivising him, and decivilising him'.[9] The revolution allowed their escape from the language and culture of the 'mother country'. Their liberation came from attacking not just these two aspects, but also the very roots of political rationality. A Hesballah leader said:

> What this meant for us was that we were free to reason out for ourselves what is right. That is our principal and significant difference with the West. We are no longer constrained to one type of thinking. Hesballah will think deeply about a problem; and decide what is right. We will then act on what we believe is right, because it is right – even if, in the short-term and beyond, it carries a price, and does not achieve immediate results. We do it, because our reasoning tells us that this is the right thing to do.

This sense of a break with past patterns of thought similarly underpins the Hamas perspective that it will not acquiesce to western ground rules. If those ground rules exclude, as doctrine, Islamist thinking – if it is just an 'ends and means discussion' on western terms – then 'What is there to talk about?', as one Hamas leader wryly noted.

In the West, Qutb argued, the pattern and organisation of an atomised modern society had also adversely impacted on the physiological and mental state of Muslims and humans generally. The West's privileging of materialism – of community as defined as no more than the sum of its individual parts – and of nature as an objectified particular, had led to losing the broad view. Qutb accused the West of pursuing material well-being to the extreme; of pursuing individualism to the extreme, and of pursuing its economic and political interests to the extreme. Western instrumental thinking was responsible for tipping society towards this imbalance, he argued.

The West had capsized: if civilisation is held to progress largely by virtue of its technical domination of nature, it regresses in cultural terms, and both thought and experience become impoverished, Qutb suggested. This represented the tyranny of the twenty-first century, which Slavoj Žižek characterised in this way: the ultimate victims of positivism are not, as intended, the 'confusing' metaphysical notions that positivists so abhorred, but facts themselves. In this way, science functions as a social force, as an ideological institution: its function is to provide certainty, to be a point of reference on which one can rely, and to provide hope. The radical positivist's pursuit of secularisation transforms man into an apathetic creature with no great passion or commitment – and indeed life itself into an abstract anaemic process.[10]

Žižek continues:

> Science today effectively does compete with religion, insofar as it serves two properly ideological needs, those for hope and those for censorship, which were traditionally taken care of by religion. To quote John Gray: Silence alone has the power to silence heretics. Today it is the only institution that can claim authority. Like the Church in the past, it has the power to destroy, or marginalise, independent thinkers ... From the standpoint of anyone who values freedom of thought, this may be unfortunate, but is undoubtedly the chief source of science's appeal. For us, science is a refuge from uncertainties, promising – and in some measure delivering – the miracle of freedom from thought, while churches have become sanctuaries for doubt.[11]

The nation-state, the demand for Muslim societies to reform, and fundamentalist positivism all impacted on Islam in a number of disastrous and brutal ways: but the way in which the nation-state was engineered in the Middle East in the last century only added to the this sense of unfolding tragedy.

There the new national frontiers drawn by the colonists deliberately bore no resemblance to the ethnic distributions on the ground. The British and French colonists, for example, created the state of Iraq along lines that did not match any ethnic boundaries. It was a deliberate choice to make a hotchpotch state. Instead of following ethnic distribution, evidence suggests that the British regularly and intentionally misaligned the map in a conscious policy of colonial exploitation, repeated throughout the empire, that leveraged minority ethnicities in a bid to facilitate colonial rule.

By empowering the minorities, the British acquired a weakened state with the potential to play one minority against another. The colonial power could then co-opt a dependent elite to front for the British in wielding power. The authors of this strategy knew that were British support at any time to be removed, their co-opted minority community would be unlikely to survive alone for long. They would soon fall victim to other more populous ethnic groupings. This fear bound the colonial administration and the British colonialists together.

Re-thinking the Nation-state

With this experience of the nation-state and of the associated western impulse of militant nationalism, too, it is not surprising that Muslims began to analyse the factors that had given rise to the secular instinct of nationalism. In reflecting on this, they recalled that nationalism had been the offspring of the demise of the sacral culture that had preceded it.

The Umma historically had been imaginable largely through the medium of a sacred language and a written script. Members, drawn from very different parts of the vast territorial stretch in which the Umma existed, knowing nothing of each other's languages, nonetheless understood each other's processes of thought from their understanding of the common values of the Qur'an. It was a tradition where states were defined by centres, borders were porous and indistinct, and sovereignties faded imperceptibly into one another. Hence, paradoxically enough, the ease with which pre-modern empires were able to sustain their rule over immensely heterogeneous, and often not even contiguous populations for long periods of time.[12]

If nationalism and the malignant characteristics of the western nation-state could be understood by aligning them, not with a self-consciously held political ideology of nationalism, but with the various religious and political processes that preceded the rise of eighteenth-century nationalism – then those very contrary processes – the sacral community – to which the nationalist impulse was a response, might offer Islamists a solution to the intrusion of the western nation-state into Muslim societies.

In other words, Islamists could find in the traditional communities of religion that pre-dated the rise of the nation-state the possibility of some answers to how to respond to the nation-state today.

One Islamist thinker, who describes himself as close to Hesballah and has spent a lot of time working through the ways in which Islamists should respond to western manifestation of state power, suggested that the Islamist answer had been to examine the possibilities for creating a different organisational structure to western hierarchy, through what has been termed a 'rhizome structure' – a horizontally mobilising and unifying networked structure – similar to the matted root structure of a horizontally colonising plant.

Earlier another Hesballah member described 'communities of capability' as a form of resistance to western power that can act as a pole around which Muslims can unify – rather than stay locked into the nation-state paradigm – and which could challenge the power of the western state from an alternative organisational and structural platform.[13]

These 'communities of capability' are not seeking to regress to a less efficient organisational form, but rather to seek freedom from hierarchy – whether western, or from Arab leaderships – to escape from vulnerability, dependency and asymmetry of power – through the adoption of flat, decentralised networks.

> We conceived of the so-called 'flat' organisational structure initially for defensive reasons. Hesballah's first objective was to mount a resistance against the Israeli occupation of Lebanon [in 1982] and to the US actions in Lebanon at that time. The 'flat' structure was designed for resistance, but gradually it began to serve also the movement's social requirements which evolved as an integral component of a wider resistance.
>
> Of course, the political dimension of the 'flat' structure derived from Ayatollah Khomeini's conception of the Revolution whose objective was to empower the 'dispossessed'' – a rallying call formulated from Ali Shariati's translation into Farsi of Fanon's The Wretched of the Earth. The flat networked structure allowed the masses to be organised for political action, while offering some protection from the depredations of the secret police.
>
> The Iranian Revolution created new identities, and Islamic concepts acquired new meanings. At that time, the legitimacy of the nation-state had been utterly destroyed by its association with the Shah and with western

interests. We started to construct an identity around basic social structures such as family, clans and the community and then from this base, developed the ideology and leadership for the movement. Of course the structure is not completely flat as Shi'ism has a traditional leadership (through its seminaries and its collegiate senior leadership).

The 'flattish' communities linked by social mechanisms, and an ideology of shared values and of resistance, have proved to be also an effective mechanism for mobilisation and political activism that have yielded benefits well beyond the original defensive motivation.

The Islamist network of horizontally linked communities confronts western hierarchical structuralism, with its rigid lines of control, with a network of cells that can change shape and evolve. Traditional western state leverage is at its most effective when brow-beating the type of weak nation-states that the West deliberately scattered in its former colonies. Western states, however, have little purchase on horizontal networks – which, as non-state actors, tend to be more immune from the collective instruments of western control such as the UN Security Council or international agencies and organisations.

Western inability to find the fulcrum to impose its will on low-tech networked communities through legal conventions, and an international system based on the principle of the community of nation-states, designed to give an inbuilt advantage to the more powerful nation-states, naturally undermines the credibility of this power. The perceived failure of the system to impose its will or to crush such networks is a catalyst prompting others to challenge it too, sensing that western power is not invincible – and momentum evolves.

There is some resonance between these contemporary evolving concepts of flatter organisational structures with the Ottoman millet system in its pre-nineteenth-century form: different confessional and ethnic groups within the empire were granted considerable independence and the right to self-regulation. They also enjoyed a measure of autonomy, in that these quasi-independent groups maintained their own taxing and spending powers. This type of loose autonomy had a particular virtue in accommodating ethnic and confessional communities that were spread across a number of formal jurisdictions – and often were not contiguous.

Of course this system evolved under the Ottomans to solve the problem of coexistence with the non-Muslim confessional elements and a multitude of ethnicities within an empire that was explicitly Sunni. It was, therefore, to the extent that the Caliph was at the apex of this network of semi-autonomous groups, a semi-flat and two-tier arrangement – with the Sunnis occupying the top tier.

It is possible to foresee a re-thinking of the traditional sacral community with God at its apex, acting as an informal model loosely connected to the legitimacy of the Umma, and characterised by networked, semi-autonomous Islamist movements operating not under a Caliph – at least for the immediate future – but under poles of Muslim leadership – the homologue of the 'centres' of the earlier era. To a certain extent this arrangement already exists – albeit at a very informal level.

A more decentralised, networked order, one Hesballah interlocutor suggested, will result in a global society with less stratification in terms of power, less disparity of wealth within communities. With state power decentralised and diffused to the local level, a lower capacity for major conventional conflict becomes possible: reducing the influence of the exploitative and competitive tendency of the hierarchical system will also reduce instability, he foresaw.

'Openness' Inverted

When Bergson formulated the term 'open' society in the 1930s and conjoined it irreversibly in the minds of most westerners to their ordained order-from-market-exchange approach, Bergson was marching in step with the western conviction that history's progress towards its culmination represented God's will, or, for the secularists, the fulfilment of human nature with the advance of science and technology. Those who try to thwart it, such as Islamists, are fighting God's will, or are a reactionary force seeking to smother the 'natural' human instincts and aspirations towards an 'open' society.

Bergson of course, in defining 'openness', simultaneously defined the 'other'. The 'other' was the 'closed' society, characterised most usually by static religion that arises as a kind of mental habit, which binds human intelligence to the instinctive drive for solidarity and continuity: it keeps people and societies immobile.

It was not Bergson, but Popper who turned these themes into a Manichaean struggle. In his *The Open Society and its Enemies*, he presented a protracted duel between the 'good' open society and the forces of reaction, religion and traditional values, engaged in a perpetual struggle to smother 'freedom'. It was, as we noted earlier, a Cromwellian demand for the personal latitude required to encourage a then nascent capitalism and 'liberal' polity to thrive.

As the 'open society' irretrievably was defined by Popper for Americans as American society – his contrary formulation, its opposing category, was first to be symbolised by Marxism, and now is symbolised for most Americans by an Islamism that is seen and presented as the archetypal 'closed' society.

It follows from the juxtaposition of these opposing categories that not only does Islamism become, by definition, a 'force of reaction' attempting to smother western freedoms; but it is also a movement destined to fail. 'Our enemies', said Oliver Cromwell, 'are all the wicked men of the world, whether at home or abroad. Yea, act well, and be convinced what is God's interest and but prosecute it ... all the interests in Christendom are the same as yours.'[14]

Behind this lies the Christian view of history as a movement, not necessarily linear – with its successes and reverses – but a process within which is contained a purpose, and an inevitability of culmination of purpose. The secularist version drawn from these roots lacks the certainty of culmination, but sees advances in science and technology also as part of a movement of inevitable progress leading towards a universal goal.

In short, God is a Liberal: He created human nature in such a way that the market mechanism of political and economic life is the better fit for human nature. Popper and most westerners believe that it is a better fit than any competing economic or political system that Islamists may care to devise. The collapse of the Soviet Union represented the last attempt by a powerful mass movement to organise itself on any other basis than free market capitalism. The Soviet defeat proved the futility of trying to oppose the system once and for all, Francis Fukuyama argued – taking Popper to his logical conclusion.

It is plainly not logical from this perspective to waste much time in trying to understand Islamism if its demise is a Darwinian inevitability. It is simply necessary to step on those 'ants' of Bergson's metaphor that are guided by static religion – each individual fulfilling his or her allotted role in the anthill – in an allegory that, in contemporary visualisation, alludes to totalitarianism.

More optimistic westerners take a longer historical perspective: Catholicism had a long and bitter history of opposing the values of the open society before finally making peace with it. In the same way, they hope to see a growing pluralism take shape within Islam that will allow it to take its place within a dynamic and open western community of nations.

From this latter hope derive European policies to create 'moderate' Muslim leaders around whom Islam can be returned to docility and plurality, much as the Catholic Church, after bitter religious and political conflicts with the Anglo-Saxon world, also 'succumbed to the inevitability' of the free market exchange system – and understood the futility of opposition. The Catholic Church abandoned its opposition to pluralism in 1965, when it formally accepted that freedom of religion was a moral principle. It became 'tolerant'.

Popper, however, in his dichotomous framing of open and closed societies, omitted one key aspect from Bergson's original analysis. Were Ali Shariati, Khomeini or any of the other main Islamist leaders to be asked about Bergson's labelling of static religion as a passive force that holds society immobile in its precepts and traditions, they could not agree more! The entire Islamist struggle and revolution, as we have argued in these pages, has been about this issue precisely: how to turn Islam into a dynamic, open and forward-looking religion.

That the Iranian Revolution which marked the watershed step in the recovery of Shi'i Islam as a dynamic and revolutionary force, together with the import of this change for Sunnis, have both passed almost unnoticed in the West, is powerful testimony to the power of a good metaphor.

The answer to this 'blindness' or disinclination to 'try to understand' in respect to Islamism no doubt is partly due to the powerful mechanics of an antonymic metaphor that placed 'open' in direct conflict with 'closed'. The force of this simple construct, and one rooted in ancient myths that continue to resonate powerfully, has produced a western view of Islamism that is too mechanically simplistic and rigid to step beyond its hubris – the conviction of the inevitability of failure of any challenge to its continuing universal prevalence – and the complete lack of necessity of trying to understand it.

Dynamic Religion as Catalyst of Social Change

What Bergson also noted – and missing from Popper's sequel to his typology – was that the other side to regressive human behaviour – of taking refuge in instinct – was an openness to learning and change that pulls humanity way from the closed world of tradition and pattern. And it is the pulling away from this tradition that characterised the very ethos and mission of the Iranian Revolution. Bergson's 'drive for change' as the defining quality of the open society places the revolution as a singular symbol of the dynamic of our era.

He also said that open societies are called into being by ideals and aspirations, and noted that modern western industrial society contained many features of a closed society. In short, his writing was much more nuanced than the simple metaphor for which he is mainly celebrated. Bergson also added a further category of impetus towards the open society, and one that was dropped from Popper's subsequent appropriation of Bergson's typology

– Bergson identified dynamic religion as a key motor driving people forward to embrace change.

Popper's missing element – Bergson's characterisation of dynamic religion – puts into question the entire construct of the West as the 'open' society and Islam as the archetypal 'closed' society. If 'openness' is, as Bergson affirms, attachment to 'ideals and aspirations', then it is Islam with its aspiration for justice that can be called open and dynamic, while the West, which holds fast to the traditional myths of the natural order and progress, and is delimited by its instrumental thinking, is the society that might be termed 'closed'. In other words, Popper's Manichaean construct can be inverted as soon as the category of dynamic religion is re-inserted as the missing element from Bergson's original formulation.

Interestingly, gnosis or intuitive insight and knowledge, especially Catholic mysticism, was for Bergson the characteristic expression of dynamic religion – a view, as we saw in the chapter on political Shi'ism, that was shared by the Iranian leadership. In his final address to the Iranian people, Khomeini begged Iranians to continue the study of the field of knowledge known as 'irfan' (theoretical gnosis) since there could be no truly Islamic Revolution unless there was also a spiritual reformation.

It was this intuitively imaginative spiritual leadership of the Imams that had made Islam the dynamic force that had energised and mobilised the world in the seventh and eighth centuries, and which Khomeini saw was as necessary today in order to drag society back from the precipice of its present materialism.

Khomeini, Shariati and Qutb were all students of intuitive reasoning, or theoretical mysticism; Iran has a long history of gnosis, which is in the process of revival, as is Sufi thought in the Sunni world. As Bergson suggested might occur, its re-emergence is proving to be an important component of dynamism.

For those in the West accustomed only to view the Islamist revolutionary leadership through their own tradition of dogmatic puritanism, it can be a surprise to discover the vogue among Iranian revolutionaries for the mystical poetry of Islam. In expressing the aspiration of the soul towards God – divine love

– these poets cannot easily impart these feelings to other men, as Ibn Arabi noted, they can only express them symbolically. Arabi was a key influence on both Qutb and Khomeini. Al-Arabi and Jalaluddin Rumi, whose poetry is now widely read in the West, often expressed this aspiration through the erotic and bacchanalian symbolism of love for a woman. 'Drink wine! That it may set you free from yourself', is Arabi's message, urging loss of 'self' in the rapture of divine contemplation. This was symbolic, rather than intended as a behaviour that he expected to be followed mechanically. It is to such elements that Bergson probably refers when he tries to capture the quality of 'dynamism' in religion.

Inverting the Popper typology in relation to its usual meaning, as we have just done, serves to highlight the parallel and curious inversion that religion has become the principal site from which it is possible to deploy critical doubts about today's western society. Islam has emerged as a site, also within western societies, where Muslims and non-Muslims find a platform from which to mount resistance.

A further inversion is that, while the West is overwhelming physically powerful, its narrative is no longer that of the majority in the world. The myths on which it rests, and the legitimacy of its vision, are being questioned and challenged by an alternative meta-narrative – and by much of the rest of the world. As de Gaulle noted in respect to the fading legitimacy of constitutions: a rose only lasts as long as it lasts.

We have argued that the idea of the invisible hand in economics is a myth: free markets, where they existed, were the product of massive state action. We have also argued that the attempt to engineer free markets around the world, far from bringing stability and peace, brought terror, massacre and dislocation. We have also held that the connection between establishing a market structure and bringing democracy is false: they are competitors.

We have contended that it is also an illusion to view the nation-state as synonymous with 'democracy', by which is meant genuine participatory politics; it was conceived to deliver a powerful and armed elite, strong enough to force through the social changes demanded by the free market and free trade mechanisms.

And we have argued that the dominant process of thinking – instrumental rationality – whatever its scientific achievement, has not been as G.K. Chesterton noted, an unalloyed freeing of the intellect. These critics of religion start by denouncing religion as the reactionary force that threatens to smother human freedom, but then feel compelled to sacrifice the very existence of humanity to the non-existence of God. What are we to say of the fanatic who wrecks the world out of hatred for the 'other', who forsakes freedom itself, thus sacrificing precisely what they sought to defend? 'The secularists have not wrecked divine things; but the secularists have wrecked secular things, if that is any comfort to them.'[15]

In this chapter, we have continued with the argument that the conflict between Islam and the West is at its core a religious one, arising from processes and ideas that evolved during the religious wars of Europe. It is not therefore a struggle between Christianity and Islam as such – since the ideas and processes that can be traced down to the eruption of the present conflict themselves initially emanated from the Protestant and puritan struggle with another sacral community, namely Roman Catholicism, and were later extended to Islam. But neither is it an exclusively Protestant creation, as many of these themes – such as seeing history as a teleological process, apocalyptic expectations, and the belief in a transformation and redemption that can be brought about by human action – go to the roots of Christianity. At issue, as the Iranian cleric suggested, is the essence of man.

The question posed in the introduction, and to which we return in the last chapter, is what to do to prevent deterioration: the answer given by the cleric in Qom was that finding the path to coexistence requires first that the West should begin with some introspection. Like Michel Foucault, he believes that the first step in any process is renewal. Western thinkers need to continue critically to examine what the West is now, how it became what it is, and why this present state came about. From this critical re-examination, and by re-visiting original resources, it should be possible to find the energies of renewal – and, from new thinking, a different path to coexistence with Islamism. It is, in essence, a call to think about thinking – that is, thinking more about thinking, rather than re-thinking 'policies' – which would signify little change from 'ends and means' instrumentalism, and western terms.

From these arguments it follows that both western options that fall out from the false dialectic of an 'open' West versus 'closed' Islam are misconceived. The Islamist principle of a collective experience of the attainment of ethical living, we have argued, is irreconcilable with a system which holds to individuals' selfish pursuit of desires and appetites interacting to the benefit of all. Islamism can therefore reconcile into the western schema, not by discovering 'tolerance' but only through abandoning its central tenet. This seems an improbable outcome.

Similarly, to try to enforce a private and personal 'lifestyle choice' on Muslims in place of the collective culture necessary to sustain a just community represents, as we have argued, nothing less than an attempt to undo the last 100 years of Muslim history. It may have limited success, were enough pressure applied to particular vulnerable communities, but undoing the history of Islamism by setting up western models of so called 'moderation' that are simulacra of Christian experience, is hardly likely to reverse recent Islamic history.

We have also argued that the Islamist Revolution is about creating a dynamic and forward-looking religion that is in the process of evolving distinct ideas about the individual, about relationships within a society, about relationships between the community and its government. It has substance, it has ideas and it has force. It is not possible for guardians of a fading meta-narrative simply to reverse any feelings of vulnerability that they may experience from a rising rival narrative by a show of military force. And any attempt to do so is more likely to convey a whiff of a defensiveness and weakness, rather than to signal strength, as intended.

In the next two chapters we draw on two mainstream Islamist movements, first to illustrate how Hesballah has succeeded in rescuing culture from being a set of personal and private 'idiosyncrasies', to re-politicise it in a novel fashion – as a collective force, and as a tool with which to mass mobilise for resistance. In the subsequent chapter, drawing on the Hamas example, we argue that Hamas has used armed resistance as a psychological tool to facilitate objectives other than simply the defeat of the enemy.

Part III

6

A CULTURE OF WILLPOWER AND REASON

Most accounts of Hesballah and of the Shi'i of Lebanon 'awakening' begin with either the arrival in Lebanon of Musa al-Sadr, the charismatic cleric from Iraq, in 1959, or they begin with Israel's first invasion in 1978. But it is simply not possible to understand either the Shi'i of Lebanon or Hesballah by this approach. They did not just 'arrive' in the 1960s and 1970s. And the Shi'i experienced not one, but several political 'awakenings' from the late 1950s onwards – neither the Israeli invasion, nor Musa al-Sadr, nor the Iranian Revolution should be viewed as the unique starting point for Lebanese Shi'i political assertion.

Mount Amil, the mountainous range in the south of Lebanon, has been a centre of refuge and of Shi'i learning from at least the tenth and eleventh centuries. It was to here that Iran and Najaf turned in the sixteenth century for their scholarship. The links between Iran, Najaf in Iraq and Syria through Shi'i scholars and clerics is therefore more than 500 years old.

But the Shi'i need also to be understood as the perennial victims of one slaughter after another throughout history, and of a history of persecution by Sunni Arab kings and caliphs, Christian crusaders and the Ottomans. Throughout this history, they have never had powerful patronage or an external power to protect them. History has bequeathed to the Shi'i, not just in Lebanon, but everywhere, a strong sense of vulnerability to the intervention of strong powers. It has also bequeathed a powerful sense of the Shi'i as a common family, wherever they may live.

It is with this understanding that the history of Hesballah must be seen. The Christians of Lebanon have always had recourse to the West for support in their political struggles, and the Sunni Muslims have been always able to call on strong regional Sunni powers to intervene – and now enjoy the patronage of the United States. The political history of the Shi'i – until their recent mobilisation – has been one of persecution and of political and social marginalisation. The Shi'i remain very conscious of this, and feel their vulnerability – despite their successes in religious renewal and political and social mobilisation.

In essence, the political history of Lebanon has been one of a series of crises marking a path towards a more equitable system of power-sharing: behind this jostling for power between the fourteen confessions that make up Lebanon stands the bigger issue of which national identity will be the one that ultimately Lebanon will follow: a western-oriented and cosmopolitan one that preserves a Christian tradition, or one that looks more closely to Lebanon's geographical location as part of an Arab and Islamic region from whose political dynamics it would be an illusion to believe Lebanon can separate. It is within this Lebanese political context that the marginalisation of the Shi'i in Lebanon, and the rise of Hesballah needs to be understood.

The various sectarian competing histories of Lebanon often lay claim to having shaped the character of Lebanon by virtue of their historic presence and role, to which other 'blow-ins' cannot lay claim. The reality is that historic Lebanon – the mountainous coastal ridge known as Mount Lebanon – has been home to minorities who have been the victims of persecution for a very long time.

For more than a thousand years, from 632 until the end of the First European War in 1918, Syria, of which Mount Lebanon formed a part, was under Islamic jurisdiction as a part of the territory of a succession of Islamic empires. The only exception was the period between 1098 and 1291, when western Crusaders held sway.

At some point between the tenth and eleventh centuries, the Syrian and Christian sect of the Maronites moved from Syria to gather in the heights of the northern portion of the Mount Lebanon ridge. It was at about this time that the Druze emerged as a separate sect of Islam, concentrated along the southern spine of Mount Lebanon and in the southern Beqa'a Valley. The Druze is a sect, derived from the Isma'ili creed, that is widely regarded as not being truly Muslim. The early history of Lebanon was largely one of rivalry and clashes between these two tribal communities – Druze and Maronite – then more closely equivalent in numbers that at present, over their claims to pre-eminence over the religious and political character of the Mount Lebanon range that both occupied.

The Shi'i were already present to the south of Mount Lebanon and in the Beka'a by 874; but their territories remained separate, as a part of Greater Syria, and were included in Lebanon only in 1920.

Little is known about the spread of Shi'ism in the south from the earliest times, but it is probable that Shi'i became numerous in Mount Amil, the hill country that lies inland from Sidon and Tyre, from the tenth century. By this time, Shi'ism was pre-eminent in Greater Syria as a whole. In Aleppo, an important religious centre in the north of Syria, a Shi'i dynasty ruled, and most of the Muslim population of Greater Syria, was Shi'i at this time. Greater Syria or Bilad al-Sham then included all of historic Palestine and Jordan as well as what today constitutes Syria and Lebanon. All these territories then were mostly Shi'i.

The conquest of Syria in 1070 marked the turning of the tide for the Shi'i. The Sunni Turkish tribal conquest of Syria and the subsequent arrival of the Crusaders were followed by Salahidin's recovery of Crusader-occupied territories. Spurred on by the anti-Shi'i doctrines of Ahmad Ibn Tamiyya (d. 1328), four military expeditions 'to eradicate the Shi'i heresy' were mounted by the Mamlukes in northern Lebanon between 1292 and 1305. The Shi'i were being gradually eliminated and marginalised in order to impose conformity with the beliefs of the rulers.

Throughout this period of persecution the Shi'i were projected as non-orthodox and criticised as an ideology of 'rejectionism' by Sunni political rulers. The proclivity for dissent in Shi'i political thought was deemed threatening by the Sunni authorities.

By the fourteenth century, the Shi'i were no longer in a majority among the Muslims of Greater Syria. They had been largely removed from northern Syria – either they had been killed, fled or converted to the Sunni sect – but they continued to be present in Damascus and Aleppo.[1] It seems that Mount Amil became a centre of Shi'i learning following the Crusades, when Shi'i were driven from Nablus in Palestine and Amman in Jordan – until then predominantly Shi'i cities – to take refuge in Mount Amil.

In spite of attrition and persecution, the high tradition of Shi'i learning survived in the small market towns and villages of Mount Amil. The persistence of such a tradition in poor rural districts is not surprising. The survival in Mount Amil of a profoundly articulated creed and an impressive body of jurisdiction reflected the depth of conviction that has always marked the Shi'i, as did the existence of the shrine cities of Iraq, which exercised their influence on Amil from afar.[2]

The *madrassas* (institutes of Islamic learning) reached their zenith in Amil in the fifteenth and sixteenth centuries. It was during this period that the migration of Shi'i scholars to Iran, Iraq and Mecca began. As the Safavi dynasty (1501–1722) began the imposed conversion of Persia from Sunni Islam to Shi'ism, the Safavi dynasty's leaders turned to the Shi'i of Mount Amil for theological expertise and to help in the establishment of new seminaries throughout Persia. Thus began the close association between the Shi'i scholars of south Lebanon with Iran and the Shi'i seminaries of Najaf in Iraq that arose during the mid-sixteenth-century and continues in the present.

Institutionalising a Culture of Sectarianism

The modern modalities of Lebanese sectarianism were well established before the modern state of Lebanon came into being in 1943. In 1841 the Ottomans had established a confessional council of ten members (three Maronite, three Druze, one Greek Catholic, one Greek Orthodox, one Shi'i and one Sunni) that represented Lebanon's divergent identity.

In 1860, after Maronite workers rose up against their Druze landlords, leading to the deaths of as many as 11,000 Maronites and the burning of more than 200 villages, the Ottomans, under pressure from France, which was concerned for the well-being of its Maronite allies, established a representational council composed on similar confessional lines. This marked the first European intervention in Lebanon since the Crusades.

The historian Augustus Richard Norton noted that while these dynamics were well entrenched before independence in 1943:

> ... there were periodic readjustments both in the ratios of confessional representation and the allocation of government posts. However since [1943] there have been only modest adjustments, despite the fact that the confessional birth rate differentials have significantly changed Lebanon's demographic profile.[3]

The state of Lebanon from inception therefore lacked two essential ingredients to be a success: it was shaped without any underlying political accord, and it inherited and entrenched a pattern of uneven and accelerating social and economic disparity that was also reflected in differential rates of population growth. Not surprisingly, those elements enjoying the greatest economic advantage, such as the Maronites and the Sunni middle classes of Beirut, have experienced diminished birth-rates, whereas those communities in deprived regions maintained higher birth rates.

In all of this, unlike the Sunni Muslim traders of the coastal region and the Druze, who had had a political role in the historic Mount Lebanon, the Shi'i were at best marginal. In Ottoman times, the community had been the victim of Maronite and of Druze expansion, and they were still treated as 'lesser Arabs'.

Arab nationalism, which defined regional identity for a long period until the rise of Islamism, at its heart is a Sunni phenomenon and has held an inherent bias against the Shi'i (who comprise 15 per cent of Muslims globally), who were viewed as having divided the Muslim family.

Shi'i have never been well represented in the bureaucracy or military corps of an Arab state. In Lebanon, the seminaries, the libraries and the seats of learning in the south that the Safavi dynasty called upon when it began its conversion of Persia to Shi'ism in 1501, were subsequently ravaged by Ottoman forces sent to destroy this centre of Shi'i culture. They dispersed the more eminent among the local scholars and ransacked their libraries. Their Shi'i co-religionists in what is now Turkey fared worse under the Ottomans, who simply put them all to the sword, sparing only the Alawi sect of Shi'ism, which still survives in Anatolia.

In Lebanon, the Shi'i were also politically marginalised by both the Christians and the Sunni merchant classes who supported the Christians. The 1932 census – the basis for the allocation of parliamentary seats – put the Shi'i at 17 per cent of the population. On this basis they were allocated ten out of the 55 seats in Parliament; but the 1932 census was highly politicised and undertaken so as to ensure a Christian majority.[4] Many Shi'i were not counted.

At this time, the rural areas in which the Shi'i were concentrated were in decline and were dominated by hereditary feudal landlords who occupied most of the Shi'i parliamentary seats, and displayed little interest in their vassal workers. Living conditions in Shi'i villages were atrocious compared to standards elsewhere. By 1943, the Southern Lebanon district, which consisted of 300 mostly Shi'i villages, contained no hospitals and no irrigation schemes. Poverty and illiteracy were the norm in Shi'i rural communities.

The sectarian basis to the state decreed that each sect was responsible separately for establishing and running social institutions such as schools and hospitals, rather than having institutions of a common Lebanese identity. The sect – based on its political clout more than community need – therefore became the vehicle for access to state funding. Political under-representation in such a system exacerbated mal-distribution of resources and acted as a multiplier of poverty in a politically marginalised community such as the Shi'i.

In the early 1970s, Beirut and the surrounding Mount Lebanon had 64 per cent of private primary education facilities; 73 per cent of secondary educational institutions and all the university teaching; while 65 per cent of all doctors worked in Beirut, which accounted for only 27 per cent of the population.

As the rural areas languished, the economic and structural development of Beirut continued apace thanks largely to the Maronite and urban Sunni links into the network of western capital. After a brief civil war in 1958, Beirut had blossomed as the undisputed centre of the financial network linking the industrial world with the oil-producing nations of the Gulf. But the rapid urbanisation that came with incorporation into the capitalist economy further exacerbated disparities within Lebanon. Again it was the Shi'i who suffered disproportionately.

Economic growth in Beirut prompted a mass migration of rural Shi'i to Beirut. By 1973 only 40 per cent of Shi'i remained in rural areas and the Shi'i constituted 29 per cent of the population of Beirut.[5] Most of these newly urbanised Shi'i settled in a ring of suburbs aptly known as the 'misery belt' of Beirut.

The several hundred thousand Shi'i who settled in and around Beirut in the 'misery belt' were never assimilated into an urban 'Lebanese' identity. Rather, the poverty and lack of social provision reinforced the confessional Shi'i identity. This collective consciousness was enhanced by the widespread – and not unjustified – belief that the Shi'i had suffered the costs of the continuing conflict in Lebanon far more grievously than other groups. The Shi'i were forcefully displaced from their homes in the south on two occasions following the Israeli invasions of southern Lebanon in 1978 and 1982, as well as being ethnically cleansed from Christian enclaves during the civil war.

More important was the bigotry with which these Shi'i migrants to Beirut were received. Largely tenant farmers, sharecroppers and agricultural labourers, they become the 'dirty Chiclet vendors'[6] on the streets of Beirut. Suave Beirut citizens referred to 'those people' with unmistakeable disdain and contempt. In a study of Burj Hammud, a Beirut suburb, the Shi'i were described as dirty, untrustworthy, rapacious and a sexual threat to Christian women.[7]

The Shi'i Mobilise

Against the background of this rupture of Shi'i relations with their village homes, and the rupture of traditional relations with both the feudal landlords and the 'learned Shi'i families' who were also in political decline, and with the frustration of their expectations, the Shi'i were open to social and political mobilisation.

They lacked, however, the charisma, the vision and the energising quality of a revolutionary leader to translate the readiness of the people to discard old and worn-out patterns of behaviour into fresh thinking about new ways of living and new ways of envisaging the future. In 1959, the leadership, the ideology and the charisma arrived in the south of Lebanon in the person of Musa Sadr.

Musa al-Sadr was born in Iran in 1928, the son of an Ayatollah. The al-Sadr family, as we saw in an earlier chapter, was noted for its intellectual brilliance and had formed the epicentre of the Najaf 'nexus'. Musa al-Sadr had not originally intended to become a cleric, hoping instead to pursue a secular career, but his father, fearing for the future of Shi'ism in Iran, prevailed upon him to discard his original plans and to study law. One year after his father's death in 1953, he moved to Najaf in Iraq – a move that shaped his thinking about the future of Shi'ism and also set the course for the coming revolution in southern Lebanon.

It was this novel construct of Shi'ism from Najaf that Musa al-Sadr brought to Lebanon in 1958. His great-great grandfather had been born in south Lebanon, but following an anti-Ottoman riot in which his two sons were killed, he had left Lebanon for Najaf. On the face of it, Musa al-Sadr was an improbable leader for the Lebanese Shi'i: he was without patrons in Lebanon although his family connections in Iran and Iraq were complex and extensive.

He was a new kind of leader, an activist cleric engaged in the life of his community. He was tall and handsome with piercing green eyes. He spoke several languages and was as conversant with western thought as he was with Shi'i theology.

He succeeded in giving the Shi'i a new political identity and in mobilising them politically. There had been episodes of Shi'i protest and labour unrest during the late 1950s and early 1960s, but Sadr's pattern of mobilisation followed the Najaf inversion of tradition and historic practice, taking Shi'ism from being a force for passivity and immobilism, to being the instrument for action, energy and change.

The esoteric language of Shi'ism was turned into an ideology that resonated with everyday concerns of human welfare, and which also called up the vital human energy of resistance, which inspired the Shi'i community to an act of revolt. By organising politically and rallying behind their own militias they were able to wrest control of their destiny to become models for the Shi'i awakening and a challenge to a Lebanese political and social structure that had ignored and marginalised them.

Musa Sadr, Ayatollah Fadlallah and others helped insert practical social provision as a key component of an Islamist identity among the Shi'i in Lebanon. The extensive social and welfare services which these two clerics inaugurated helped to provide the services that south Lebanon sorely lacked, but these organisations also became vehicles for consciousness-raising among the Shi'i and the means to create a 'culture of resistance'. For Hesballah, this legacy continues to be reflected in its extensive contemporary social programmes.

By 1976, two years before the Iranian Revolution, Fadlallah was outlining the intellectual and psychological changes that would move the Islamists from the traditional Shi'i posture of passive acquiescence in the face of their history of economic marginalisation to one that embraced economic success and modern technology. Fadlallah argued the case on its own merits, but advocated this shift also on the basis of the desirability of the political strength that it brought – as building-blocks to mobilisation and resistance.

He endorsed force and power: force, he held, enables a man to be himself and not someone else, and enables him to seize control of his life:

> Force means that the world gives you its resources and its wealth; conversely, in conditions of weakness; a man's life degenerates, his energies are wasted; he becomes subject to something that resembles suffocation or paralysis. History, the history of war and peace, of science and wealth, is the history of the strong.[8]

This was revolutionary. Since its inception, Shi'i thought had never viewed the acquisition of power as a prerequisite of a good and pious life – on the contrary, asceticism had been seen as the appropriate response of the spiritual Shi'i towards the 'narcissism of man and the tyranny of wealth – man's biggest idol'.[9]

In the West, Hesballah's social programme, labelled as the movement's 'charitable activities' and 'financed by Iran', is dismissed as a blatant buying of political support for the movement. This is a flawed reading: their programme too is about mobilisation. It is about creating 'communities of resilience and of volition' and about self-reliance in defence. 'The pious strong' man is more meritorious than the 'pious weak' man, Fadlallah wrote: it is not only by words that men forbid evil, but through armed power as well.

The aim, as Ayatollah Fadlallah described during Lebanon's civil war, was to create a 'human state' that would provide the resources for people to help themselves and to assist one another. In contrast to the western conception of the nation-state as an instrument of free market economics, Fadlallah posited the 'human state'. It was to be constructed around human values and would implement the norms of a just community.

Musa al-Sadr's time in Lebanon, until his trip to Libya in 1978 – during or after which he disappeared without trace, thereafter becoming known as the 'vanished Imam' – coincided with the outset of a pivotal period in Lebanese relations with Israel. In 1968, the Palestine Liberation Organisation (PLO) had begun making military raids into Israel from south Lebanon. By the early 1970s Lebanon had become the PLO's main and only platform for launching attacks on Israel, following the PLO expulsion from Jordan.

Towards a Shi'i Military Defence

As Israeli reprisals into south Lebanon intensified in response to these PLO raids, Musa al-Sadr demanded protection for the Shi'i of the south. The Shi'i had begun to abandon their villages and to move north to escape the war zone. Sadr responded by establishing training camps in order that the Shi'i could learn how to defend themselves. He established ties with the Palestinians, but relations eroded and became increasingly tense as Shi'i suffering grew.

Under the pressure of Israeli attacks and the activities of the Palestinian commandos, the bitter grievances of Lebanon's confessional groups erupted and civil war broke out in 1975. Sadr and his followers started their own militia called Amal, which was trained and supplied by the PLO.

The year 1979 saw the overthrow of the Shah and the onset of the Iranian Revolution. The revolution had an electric effect on Shi'i everywhere, but for those in Lebanon – as Grand Ayatollah Fadlallah pointed out at the time – it underpinned the incipient mobilisation of the Shi'i with a huge sense of empowerment: that if they organised, and if they planned, and were determined, they could achieve great victories against the odds.

So, when Israel invaded Lebanon again in 1982, the resistance that ultimately emerged to defeat Israel and to force its withdrawal in 2000 was a Shi'i community – with Hesballah as its core – that was mobilising, and that had been motivated and inspired by the Iranian Revolution.

At the outset, 'they [Hesballah] were very amateur, foolhardy in many ways, but very brave. They just walked into the line of fire and were cut down very badly. It was just like watching the Iranian assaults against Iraq',[10] noted a commentator on Hesballah's early military efforts after the unveiling of its military wing in 1985.

By mid-1986, the Islamic Resistance of Hesballah understood that it needed to evolve, and to develop new tactics if it was to be successful against the Israelis. It could not remain as an armed vanguard within a coalition of guerillas and continue the conflict in isolation from the support of the people: not only was the movement suffering severe casualties in some engagements, but its rapid growth in the Beqa'a Valley along the border with Syria, and in Beirut, had brought the group into conflict with Amal and with Syria. In 1987, Syrian troops in Beirut had clashed directly with Hesballah, but, more seriously, in 1988 open war erupted between Hesballah and Amal, prompted by the latter's fears that Hesballah was encroaching on Amal's support base among the Shi'i.

Even in its relations with the local population in the south, there had been strains caused both by Hesballah's imposition of Islamic restrictions on traditional activities such as playing backgammon, and by Israeli reprisals against resistance operations that seemed to the local inhabitants to be foolhardy and destined to fail. It was not that the local Shi'i objected to resistance, it was that they wanted it to be effective and not lead to disproportionate pain for the civilian population in pursuing operations against the occupiers.

At the outset, resistance to the Israeli occupation had comprised a collective of locally based Shi'i groups operating largely autonomously and under local leadership. It is estimated that there may have been up to 18–24 different components to this somewhat chaotic early resistance, which was dominated by Amal, the largest movement.

In many cases there was overlap of membership, with fighters having two or more allegiances to different resistance groupings; thus during the 1983–88 period of hostage-taking in Lebanon, responsibility for actions was often falsely attributed, or misleadingly attributed to movements based on the overlap of membership. Hesballah has consistently denied involvement in the hostage-taking in Lebanon of the early 1980s.

Hesballah responded to this relative anarchy by reforming its military arm. It was really only in 1987, however, that it began disentangle its membership from the general resistance mix, to introduce a strict cell structure, and to impose secrecy regarding its military structure and operations, which remains its hallmark to this day. Even today, a person's membership of the Hesballah military arm is not known to their family or to close colleagues in Hesballah. And it was only in 1991 – after the conflict with Amal had ended in 1989 – that it can be said that the Islamic Resistance Movement finally emerged as the forerunner of the modern Hesballah military force.

To understand the changes that took place after 1991 that transformed the performance of Hesballah as a military resistance, it is necessary to understand that its essence lay not just.in the organisational changes and the acquisition of expertise, but in creating a psychology of willpower; entrenching a culture of resistance and steadfastness within the community; instilling the willingness to sacrifice on behalf of the community; and engaging in deep study of the enemy.

Western observers frequently look for some pivotal technical or organisational change that can explain Hesballah's military successes. Certainly, it is true that Hesballah has evolved an organisational structure that is very different from western military models, and it is true also that it now has the experts and experience that it did not have earlier. It is true, too, that it has highly skilled specialised units and sophisticated equipment that it deploys in novel ways; but underlying its success, as any Hesballah military commander will be quick to explain, is the morale and willpower of its fighters.

Hesballah's methodology has been one of a careful building of a strategy to change their situation. One Hesballah member described it as a 'revolution that understands its boundaries; a revolution that comprehends that failure to recognise the existence of boundaries can lead to disaster: it is therefore a revolution that understands the need to bring people on board. This is the boundary that must be respected.'

The speaker added that:

> ... respecting this need for patience – of not moving quicker than the readiness, the mobilisation, and the state of consciousness of people permits – means that the movement avoids committing to short-term objectives. The psychological preparation is in terms of patience – not expecting results tomorrow; of casting the victories that do come as a foretelling of further victory.

In this conversation, another Hesballah senior leader with long experience of formulating the movement's military strategy outlined the essential ingredients of this revolution: 'building the ideology, building the communities of resistance who embrace this ideology and providing the charismatic leadership that can cast its spell over people; but whose task is to protect and strengthen the community'.

Hesballah defines its progress of awakening consciousness in terms of collective cohesion and development: 'Its aim is to create communities of capability that have the resilience to resist.' Underlying this approach, the Hesballah member said, lie a number of principles: a strengthening of the psyche of the individual through the study of philosophy – all military commanders attend classes in philosophy – and the practice of critical thinking. It reflects Imam Khomeini's call to replace the 'colonised brain' with the 'independent brain'. Its purpose is to build an inner self-assurance and resilience. This 'equilibrium' enables him or her to avoid the swings of sentiment from despair to over-confidence that can weaken an individual facing intense psychological warfare from his or her enemy.

Liberating Thinking

Hesballah's programme in microcosm can be viewed as a version of the Habermassian concept of recovery of the public sphere from institutional moulding – or in this case, from western thinking: Jürgen Habermas saw the capacity to use one's reason and to think critically in associations of private citizens as the genesis of a culture that would evolve to express their genuine needs and their interests – free from the pervasive moulding of instrumental thinking.

By this, Hesballah means to free Muslims from the concept that theory – and therefore 'truths' – are just the correct mirroring of an independent realm of 'facts'. This is the westernised mindset that sees facts as fixed, given and unalterable, and which believes that from these 'facts', be they properties of a natural element or social or economic findings, it is always possible to determine the 'natural laws' that accurately mirror the array of facts.

Islamists see this type of atomised and empirical study of only those elements of the universe which are readily measurable – to the exclusion of other types of reasoning – to have been the cause of instrumentalism. It was this manner of thinking that led the West towards 'social Darwinism', racism and to the Nazi scientific experiments on humans – all done in the absolute belief in this realm of 'natural laws'. Islamists would argue that truth lies in a deeper understanding of human values and the nature of reality.

Hesballah's policy also symbolises a step in the Islamist progress of redefining the individual by abandoning the 'culturalisation' of politics in which problems of injustice, exploitation and inequality are effectively anaesthetised as political issues by a change in what issues such as inequality and oppression signify in the contemporary western world.

Instead of being 'just causes', demanding the response of political protest or resistance, they are de-politicised and held to be 'cultural differences': these differences are held to result from the lifestyle 'choices' that have led an individual to embrace the way of life in which he or she finds him or herself.

Such 'cultural' differences as, for example the former position of the Shi'i as the objects of disdain and discrimination by other Lebanese, were neutralised as something 'natural', something given, which could not be overcome. They were simply the workings of 'natural laws' producing their inevitable results. This was not something that could be overcome; just as natural evolution produced its tragedies, these consequences had to be 'tolerated'. The mark of contemporary civilisation is 'toleration' – as the appropriate response to those held fast, in Popper's model, by their 'static' culture and instincts.

Hesballah's first response to this de-politicisation of culture has been to promote a strengthening of the psyche through cultivating the reasoning and critical faculties of the individual – to give him or her, an 'independent brain'.

The second step was to invert the mechanism of opposition between the collective and the individual – created through the western demand for the personalisation of culture – as the only basis for 'toleration' in a plural society that respects individual 'rights'. In an 'open society' the individual 'elevates' himself or herself above his or her particular culture.

Hesballah uses its social and community activities precisely to re-politicise culture: by stressing the collective community as a set of values, norms and role models that can be emulated by Shi'i living their day-to-day lives, Hesballah extricates the individual from 'culture as private beliefs and idiosyncrasies' that has no political significance. Instead it articulates the collective norms – Imam Hussein's martyrdom in pursuit of justice, for example – that politicise a collective culture as a site for resistance.

Hesballah recalls the embattled scholar Ibn Mubarak in the eighth century who, as we noted earlier, recreated the early community of the Prophet for his band of warriors with his accounts of martyrdom of those heroes of the early wars of Islam. Ibn Mubarak also placed the emphasis on the collective norms of the fighters' intention in jihad, as well as the striving, sacrifice and volunteering of the many individuals who comprised it. Other themes that echo today in terms of leadership were the narration of Ibn Mubarak's strength and self-control, as well as the empathy that existed between him and his comrades in arms, modelled on relations among the companions of the Prophet.[11]

Hesballah's strengthening of the individual also comes from contemplation within him or her of the concept of God's attribute of 'power', and through a personal 'drawing' on this attribute, the acquisition of an inner mental 'strength', a Hesballah Sheikh explained. This quality enables a person to contrive the willpower and spirit with which to confront and overcome disproportionate force used against him or her. This type of mental preparation was conceptualised in Imam Hussein's call for a 'victory of blood versus the victory of the sword' – in other words, in cultivating the spirit and political determination to stand against a superior force.

From the same attribute of 'mental strengthening', the Sheikh suggested, it was possible to cultivate a steadfastness and resilience that 'will drive a superior adversary to despair at being able to inflict a psychological defeat'.

Fourth, Hesballah adopts a practice of charismatic leadership that protects against abuse of office, and which develops a commitment to honourable conduct. This doctrine aims to draw on each individual's personal skills and capabilities in order to construct a strong and cohesive community. Such strong communities can serve as a wider model for others, he noted.

The movement fortifies the community by strengthening 'the individual as a human being and by fortifying the relations of this human being with his immediate fellow human beings – be they in the framework of the family, the neighbourhood, the tribe, the clan or the nation'.[12] It also strengthens it psychologically by holding aloft and extolling role models drawn from the narrative of Islam. Cultural identity-building includes a wide repertoire of Hesballah freedom music, poetry and visual links to connect people to values that these role models personify.

The movement also emphasises icons and deeds drawn from within their own community – often these are martyrs who are revered as representing certain key values in building community resilience. Additionally, Hesballah tries to create direct personal connection between individuals and those icons by linking people's personal roles within the community – however humble – to the values exhibited by the icon. Building individual self-esteem is seen as an element of developing resilience, and as a stepping stone to wider mobilisation.

In practical terms, one activist described it as a 'process of personal coaching of individuals' as well as small teams working with groups. In this aspect, Hesballah is echoing the work of the small teams of trainers used by the civil rights movement in the United States to mobilise the community for the campaign. Hesballah's aim is to strengthen each individual's ability to contribute to the community. This may mean helping him set up in business or it may mean training him as a member of an elite military militia.

Setting an individual member of the community on his feet is a part of the wider objective of enabling an individual to give, and to experience, respect reciprocated within a just community. One of the demands of the Prophet was that humans treat each other with respect: to receive respect from friends, to receive respect as a father or mother, as a husband or wife or as a businessman or woman. Respect is viewed as an important antidote to the de-humanisation and alienation of contemporary society.

The first stage is to create self-respect by developing self-reliance and self-knowledge, and then to entrust young people with the exercise of responsibility and of leadership. Providing individuals with respect from the community – making them feel valued and needed – is perceived as fortifying them and building 'resilience'. Community cohesion is developed from the concept of service owed to the community as a direct response to the giving of that respect from a process of what Hesballah members call 'networking', and from a carefully constructed psychological development of community *ésprit*.

Networking, a Hesballah senior leader explained, is the process of encouraging the exchange of favours – however small – between members of the community. The offering of some small service to another without charge, and receiving a different service in return, builds the ligaments of a community and inculcates a sense of wider social duty beyond that of individual duty.

It represents the Qur'anic concept outlined earlier, whereby a habit of giving a proportion of one's wealth to others and the offering of service to the community foster 'detachment' from material possessions, and also inculcate the ideals of selflessness and sacrifice into the community. It represents an attempt to transpose the norms of a just community into the life of contemporary Shi'i living in Lebanon today.

The objective is the channelling of energy – both positive energy as well as anger – into socially and politically useful endeavours. 'Lately [since the 2006 war] we have spent a lot of time on anger management. We want to turn this anger from a destructive course into something politically useful – building resistance perhaps – or into some socially constructive activity', one community activist said.

A Culture of Resistance and a Psychology of Willpower

These bottom-up community strengthening measures also underlie Hesballah's military doctrine. Far from the western image of a movement that is so regimented – or totalitarian, as Hesballah's detractors describe it – that there is no room for personal initiative or autonomy, Hesballah's doctrine is one that encourages personal responsibility and initiative, and stresses service to the community. Its ethos is self-discipline rather than the unthinking corporate discipline of totalitarianism.

In the conflict with Israel in 2006, a Hesballah military commander explained that 'the commanders of the small militia units that operated in villages had almost complete autonomy – within the parameters of the overall plan that had been developed before the war began'. These units also 'networked' with neighbouring units at their own discretion.

The military command structure of the movement was changed after 1989 to reflect this autonomy: most of the units are part-time locally based militia, assisted by village self-defence units. There is a small, but highly professional, full-time brigade of combat soldiers who in small numbers reinforce the militia, and there are reserve units and specialised units, but the key aspect is that all these elements operate to a high degree of networked autonomy within the parameters of various pre-agreed contingency plans of operational action.

Hesballah has deliberately avoided the dangers of becoming oversized and visible. Its 'flat' network of small, highly professional militia working on their own terrain has resulted in an effective military machine that is almost 'invisible' on the ground.

The parameters of action within which the combat units operate are planned by a military leadership that also includes local political leaders. There are regional and specialised unit commanders, but Hesballah has almost entirely eliminated the middle layers of 'command and control' on which western military units depend.

These intermediary levels were removed many years ago because Hesballah saw that when they deployed in conventional western military structures, it was very easy for the enemy to detect them; but, more importantly this flexibility also allowed units a relatively free hand in making their own decisions based on the circumstances locally, without the need to report continually up a chain of command or to await instructions. Local units are assumed to be in a better position to judge their operations than their leaders in Beirut and have the authority to act.

Leadership – so pivotal in such a structure that delegates so much responsibility to unit commanders – in Hesballah's doctrine is a quality that is innate to the individual: it is essentially a quality of personal charisma; and of character traits such as integrity, authenticity and reliability that induce others to follow him or her. There is however another intangible quality to leadership that the movement esteems – the ability to mobilise, to 'cast a spell' over an individual or a community – in one sense, a sort of mystical quality to leadership.

The role of a leader in mobilising and raising the revolutionary consciousness of people is given enormous significance. Sayyed Hassan Nasrallah's speeches are listened to with rapt attention across the Muslim and Arab world. He is viewed as one of the best orators – using a careful mix of styles that combines the vernacular of the ordinary man with philosophic and intellectual content. His speeches differ in another way: there is realism, and there are no flowery claims of achievement. He explains policy carefully and then sets out to answer criticism frankly. In this his style is virtually unique in the Arab world.

At the cadre levels, leadership involves a process of selection by peers – an identification of leadership by fellow colleagues, rather than the western-style selection of management qualities from above. 'The purpose of leadership is to develop qualities of character among those they lead, establish a framework of values that will impel young people into responsibility for their actions and fortify the community', a former Hesballah military leader with responsibility for training the militia said. This represents a contrast with the western definition of leadership as being 'the possession' of the knowledge, training and professional skills to qualify for leadership.

The conflict in Lebanon in the summer of 2006 that resulted in a mainstream Islamist movement, Hesballah, gaining dominance on the ground against a superior military force, obtaining mastery of the intelligence war, and delivering a political victory, demonstrated Hesballah's success in using a carefully prepared guerilla strategy in an engagement with an open and defined enemy using heavy weapons over a large geographic area, over a period that was long enough to secure their goals.

Hesballah in 2006 provided the model for the evolution of asymmetrical warfare applied strategically over a wide area, with units at times slipping away from the combat zone with their weapons, only to reappear in villages that Israeli troops thought they had taken, in order to initiate attacks behind the Israeli front lines. In the past, its operations would have been characterised by surprise – a key element to Hesballah's strategy – and a contact with the enemy, limited both in geographical terms as well as in its short duration.

The strategy in 2006 was simple: to ignore western air superiority. Since the Israeli withdrawal in 2000, Hesballah had begun preparing a network of underground tunnels and posts to ride out the expected aerial bombing campaign in underground protected bunkers up to 40 metres beneath the ground. When the initial air attack was complete, however many days that took, they emerged from the underground bunkers to mount a prolonged rocket and missile attack on the enemy.

In this case, it is the word 'prolonged' that is key: the rockets and missiles were not expected to cause real damage to Israel or to break the Israelis psychologically; but of course the prolonged assault did have its impact on morale – however little actual damage was inflicted.[13] Hesballah had calculated that, from the time of firing until the Israeli Air Force was able to identify and deploy fighters to take out the mobile rockets was 90 seconds. Through years of diligent training, Hesballah rocket teams had learned to deploy, fire and safely conceal their mobile launchers in less than 60 seconds, with the result that neither artillery nor air attack could stop Hesballah's continued rocket fire at Israel. Israel proved largely unable to deplete Hesballah's inventory of missiles and rockets during the war.

The purpose of prolonged missile and rocket attack, however, was to force the adversary – frustrated by his inability to bomb the enemy into halting the attack – to commit troops on the ground. It was during this last, and critical, phase, with the adversary exposed on the ground, that a dedicated, well-trained and well-led guerilla force with intimate knowledge of appropriate terrain could – and did – inflict enormous pain on Israel's modern military establishment – and defeat it.

In the hilly terrain of south Lebanon, it was not the tanks of Israel's army that protected the foot soldiers; it was the infantry, the exposed men on foot, who ended up – inverting the whole rationale for armour – having to protect their tanks from Hesballah's effective hand-launched missile attacks. In the event, Israel lost both large numbers of tanks and troops.

The price for Hesballah, of course, was an air attack that caused heavy damage to civilian superstructure and civilian casualties throughout Lebanon; but a Shi'i community such as that of south Lebanon has proved to possess the inner resources to overcome such losses. The losses to Hesballah's fighting force in any case were small in comparison – perhaps less than 200 men.

The outcome was the endorsement of Hesballah's flat, networking of autonomous units, using deliberately low-tech systems, combined with its episodic and unexpected deployment of small specialised units using high-tech weapons to maintain the psychological edge. But the outcome also reflected Hesballah's mastery of intelligence, and of the public relations war; many Israeli journalists and commentators noted publicly during the conflict, that they preferred to rely on Hesballah's account of events to that of the Israeli Defence Force.

Despite the damage done to Lebanon's infrastructure and the heavy civilian casualties, the leader of Hesballah, Sayyed Hassan Nasrallah, summed up his perception of the outcome in a victory speech on 25 September 2006: 'You are today sending an extremely important serious political and moral message ... to the entire world ... do not underplay the victory ... your steadfastness and resistance exposed the United States, and raised the level of peoples' consciousness.'

The Value of Resistance and Struggle

This Hesballah victory, in the estimation of its leader, showed the people of the Muslim world that the strategy employed by pro-western Arab and Muslim governments – a policy viewed as appeasing US interests – on the grounds that there is simply no alternative except to acquiesce to US political and military power – is not the only one.

Hesballah, resistance in Iraq and Afghanistan, and, in a different context, Hamas, have shown Muslims that there is an alternative: armed defiance as a part of a wider resistance, mounted asymmetrically against overwhelming conventional western military power. The Hesballah victory provides one element of asymmetrical resistance – the model of military success – of defying western military hegemony in the region, and thereby undermining also its political stature and narrative in the region.

The philosophy of resistance espoused by Hesballah is derived from the same principles that underlie its social programme:

> When we talk about justice, human rights or human welfare we need to note the definition and perspective from which we approach them. We must show how Islam gives these values innate value and importance.
>
> Islam recognises these values as being essential values. The respect of man, his dignity and his life, are all aspects of Islam, they are not tools to be used by politicians to control man.
>
> We see huge difference between the western and the Islamic universal view. In western thought, politics and governance are regarded as 'ends'; and values are the 'means' of policy. In Islam, however, it is quite the opposite: it is politics which is at the service of spreading human values and ethics.
>
> If we go back in history and read about the Prophet and his family, we see that they were never ready to sacrifice values for the sake of power. If you observe that today the Shi'i and Muslims generally regard figures such as Imam Ali or Imam Hussein as role models for revolutionary movements, it is because they put human values above politics.
>
> Today the ceremony of 'Ashura' (the Shi'i annual commemoration of Imam Hussein's martyrdom) offers to every Muslim a model and path for resistance and the struggle against injustice. This impulse emerges from Ashura's insistence that human dignity and human values transcend all else. The message of Ashura is that human values are so vital that a leader such as Imam Hussein, the Prophet's grandson, was willing to sacrifice himself for them, rejecting compromise on principles – even at the cost of his own death.

The main logic to resistance and struggle in Islam is defined by precisely these noble values: at no level can man and his values be eliminated. It is these considerations that determine both when and where a Muslim may go to war, and also define the terms on which peace is established. Decisions of war and peace are carefully calibrated by these values. The issue of when to make peace, and when to go to war, therefore, is no mere political expedient: it is a matter of principle and doctrine.

Our conception of martyrdom should be understood similarly. Martyrdom is not a committing of suicide. When our essential values and principles are at stake, or are infringed, we offer our human body as a sacrifice; its spirit, nevertheless, remains to preserve these values.

Jihadist groups such as al-Qae'da practise no popular mobilisation of this nature; their form of 'shock and outrage' consciousness-building, which envisages no preparation of people, is intended to foster hostility and overwhelming feelings of anger, and a desire for revenge rather than the 'awareness, and not hostility' that Sayyed Hassan Nasrallah identified as his desired outcome from Hesballah's military conflict in the summer of 2006.

Al-Qa'eda tactics, a reflection of its sense of powerlessness in a global context, are condemned as unjust by the overwhelming majority of Muslims. Their actions, which, by their nature, entail unpredictable outcomes – including counter-productive ones – have resulted in creating victims, often innocent victims, whose deaths are viewed as morally unjust by the vast majority of Muslims.

Hesballah, by contrast, took on directly a western conventional military machine and prevailed – something, as its critics frequently point out, al-Qa'eda so far has failed to do. That such an outcome has been achieved by a mainstream political movement that stands in elections, is accountable to its constituency, and shows real concern for the welfare of fellow Muslims – unlike that of some jihadists – has not been lost on public sentiment.

Movements such as Hamas and Hesballah look on the results of al-Qa'eda-type uncontrolled, and uncontrollable, unleashing of emotion and of dynamics of mindless violence as purely destructive and inimical to the creation of any improvement in society. They see it as the type of uncontrolled revolution that ends by consuming its own authors: they view these tactics as a recipe for unrestrained turmoil and conflict between Muslims.

There are few issues more sensitive to the Shi'i than the emergence of radical Sunni groups that view the Shi'i as heretics. The Shi'i comprise perhaps 15 per cent of all Muslims today, and therefore feel themselves to be particularly vulnerable to those Sunnis who declare Shi'i to be unbelievers who should be put to death.

Internal Ideological Warfare

The Shi'i rejection of Sunni power following the martyrdom of Hussein in 680 CE led some Sunnis to brand the Shi'i as an errant interpretation of Islam, and within a few years of Ali's death a sect of Islam, the Khawarij, had already set about massacring any Shi'i that they could find. Sunni political leaders, however, worried less about the Shi'i as a theological threat than as a political threat.

These caliphs and kings imprisoned and killed Shi'i imams; Sunni jurists were encouraged to formulate a Sunni orthodoxy intended to marginalise and exclude the Shi'i, and to contain their appeal. By the end of the tenth century, Shi'i were being killed, and even burnt alive. When the Byzantine-Turkish forces invaded the Middle East in 971, the first reaction of the Sunnis was to blame the Shi'i. Shi'i houses were torched and the inhabitants attacked and killed. By the middle of the eleventh century, persecuting the Shi'i had become a custom, a pattern of behaviour that would be repeated down the centuries – to the present day.

Today anti-Shi'i sentiment is focused mainly among certain Sunni groups of a Salafist orientation, and in al-Qa'eda. Some of these anti-Shi'i jihadist movements call openly on their websites for Muslims to kill the Shi'i – and also to assassinate those Sunnis such as the leaders of Hamas who have relations with Shi'i movements such as Hesballah, which these websites usually describe as 'the Party of the Devil'.

A member of the top Hamas leadership banged his fist hard on the table to emphasise this point: 'Usama bin Laden may have

been a disaster for you; but he has been a catastrophe for us',
he said.

> The situation of Muslims everywhere has deteriorated as a result of the
> 'War on Terror'; it is worse for Muslims in Cairo as much as it is in Paris,
> and in the Palestinian territories it has allowed Israel to unleash massive
> military action against us.

Sayyed Nawaf Mousawi, one of Hesballah's chief political
strategists, was explicit on the dangers that the Sunni jihadi groups
such as al-Qa'eda pose to a Shi'i movement such as Hesballah.
Hesballah, he noted was highly vulnerable to what he described
as the 'khawarij trend'.

Sayyed Mousawi underlined that the many modern counterparts
to this early bloody trend of sectarian hatred had 'marked
Hesballah leaders for assassination'. Sayyed Mousawi said that
such movements, including al-Qa'eda, 'actually represent a greater
danger to my people and to the Palestinian population than they
do to western interests – great though that may be. This is the real
danger. This is the danger that needs to be recognised.'

The reason for such targeting, Sayyed Mousawi explained, is
the paradox that 'the jihadists think we are too moderate, too
willing to participate in democratic processes – which they view
as just another colonialist plot promoted by the Americans to
dominate our region', whereas the Americans attack us because
'they see us as a threat to their hegemony'.

'Would the United States devote so much time, attention and
effort to Lebanon – were it not for the existence of Hesballah
there?', a Hesballah leader asked. 'If Lebanon was only Siniora,
Jumblatt and Geagea [Lebanese political leaders of different
confessional faiths], would the US bother with Lebanon at all?'

The United States 'bothers' about Hesballah for the same
reasons that most European governments bother – because they
view Hesballah through the optic of Israel. Hesballah leaders
say – time and time again – that when Europeans come to talk
with them, their questioning invariably remains Israeli-centric.
These visitors define Hesballah as the opposite 'other' to Israel.
As a consequence, their focus is on disarming the movement and

attempting to domesticate and weaken it by making all its parts subordinate to a strengthened central government in Beirut.

It is of course an old story: it is Turkey again. In Turkey, and in other parts of the Muslim world, the institutions of Islam were 'nationalised' and its office holders became civil servants and the docile dependents of government, whereupon they quietly nodded off to sleep. As we saw in the last chapter, the nation-state has always been viewed by the West as an instrument by which to enforce its norms.

But it is a model that simply has never worked in Lebanon. The Lebanese government has always been a power-sharing arrangement struck as a balance between each confession's separate power and strength. This is one of the reasons Lebanon has such a long history of external interference – as one or other confessional group has attempted to leverage its position against the other confessional groups by calling on the support of an external patron. This has been the case for the last five hundred years, and is unlikely to change in the foreseeable future.

The habit of viewing Hesballah as the opposite 'other' to Israel has obscured any deeper western understanding of this movement being at the forefront of thinking about the evolution of Muslim communities. Were policy-makers able to step beyond their limited optic, they would see, as we have argued here, an Islamist community that functions as an experimental model of how a just, equitable and compassionate community of Muslims might still function in a state, Lebanon, that is dominated by western values.

It is, in the microcosm of the Shi'i in a westernised Lebanon, playing out the ideology, the social structures and human content for what might well shape the future at the macrocosm. This is a process that has led Hesballah leaders to redefine the meaning of community, culture, economic activity and individualism in novel ways, and just as Hesballah is a continuing experiment within a larger Lebanon, so too Hesballah offers insights and one of the most creative models to the Muslim world. In the longer term, its relationship to Israel may become a footnote to this more significant story.

7

REFUSING SUBSERVIENCE

When Edward Said drew attention to Sigmund Freud's provocative reminder that Judaism's founder was a non-Jew, and that Judaism begins in the realm of Egyptian, non-Jewish monotheism, Said surmised that Freud's intent was deliberately to 'open out' Jewish identity to the true diversity of its history.[1]

He noted in his talk that even the science of archaeology had been utilised by Israel as an array of 'facts' from which a new 'natural right' could be empirically deduced to consolidate a Jewish state:

> Thus archaeology becomes the royal road to Jewish-Israeli identity, one in which the claim is repeatedly made that in the present-day land of Israel, the Bible is materially realised thanks to archaeology. History is given flesh and bones; the past is recovered, and put in dynastic order.[2]

Said quotes from Nadia Abu el-Haj's history of the colonial archaeological exploration in Palestine.[3] Abu el-Haj, he notes, linked the practice of archaeology to the same nationalist objectives as we saw in Turkey: to enable a strong unitary state with intent to possess the land through settlement, cleansing and the replacement of Arab place names with new Hebrew nomenclature – just as Ataturk had erased the Kurdish and Armenian existence from the villages of Anatolia. It followed a pattern of vibrant exclusionary European nationalism that had leveraged national states around a single ethnicity or religious group since the nineteenth century.

This deliberate deconstruction of Palestinian cultural history eventually gave rise to the gradual emergence of a Palestinian archaeology. This had been spurred, at least in part, by the emergence of revisionist history in Israel in the 1980s, which provided an historical account of the deliberate destruction and the removal of Palestinian towns and villages in the conflict of 1948 drawn from contemporary Jewish sources. The emergence of a Palestinian archaeology was perceived as a 'resistance of archaeology' and as a defiant response to a deliberate effort to undercut Palestinian identity.

A particular kind of colonial settlement – settlement facts on the ground – was inferred from this realm of discrete archaeological remnants. And the latter served as the fragments from which a sort of spatial biography was assembled. It was from these 'facts' that a Jewish state was deduced, as if from a 'natural ordering' of historical facts, to become the Jewish national home.[4]

This 'positivist' scientificity resonated well with the Christian meme of the Americans' own history of settlement and ethnic clearing in the new colonies of North America: 'We are the particular chosen people – the Israel of our time; we bear the ark of the liberties of the world', Herman Melville wrote in White Jacket [5] in 1850, well before the founding of the Israeli state.

In the same lecture, Edward Said quoted Frantz Fanon's dissection of the effect of European colonialism on the psyche of Algerian natives as key to an understanding of the consequences of Israel's exclusionary nationalist thinking. The reference by Said to Fanon underlines the point that so many of the Islamist thinkers who have made their mark ideologically were deeply influenced by Fanon's powerful analysis: from Qutb to Ali Shariati, the mobiliser and ideologue of the Iranian Revolution; from Ayatollah Fadlallah and Musa al-Sadr, the mentors who had such an impact on the evolution of Hesballah's thinking – all were Fanonists of one type or another.

Thus when Palestinians look back on the people who arrived from abroad to take and settle their land, they see little difference between these more recent arrivals and the French colonists who occupied Fanon's Algeria: they were all white Europeans who claimed a superior title to the land over the non-European natives.

Benedict Anderson gives an example as typical of the colonial 'policy on barbarians' formulated by the early nineteenth-century Colombian 'liberal' Pedro Fermin de Vargas:

> To expand our agriculture it would be necessary to hispanicise our Indians. Their idleness, stupidity, and indifference towards normal endeavours causes one to think that they come from a degenerate race which deteriorates in proportion to the distance from its origin ... it would be very desirable that the Indians be extinguished, by miscegenation with the whites, declaring them free of tribute and other charges, and giving them private property.[6]

Such attitudes, however, were not uncommon in their disdain for inferior races and this pattern was duplicated, as we saw, in the German attitudes adopted in Turkey and in Algeria too. Anderson notes:

> the condescending cruelty, and the cosmic optimism [of this proposal]: the Indian is ultimately redeemable – but, rather than exterminating them by gun and microbe as his [Vargas'] heirs in Brazil, Argentina and the United States began to do soon after – he is [to be redeemed] by impregnation with white 'civilised' semen, and the acquisition of private property – like everyone else.[7]

Europeans took the land in Algeria based on the same European 'redeeming' mission that formed the central theme of earlier chapters in this book. Israeli claims to 'special rights' and a superior title to land that had been occupied by non-Europeans are also framed around its 'civilised' status – 'the only democracy in the Middle East' – and also by special 'Jewish rights' derived as natural human rights from historical facts that had been 'recovered' and given flesh and bones by a science that facilitated what Edward Said called a 'sealed off' Jewish-Israeli identity.

Liberalism and Rights

Early in 2007, a human rights organisation working for Arab minority rights in Israel, Adalah, proposed a draft constitution for the state of Israel – which has no constitution.[8] The purpose of the draft, according to Professor Dwairy, Adalah's chair, was:

> to propose a democratic constitution, which respects the freedoms of the individual and the rights of all groups in equal measure, gives proper weight

to the historical injustices committed against Arab citizens of Israel, and deals seriously with the social and economic rights of all.[9]

Israelis reacted with anger and outrage to a proposal that would allow the Jewish majority to maintain its character through educational and cultural institutions, but which insisted that, as long as Israel is defined as a Jewish state, its laws will always fall short of the basic democratic principle of the right of all its citizens to full equality – a principle which, if implemented, would bring about an end to the injustice of structural discrimination against Arab citizens of Israel, and the exclusion of the Arab minority based on the definition of the state as 'Jewish'.

Not long after its publication, Israeli newspapers reported that a senior security official had warned the Prime Minister that the radicalisation of Arab citizens posed a 'strategic threat' to Israel's existence, adding that 'the proliferation of the visionary documents published by the different Arab elites in Israel is particularly worrisome, [since] the documents are united by their conception of Israel as a state for all its citizens and not a Jewish state.'[10]

This event barely made a ripple in the western press, but in microcosm it reflected the 'illiberality' of western and Israeli 'liberalism' – and the anxiety and fear that surrounds those whom the West defines as 'aliens', whether they are migrants, asylum seekers, or 'Muslim extremists' or 'Arabs'. The sense of injustice which these 'aliens' may feel – as a de-cultured and discriminated-against minority – is dismissed as a natural, but a nonetheless threatening response, stemming from their inability to rise above their static cultural instincts. They are classified as one of those reactionary forces in the grip of traditional values, unable to embrace 'tolerance', which must be suppressed before they overwhelm and smother the 'open' society.

One senior Hamas leader said that armed resistance was not simply a tool that they used in response to coercive force used against them; he emphasised that it was to 'defend our people's rights and to force Israel and the international community to accept that our narrative of 1948, and our Palestinian rights, are of no less value than the rights or narrative of any other'. His statement was, in one sense, a protest against the racialisation of inequality.

It reflects also Isaiah Berlin's warnings about a collective whose feelings have been deeply outraged by historical events. 'To be the object of contempt or patronising tolerance', he wrote, 'is one of the most traumatic experiences that individuals or societies can suffer.'[11] It is indeed one of the great wells of human despair, rooted in powerlessness and marginalisation that can no longer be contained within national boundaries.

When the leader of Hamas, Khaled Mesha'al, was asked about these feelings in an interview in 2008, he responded:

> Let me give you some images that express how I feel about my land. Although I lived in a village for only 11 years, it still has a powerful influence on my life. Those years are to me as the roots are to a tree. My greatest delight is to open the window and see the trees, and the sun as it rises or sets. My greatest delight is to go to the park, and as I sit on the earth, I recall the smell of the soil of Palestine, the soil of Silwad.
>
> This feeling of belonging to one's homeland, I believe, comes naturally to every human being. What is unnatural is when a person is cut off from that sense of belonging. And that is how I now live – and so do millions of Palestinians. And there is another dimension to this. Your belonging to the land is also a belonging to your history. As the proverb says, 'He who has no past has no present.' Where are your roots? What do you belong to? What is your identity? If you lose this, you become just a cog in a machine, or a grain of dust in the wind, without value.[12]

The response of Hamas, the Islamic Resistance Movement, to this experience has been one of resistance. Edward Said, in his London talk, had recourse to Frantz Fanon to explain the impact on the feelings of Palestinians of the secular form of nationalist Zionism. It was an appropriate allusion: Hamas' path to resistance has been different from that of Hesballah, although both have occupation as their common initial catalyst. The Hamas legacy is that of Sayyid Qutb's Egyptian Muslim Brotherhood. It was a legacy initially of vanguardism and proselytisation. It was generally a non-violent movement which practised charitable activities more out of a sense of Islamic tradition than as a political tool of mobilisation. These were Hamas' roots too, and the context from which it evolved as a revolutionary movement.

Whereas Hesballah has developed an ideological doctrine to re-politicise culture, to invert the opposition between collective and private culture and to build a social sphere around 'independent' critical reasoning, Hamas' path to resistance was to a greater extent located in the feelings and emotions of the people.

This is not to say that Hamas' resistance, as we shall see, is no more than an emotional response to violence perpetrated against them – although there is a strand in which desire for revenge still is a powerful factor. Like Hesballah, Hamas uses resistance as a tool with which to control and direct the powerful feelings which occupation and humiliation have unleashed.

In this light we shall attempt to illustrate the psychological component to resistance through the insights of Fanon and the sentiments of Palestinian fighters in prison. We shall also argue that Hamas sees resistance as the means to generate the feelings that go into building community cohesion and self-respect. It is from this base that Hamas believes that armed action will ultimately facilitate an eventual political solution in Palestine. Hamas does not believe that their armed resistance, per se, can bring about the defeat of Israel militarily. It has objectives tied to the principle of refusing subservience, and to creating a psychological balance with Israel that may eventually facilitate a political solution – and to rebuilding an ethos of respect and esteem among Palestinians.

The Emergence of an Islamist Model and Ideology in Palestine

The origins and leadership of Hamas and of the Fateh movement, to which Yasir Arafat belonged and Mahmoud Abbas belongs, both derive from the Muslim Brotherhood of Egypt. The Egyptian Muslim Brotherhood was an overtly political and charitable movement initially opposed to colonialism and the western-imposed monarchy. It eschewed the armed vanguardism of the 1970s and 1980s in Egypt that led to the assassination of President

Anwar Sadat. In the 1930s, following the influxes of Jewish settlers and the beginning of confrontation, the Palestinian question was becoming an emotional issue for ordinary Egyptians as well as for the Brotherhood. The first Palestinian Brotherhood branch was established in Gaza in the mid-1930s.

The 1948 war that resulted in the establishment of Israel split the Palestinian Muslim Brotherhood. With the annexation of the West Bank by Jordan, the members in the annexed territories adopted an essentially apolitical and educational ethos. The Brotherhood there became a sort of docile 'loyal opposition' to the Jordanian King.

In Gaza, by contrast, certain groups within the Brotherhood developed vestiges of military resistance. In parallel, secular nationalist armed resistance movements were being established in Lebanon in the shape of the Popular Front for the Liberation of Palestine (PFLP) and the Democratic Front for the Liberation of Palestine (DFLP).

From the early 1950s until the early 1980s, the Brothers eschewed military activity and patiently and almost exclusively focused on education and charitable work. This emphasis on good works became so dominant that the political strand almost disappeared from the Brotherhood's work.

In the period leading up to 1956, armed resistance virtually ceased. But with the trauma of Israeli occupation of Gaza in 1957 (which lasted for four months), two different approaches emerged among the national forces for dealing with the Israeli military occupation: while the Palestinian Communists called for passive resistance against the occupation, a few prominent Brothers formed an illicit military cell and called on their leadership to begin a strategy of armed struggle. The Brotherhood leadership vetoed the idea, however, and opted to maintain their organisational focus on education and charitable work.

In 1958, these dissidents established the National Resistance Movement, or Fateh, together with former Ba'athists and political nationalists like Yasir Arafat, and Fateh broke away from the Brotherhood.

In the period following 1967 until the early 1980s, Palestinian politics was dominated by the figure of Yasir Arafat and Fateh was the central organisation and dominant presence within the Palestinian Liberation Organisation operating from its base in Lebanon. Fateh and the PLO's political strategy tapped into secular nationalist currents: Fateh was not explicitly secular, but it was also only implicitly, rather than explicitly, Islamic. It was conceived, by Arafat at least, as a 'broad tent' movement that could accommodate most ideologies.

By the late 1970s and early 1980s, however, Fateh and the PLO were showing no success in arriving at a political resolution of the Israeli–Palestinian conflict, despite their accomplishment in building an internationally recognised organisation, and in carrying through a number of spectacular military operations.

Arafat, the central figure in both Fateh and the PLO, began signalling a readiness for compromise on the Palestinian state as early as 1973. Little headway made as a result of Arafat's hints, and his pursuit of such an opening sparked deep scepticism inside the Palestinian national movement, and popular disaffection inside his own movement, Fateh, too.

This disaffection with Arafat and his policy of signalling readiness to compromise was at its height during the Iranian Revolution of 1979, when Iranian and Palestinian revolutionaries launched street protests against PLO leaders seen to be acquiescent to Israel's claims as a state. The emotional impact of the revolution transformed sentiment among Palestinians and energised them by demonstrating what could be achieved – against all the odds and expectations.

After this landmark event, with its new ideology, a fresh generation of Palestinian leaders began to emerge, who were inspired by this thinking and the revolutionary Islamic model. This coincided with growing popular disenchantment with the Palestinian Communist and secular parties.

The Brotherhood sensed this shift and began to mobilise in the schools, mosques and universities in Gaza and the West Bank. Fateh perceived this new activism as unwanted competition, and clashes between the two movements, though quickly dampened, began.

This was a time of Israeli occupation and growing military repression in both the West Bank and Gaza. As popular feelings of resentment against the Israeli occupation swelled and became sharper, popular pressure mounted on the various Palestinian movements to react militarily to occupation.

Despite these pressures, the Brotherhood leadership – patient as always – responded to this popular clamour by counselling caution and maintaining its programme of good works. This line outraged many Brothers: there were Israeli tanks parked in the streets where they lived, and a response of simply attending to the widows and orphans seemed humiliating; and it strengthened Fateh's standing as the lead organisation of the Palestinian resistance.

Brotherhood members demanded something more: Friday sermons and concern for the poor was not enough. At first, the Muslim Brotherhood leadership relented, but only to the extent that student demonstrations were permitted. This still was not enough, and the perceived failure of will of the Brotherhood inspired one activist, Sheikh Ahmad Yasin, to contemplate a break with the direction and policy of the parent organisation.

Yasin was a charismatic man. He was a paraplegic cleric confined to a wheelchair who had spent many years in gaol; but his twinkling eyes, his piercing intellect and iron will had made him a popular figure: He was widely regarded as a fair and sympathetic mediator of personal disputes – and was sought out by Palestinians of very different political persuasions for these qualities.

As Yasin was thinking his dissident thoughts, the Muslim Brotherhood was shaken by a significant schism: Brothers influenced by the ideals and fervour of the Iranian Revolution broke away from the movement to form Islamic Jihad.

The Beginning of Armed Resistance

The Islamic Jihad walk-out catalysed the Brotherhood leadership. But it still hesitated. Ultimately it was the occupation – which under the direction of Ariel Sharon had become so aggressive – that broke the mould: finally the Brotherhood responded by forming a protective cell structure, by launching passive resistance and by committing to military action.

Under the guidance of Yasin, these three programmes were put in place and the first military cells were established no later than 1987. The period from 1984 to 1987 represented a radical shift in Brotherhood ideology towards armed resistance, led by Yasin.

The Brotherhood had resisted the early internal pressures towards armed struggle, had dissociated itself from the Brothers who founded Fateh, and even ignored the second breakaway of a faction (Islamic Jihad); but the impact of the Israeli military occupation on the lives of the Palestinians, which ultimately led to the first Palestinian Intifada, or uprising, ultimately gave birth to Hamas. The transformation was now complete, and Hamas, separated from the Brotherhood, was formed in 1987.

Initially Hamas conceived its military response to the growing challenge of harsh Israeli military occupation in terms of classical guerilla resistance. The military wing of Hamas in the period 1987 to 1992 did not resort to suicide bombers and was focused on passive resistance and street confrontations, as much as on direct attacks on occupation forces.

The twin policies of confrontation and of building the new Hamas organisation were followed throughout the first Palestinian Intifada. The use of a more organised armed wing effectively came into being during the second Intifada, after 2000, and was confined largely to it. Until February 1994, Hamas refrained from attacks that could be considered random or that purposely targeted civilians; and in 2003 Hamas offered in meetings in Cairo to revert to this posture of removing civilians from the conflict. However, this initiative was refused by Prime Minister Sharon. Since 2003 Hamas has largely abandoned suicide attacks and has focused on creating a disciplined and well-trained military structure in Gaza resembling that of Hesballah.

There is a generally accepted view in the West that the Oslo Accords, signed by Yasir Arafat and Prime Minister Rabin in 1993, placed the Palestinians on a secure path towards statehood. There is also a perception in the West that there was strong consensual support among Palestinians for the Oslo Accords process. This simply is not true.

Arafat's negotiations at Oslo divided the Palestinians completely. They had been completed in secret as part of a deception in which bogus negotiations were being conducted openly and formally, while Arafat's representatives conducted the real negotiation in secret. The other Palestinian movements were kept totally in the dark. Many of his own Central Committee in Fateh opposed the outcome; and Arafat had real difficulty in broadening his support base and in gaining legitimacy. Hamas strongly opposed the Oslo Accords and met with Arafat in Tunis to denounce his initiative. The Accords, among other aspects, gave Fateh a monopoly on political power and a monopoly on the use of violence, in return for Arafat's dismantling the organisations of his political rivals – and the suppression of resistance.

Hamas was more representative of Palestinian opinion at the time: sentiment towards the fait accompli of Oslo had been ambiguous from the start, and it was not too long before the Oslo process generally was viewed as having further weakened the Palestinian position. The terms of the agreement were widely regarded as unbalanced, and favouring the Israelis.

Hamas, Palestinian refugees in Lebanon, Syria and Jordan, along with most of the leadership in the Occupied Territories and many Palestinian intellectuals had objected to the Oslo Accords at the outset. It is probable that Arafat himself understood as early as six months after the signing of the Accord – and certainly by the time of Arafat's meeting with the Israelis in Cairo towards the end of 1993 – that the agreement with Israel was likely to fail. In February 1994, the Israeli settler Baruch Goldstein massacred 29 Palestinians praying at the Hebron mosque in the West Bank – an event which is generally held to mark the end of the political process initiated in Oslo. The massacre also triggered the beginnings of the suicide bomb attacks.

Well before the Hebron massacre, there was deep alienation from Arafat's initiative in signing the Oslo Accords which reached into all parts of Palestinian society, particularly as the Palestinian population came under continued Israeli attacks in the immediate aftermath of the Oslo Accords, as Israel took advantage of the political breakthrough to increase strict security measures in the Occupied Territories.

It subsequently became evident that Prime Minister Rabin, sensing Arafat's vulnerability to public sentiment, had ordered a security crackdown on Arafat's opponents. As aggressive Israeli military operations continued, and Palestinians experienced no tangible economic benefit from the Accords, the mood on the Palestinian street towards the end of 1993 also largely echoed that of the Fateh rejectionists and Hamas.

This background has been related in order to place Hamas as a resistance movement in a somewhat different context to that in which they are usually perceived in the West. The first point is that that their mental formation in the Brotherhood had been one of repeated reluctance to embark on armed resistance. They had inherited no direct ideology of military action, although they would all have read Sayyid Qutb's works. It was aggressive military occupation that prompted the resistance to take form; it was in essence a direct response to the feelings and sentiments of the people rather than an ideological shift. The ideology came later. The final point is that the perception of Hamas as 'spoiling' the aspirations for peace of the majority of Palestinians was and is a myth. The simple truth is one of a protracted and deep-seated conflict of view between Hamas and Fateh on what were and are the tactics most likely to achieve a genuine and just peace.

'What They Are Fighting Against ... Is Your Humanity'

It was the emotional and psychological responses to nationalist Zionism, therefore, that underlay Palestinian resistance. Mesha'al says:

> I would like first to explain how the people of this region feel and think, because the distorted stereotype of Palestinians, or Muslims, or Hamas, that is presented in the West prevents you from seeing the reality. We have two states of mind that go together: they may seem contradictory but they complement each other; and both are very human. One is a state

of compassion and love towards people who are not hostile or aggressive towards us – to all people, including the poor and those of a different religion or race. The other is of strength and steadfastness, courage and defiance in facing those that attack us. This is part of what it means to be human – a normal person is obdurate towards those who are hostile and merciful towards those who live peacefully.

This is where the concept of struggle, of jihad, of resistance comes in. This is not our attitude to everyone; we engage in struggle, jihad, resistance against the enemy who steals our land and destroys our houses, commits sacrilegious acts against our holy places, assaults children and women and kills people. It is our normal, natural right to resist, to struggle against them. All the laws given by God, and international law, give us this right. So, jihad is a response to aggression; it does not itself initiate aggression.

Sometimes in Islamic culture the term 'jihad' is applied to any exertion aimed at achieving good, in resisting the devil, in resisting evil desires, in resisting the enemy that attacks the land. It should not be directed at peaceful peoples – such aggression is not permitted in Islam. Islam does not permit the use of force to resolve political disputes within society, or between societies; but when someone uses force against you, you use force to resist them. There is no ambiguity about this.[13]

The effects of loss of freedom, whether by occupation or detention, on a human being are well known: it can lead to personality distortion and ultimately to collapse. Undermining a sense of identity is one of the key tools used by interrogators to erode a prisoner's personality and self-confidence. It is done by laughing at his ideas and values; by suggesting that they are childish and unrealistic; by implying that his heroes and leaders are flawed, and that those whom he professes to admire are in reality collaborating with his interrogators; that his colleagues have abandoned him, and that he is alone with an absurd identity that is meaningless and a source of mirth in the rest of the world.

A Palestinian in an Israeli gaol wrote about the converse to the eroding of personality and self-confidence. The human spirit can also access other resources: a sense of will and of action being the essence of physical existence and identity can also well up:

And it is just this essence that they are trying to fight against in prison during the hours, the days and the years. Not against you as a subversive political person; not against you as a religious person or as a consumer from whom they deny the material pleasures of life. You can adopt any political view that you wish, practise your religious rite, or obtain a variety of goods. The goal of the prison system is to undermine the person within you; any relationships that you have with human beings and with nature, and even to undermine your relationship with the gaoler as a human being. They will do everything to make you hate them. What they are fighting against ... is your humanity.[14]

Another prisoner emphasised collective culture among prisoners as the means to keep identity and will alive:

We have knowledge of the Prison Administrator and his plans to degrade us and to stamp on our dignity and devoid us of our humanity. The Administration wants each one of us [to be] on our own ... they do not want organisation ... the aim is breaking the prisoner and his tenacity ... to empty the prisoner of his human content and humanity.[15]

The ability to reach down within, to touch hidden seams of personal resolve, whose resuscitation proves to be such a liberating experience was apparent also to Michel Foucault during the Iranian upheavals, when he described his experience on the streets:

What Islam called forth was not the people's anger but a long immobilised form of life. And what motivated the individual revolutionary to face the Shah's armed forces was not any political commitment, but rather the life within him which refused any longer to compromise itself with coercion and violence.[16]

Humiliation, deprivation and brute force complete the process of destruction of identity. And what is practised at the individual level, holds true for a people. Colonialism, as Fanon pointed out, practises the same agenda, but on a macro scale. His contribution was to identify that psychological impact on a colonised people:

> Exploitation, tortures, raids, racism, collective liquidations ... [all] make of the native an object in the hands of the occupying nation. This object-man, without means of existing, without raison d'être, is broken in the very depth of his substance. The desire to live, to continue, becomes more and more indecisive, more and more phantom-like. It is at this stage that the well-known guilt complex appears.[17]

Fanon describes this guilt that every Palestinian understands, of being ashamed at not doing more to help a fellow Palestinian being abused at a checkpoint, of being ashamed at a parent's servility towards the occupier, and of the inevitability of being stigmatised as guilty by the authorities, as a kind of curse. 'He is made to feel inferior, but by no means convinced of his inferiority.'[18]

The origins of resistance lie, Fanon suggests, in this imposed guilt and inferiority that those deemed 'backward' and 'culturally primitive' are forced to assume because of their powerlessness against an overbearing system. But it is an inferiority that is never internalised – except, Fanon suggests, for a minority who opt to try to become 'white men' and slide into collaboration with the dominant culture. Those who are boycotted by 'civilisation', those who are demonised as having no values and therefore no identity can liberate themselves through armed resistance: armed resistance, Fanon concluded, was the psychological antidote to communal personality erosion.

A Palestinian prisoner in his twentieth year in captivity described Fanon's thesis exactly:

> The truth is that I did not plan to be a freedom fighter, and I didn't plan to be a member of a faction or a party, or even to be involved in politics. Not because these things aren't right, and not because politics is forbidden and disgusting, as some people claim, but because for me these are great and complex things. I am not intentionally a freedom fighter or a politician.
>
> I could have continued my life as a painter or a gas station attendant, as I was doing until my arrest. I could have married a relative at an early age, and she would have borne me seven or ten children. I could have bought a truck and become familiar with car dealing and currency rates. All this was possible. But I saw the horrors of the Lebanon War [the first war of 1982] and the massacres in Sabra and Shatila,[19] and they shocked me.

He continues:

> ... to stop feeling the shock and the trauma, to stop feeling the sadness of human beings, any human beings. Insensitivity in the face of horrors, any horrors, is like a nightmare for me. It's the measure of my will and of my refusal to surrender. To sense people; to sense the pain of humanity – that is the essence of civilisation. The will is the essence of the rational person. Action is his physical sense, emotion is his spiritual essence.[20]

Resistance is seen by these prisoners as an opportunity to alter their existence, to choose to struggle as a new way of living. Yet, as the prisoners' descriptions make plain, it is not simply a matter of individuals making a choice of opting for resistance. It is – as Foucault again and again hearkens back to, as a key theme of revolutionary Iran – life itself, the essence of living beings that is asserting itself in the descriptions by these Palestinian prisoners. They are united, not by a political programme, or an ideology, but by collective will. At a certain point, a man or woman will give preference to the risk of death over the certainty of having to obey.

'Palestinians feel that their life is one of struggle and resistance. When you live every day under occupation, your natural behaviour [changes] – this is what people in the West should understand', Mesha'al suggests.

> Every day, we suffer aggression, killing and siege, with houses destroyed and families homeless. We have 11,600 people held in Israeli prisons, some of them children and women, some of them elderly, a thousand of them sick. When someone sees his life destroyed and sees that the world cannot help, when we see that the United Nations can do nothing, and that there is no international will to force the Israelis to leave our land as it forced Saddam Hussein to leave Kuwait; in these circumstances, you are obliged to resist – if you want to live with dignity.
>
> If you don't, you're not behaving normally. It's just like if a person is sitting at home and suddenly a fire breaks out in the house. The natural response is to get some water and pour it on the fire. When you live in an occupied land, it's natural to take up arms to resist.

And this becomes a matter of pride for a dignified person. You feel proud that you are doing your duty, just like a person who puts a fire out – or when someone goes to rescue someone who is drowning, it is his duty but he feels proud to be doing it. So, you find that Palestinians are proud of their struggle even though it is forced upon them. We feel that this is what it means to be a man; this is what it means to do the right thing.

We, like all human beings, love life, but we love life with dignity. We do not like to live in humiliation, under oppression. Perhaps there are people who do not care how they live; they want just to live – even if it is in humiliation. People in this region – Arabs in general, and Muslims – do not want to live like that.

So, when we say, as Palestinians, as Arabs, as Muslims, that in order to free our people from injustice and occupation we are ready to die, we say this not because we hate life, no, but because we want to die so that the rest of our people can live in freedom and dignity. It is a matter of some people sacrificing themselves so that the rest of the people may live. It is because we have a responsibility – not a hatred of life, or a death wish.[21]

Armed action is only one element of Hamas' resistance. Islamist resistance is also about refusal: refusal to acquiesce to those who attempt to self-fashion a superior identity; or indeed those who claim to superior rights above those of other human beings. It is a refusal to allow the complexity of the past to be reassembled by archaeologists who seek to privilege one particular layer of history above others. It is a refusal to allow one narrative of history – Israeli Prime Minister Golda Meir's response 'How can we return the occupied territories? There is no one to return them to',[22] for example – to stand unchallenged.

A teenage Palestinian prisoner in an interview in the Youth Wing of an Israeli gaol described himself thus:

You must know that all my values and ethics are based on Islamic beliefs. I refuse any belief contradicting Islamic values. So, to describe myself and what I do: I am a person who refuses to live with indignity or to see his brother being killed, and just to stand aloof. I am someone who refuses the sacrilege of our holy places and their destruction or bombardment. I refuse also the demolition of peoples' homes. I refuse to stand aloof. We have both integrity and courage. These are ordinary qualities in an ordinary person. I do not consider it exceptional to have these qualities. Everyone should have these ordinary qualities.

Refusing Recognition

The refusal to recognise and to acknowledge special rights or a hierarchy of identity is filtered through the prism of Euro-centrism when westerners contemplate a movement such as Hamas: refusal to recognise Israel is perceived not as an act of resistance but the obduracy of fundamentalism. It is a further signal of being held fast by religious or cultural instincts – it demonstrates the inability to embrace change.

'Plainly Israel "exists", and to deny it, is obdurate perversity ... All they have to do is say those three words: We recognise Israel', an editorial board meeting at *Ha'aretz*, the Israeli daily newspaper repeatedly and wearily emphasised in a discussion with the author – with heads shaking in disbelief at Hamas' inexplicable refusal to say the three words.

Hamas is not only refusing to 'say the three words'. It refutes a Jewish-Israeli exclusionary identity, one that has never acknowledged Palestinian rights, and which has never accepted any parity of rights between the Jewish people and the Palestinian people.

Khaled Mesha'al, the political leader of Hamas, speaks of resistance as an attempt to bring about a 'balance'. He was clear that the aim of this was to effect a psychological change on the part of the occupier – rather than to inflict a military defeat in terms of conventional military tactics:

> The problem is that they believe that they can dictate to the weaker party. This is not an approach that will lead to peace. A few years ago in 2003 we were ready to be flexible. We offered a new initiative – the truce, or hudna, of 2003 – but Israel did not respond positively. It did not result well.
>
> Israel still, at this time, plainly does not feel the need to pay any price ... It wants to impose its pre-conditions of required Palestinian 'good behaviour'; it then demands the right to evaluate for itself that 'good behaviour', and thinks that is enough. It is never willing to offer gestures on

its own initiative. This unbalanced approach will fail: it needs to understand that in Hamas there is a tough negotiator; but one, that, unlike others, stands by its commitments when given. [23]

And in a later interview:

They want neither a peace based on justice nor a peace based on compromise. They want to keep the land, they want security for themselves and they want to be the masters of the whole region, without recognising the rights of Palestinians. Yasir Arafat and Mahmoud Abbas tried to pursue a compromise. Did they achieve peace with the Israelis? So, the obstacle to peace in the region is Israel – and American bias. [24]

What Hamas is doing – in dramatic fashion – is to put a finger on a key failure of the Israeli–Palestinian political process since the Oslo Accords were signed in 1993 – which is the singular omission of any clear outline of Palestinian rights.

What the Hamas leaders are stating is that while the West repeatedly honours the Jewish narrative of injustice, it feels no parallel need to recognise or acknowledge the Palestinian narrative of injustice that Palestinians feel in respect to the events of 1948, when villages and houses were destroyed, many were killed and thousands fled to refugee camps beyond Palestine's borders.

Hamas refuses recognition of Israel and persists with resistance in order to demand that recognition of this Palestinian narrative, first, should be made unequivocally; and, second, that it should take the form of an affirmation of Palestinian rights to a state on the basis of Israeli withdrawal from all Palestinian lands conquered in 1967.

To Hamas, the international demand on them for a prior recognition of an Israeli right, before Palestinian rights are recognised, seems to require from them to concede the right of a superior Jewish title to their land, while disdaining their rights as a secondary consideration to securing the Palestinian recognition of Israel.

Hamas has forcefully pointed out that the USA's insistence on recognition of Israel has never been a condition for any previous dialogue. [25] The US and its allies maintained relations with

President Abdul Nasser, President Hafez al-Assad, King Fahd Ibn Abdul Aziz and King Hussein, at a time when Egypt, Syria, Saudi Arabia, Jordan and Iran not only refused to speak with Israeli leaders, but vowed to destroy Israel.

Hamas' act of refusal therefore is not, as it is often labelled, the action of a 'spoiler', whose wrong-headedness over failing to utter 'the three words' is otherwise inexplicable. Continued resistance is intended to change the terms of debate, to shift from one party's self-assumed 'right' to occupy others' lands, to that of a negotiation based on the starting point that both parties have 'rights' and both have suffered from injustice. Only from this more balanced starting point can a solution flow.

Hamas leaders believe that a statement of Palestinian rights is more likely to facilitate a political process than undermine it. In other words, resistance is not about refusing dialogue but is a tool to change the parameters of dialogue and thereby make genuine value-modification and discussion between the parties possible. When Khaled Mesha'al said that resistance facilitates a solution by helping to create a balance, he was describing this paradigm shift:

> We in Hamas, like most of the Palestinian factions, have accepted the idea of a state with the borders of 4 June 1967.[26] However, we have said that we will not recognise Israel. Why? It is because the Palestinian people are convinced that the land which Israel occupies is their land. So, while they accept a state with the borders of 1967, they do not want to give legitimacy to those who occupied their lands 60 or 70 years ago. So, the formula is simply this: if through politics we can come to agree a Palestinian state with the borders of 1967, why should we be forced to renounce our beliefs and feelings too, by recognising Israel?[27]

Resistance for Hamas therefore is both an expression of deep-seated human emotions and Islamist principles of justice. At a human level, resistance offers those whose lands have been occupied a route to self-respect and esteem by becoming what Fanon called 'actional' – by which he means resistance to the established order, the capacity to say 'no', to refuse to adjust or adapt to the pressure to acquiesce.

At the level of justice, Islamists view these human values as standing above politics. Hamas therefore does see a solution with Israel in different terms from those of Fateh. They do not share Fateh's optimism that Palestinian weakness in contrast to Israel's strength can be counterbalanced by co-opting the international community to weigh in on the Palestinian side.

Hamas believes that only by getting the principles right, by insisting on the meaning and significance of concepts such as freedom, justice and welfare, which in the current western usage, in their view, have little reality or moral value, can a real dialogue take place. And if we want to understand and put meaning to these words, they have to be addressed from a footing of respect. Respect is therefore crucial to facilitating any successful outcome, and if there is no other alternative, then respect has to come from resistance.

In short, Hamas believes that a negotiation that centres on ethical issues such as rights and justice for Palestinians cannot be successfully concluded with Israeli negotiators who take force and power to be the dominant factors. Peace and justice can only be axioms to someone who recognises them as being definite and ultimate. Until this comes about, no dialogue will be successful, Hamas suggests.

Resistance, Dignity and Rights

A young Palestinian prisoner in an interview expressed his feelings:

> The actions that Israel takes against us; invasions; blood; killings; daily destruction: even the television – all these things make your heart bitter and hardens it. It empties it of any feelings towards others. All you think of is to empty this energy of anger into the enemy. Daily images of blood make you feel for the dead or martyred brother or friend and it enrages you. Everyone has these feelings: I know that. The psychologists say it – so I must destruct as much as I can, whether they are called civilian or military: every Jew in Palestine is a military, except the children.

It has become clearer to me in prison that it is possible to coexist with Jews; but we must not forget that our cause is not a mere problem of coexistence … it is based on the principle of liberating our homeland. We must have our freedom. When a Palestinian kills an Israeli his purpose is not the killing in itself. Killing for the sake of killing is unlawful in Islam … If our freedom is taken from us, we try to inflict as many losses as possible on our enemy. Our objective, the world must know, is not the killing itself, but our freedom.[28]

And Mesha'al notes:

As for effectiveness, any action in the world has both positive and negative results. We recognise that these operations [i.e. suicide bombings] have a negative impact, especially in terms of world public opinion; but what is the message that these operations deliver? The most important message is that the Palestinian people will never capitulate. If they do not find weapons, they will fight with their bodies. And this, I assure you, is what is going to cut the conflict short. This will compel Israel to recognise Palestinian rights.

[I can foresee a day when Muslims, Jews and Christians will live together in harmony] … That was the case in the past, and it can be so again in the future.

Mesha'al asserts. 'What matters is that occupation and aggression come to an end – and with it the ambitions on which the Zionist movement was founded.'[29]

The political leader of Hamas also emphasised that there is no problem with Jews either as individuals or collectively as a society. 'This is not the dispute: the conflict stems from behaviour – from aggressive Zionist behaviour. It is this behaviour that is unacceptable. The question of behaviour however is a political issue between us; it is not theological.'[30]

Mesha'al continued that of course there were theological differences between Jews and Muslims and that these differences will persist; but these continuing differences are not such that prevent good relations between peoples. 'My father took part in the resistance against the British Mandate in the 1930s when they occupied us. They are gone now. Of course feelings from that era persist for me, but their behaviour has ended: there remain differences between us, but we are not in conflict.'[31]

We have argued in this and the previous chapter the centrality of the idea of resistance. In Chapter 6, we argued that resistance represented a crucial concept in re-politicising culture and in inverting the emphasis from the personal to collective culture. We also argued that both the military and political requirements of resistance had been met by developing the 'independent' brain – to re-equip its members with the critical process of independent reasoning.

The importance of reasoning in the Shi'i tradition and the significance this training is given throws open to question whether the western meaning attached to religious faith is appropriate to Shi'ism. The Shi'i do not see faith in the Christian Abrahamic way as to do with unquestioning obedience. For the Shi'i, faith is a concept of knowledge of being which is derived from reasoning and intuition.

The traditional western presumption of a tension between religiosity and reason does not seem to be borne out by Shi'i experience. As one Islamist leader put it, the movement does not see Islam in the terms that Europeans view it, as a medieval religion: 'We do not see God as permitting or prohibiting each and every action. We see Islam as setting out broad principles that guide our actions.'

And in this chapter we have focused on Hamas' location of the impulse to resistance in profound human values. We have also seen that Islam recognises these values as being essential values. The respect of man, his dignity and his life are all aspects of Islam; they are not viewed as means to an end. Hamas defines resistance not as a means to a pragmatic end of 'gaining power'. They define resistance in terms of a universal Islamic view that places certain values ahead of politics. This is what sets them apart from Fateh: they mount resistance as much to insist that Israel acknowledge these principles as the foundation for negotiations, rather than seeing resistance simply as a 'means and ends' pressure point. It is not the western universal view; it is one that says that there is no point to dialogue with those who will not understand argument based on principles – those who believe only in force and power.

In the next section we consider the nature of Islamist resistance and pose the question of whether it should properly be described as 'divine violence'. We also examine the characteristics of western responses to Islamist violence and seek an explanation for these responses in the thinking that underpins secular modernism. Finally, we look at the connections between Islamist violence and the western reaction, and seek parallels from the life of the Prophet Mohammad after his migration to Medina in 622.

Part IV

8
RESISTANCE AND THE NORMALISATION OF INJUSTICE

In the ninth of his *Theses on the Philosophy of History*, Walter Benjamin refers to Paul Klee's painting, Angelus Novus, which 'shows an angel looking as though he is about to move away from something he is fixedly contemplating. His eyes are staring, his mouth is open, his wings are spread.' He goes on:

> This is how one pictures the angel of history. His face is turned toward the past. Where we perceive a chain of events: he sees one single catastrophe which keeps piling wreckage and hurls it in front of his feet. The angel would like to stay, awaken the dead, and make whole what has been smashed. But a storm is blowing in from Paradise; it has got caught in his wings with such violence that the angel can no longer close them. The storm propels him into a future to which his back is turned – whilst the pile of debris before him goes ever higher. This storm is what has been called progress.[1]

Of course western perceptions are held fast by the imagery of the violent storm blowing in from Paradise that sweeps away even the angel. It resonates with the idea of divine 'revenge' exploding in a retaliatory rage. Slavoj Žižek comments on this imagery that: 'opposite such a violent enforcement of justice stands the figure of divine justice as unjust – as an explosion of divine caprice'.[2] He adds that it is pointless to seek symbolic meaning in such acts of retribution: things are just what they are, not bearers of hidden mystical meanings. Such acts are unreasoning fury on the loose and there is no way to protect oneself, except by an answerable force.

For secular westerners, this form of 'divine violence' represents reason capsized into madness. Such divine retribution, which

Edmund Burke detected in the French Revolution, appears as something deranged, leading to the kind of politics which shears through the sedimented layers of custom and tradition in order to attain its ends; to which Žižek adds: 'Well ... gentlemen ... do you want to know what this divine violence looks like? Look at the revolutionary Terror of 1792–94. That was Divine Violence.'[3]

This divinely inspired fury of unreasoning is the phantasm by which the West 'knows' Islamic 'terrorism'. It is a professed 'love of death' which in reality is just a raging appetite for annihilation. It represents, in this portrayal, the idea that only by paying our dues in spilled blood can the corruption and excesses of the past be swept away. In Robespierre's last speech in 1794, the day before his arrest and execution, he affirmed these experiences of 'purity' amongst the revolutionaries, that sublime love for the homeland and the even more sublime love for humanity, 'without which a great revolution is just a noisy crime that destroys another crime'.[4] It is, in short, a spectre reeking of guilt, retribution and ultimate salvation.

It is also very Christian. The relation between divinity and violent retribution is drawn from Christianity's apocalyptic themes – and more directly from Saint Augustine (354–430). Augustine began as a follower of the Manichaean religion, which viewed evil as a permanent feature of the world. Whereas Mani, the founder of the Manichaean religion, believed that humans were fodder in a real war that was raging between good and evil that would go on for ever, the followers of Jesus looked forward to an 'end time' in which evil would be permanently destroyed. Saint Augustine believed that human beings were ineradicably flawed, and this doctrine of original sin, the guilt to which it gave rise, and the recurring attempts to cleanse it, became a central part of Christian orthodoxy.[5]

As the war between dark and light persisted, humans became overwhelmed with evil, and divine retribution was expected in terms of an apocalyptic event that mysteriously leads not to catastrophe, but to salvation. For modern Christians, such as G.K. Chesterton, this type of 'divine violence' flowed from people losing a grip on common sense – not being able to see things as they really are; but for the majority of secular westerners, the violence of the French Revolutionaries and Islamic 'extremists' is the same – implacable malevolence and aggression.

It is pointless, they argue, to seek or expect any 'meaning' to it: it is resentment transformed into a raging appetite for annihilation. In reality the revolutionaries of France were not bent on malevolence, as Robespierre's expressions of 'tough' love testify, but were reflecting the early Christian theme of an 'end time', transformed into secular utopianism, which would bring about a new type of human life.[6]

The need to restrain the furies of 'divinely inspired' violence, which had so devastated Europe during the Thirty Years War (1618–48), was pivotal to the writings of Thomas Hobbes in 1651, whose central theme in his widely influential Leviathan was the human insecurity from fear of violent death, and the need to tame religious 'fanaticism'. Hobbes, writing at the time of the English civil war, also advocated a social contract between the individual and a necessarily 'strong' government or monarchy, by which the latter guaranteed the individual's security in return for his or her obedience. By obeying such a government, Hobbes suggested, humans could transcend the fears and insecurities of such divinely loosed caprice and death.

Hobbes' edifice of a social contract between government and the individual – by identifying natural law with self-preservation – laid the basis for John Locke (1632–1704) to take a more optimistic view than Hobbes, and to assert the natural goodness of humanity. The inevitable pursuit of happiness and pleasure, when conducted rationally, leads naturally to harmony, he held; and in the long run, private happiness and the general welfare, coincide, through a working of the invisible hand. In his state, formed by social contract, all people were equal and independent, and none had a right to harm another's 'life, health, liberty, or possessions'.

Locke's ideas shaped western thinking over the next 300 years. The system of competitive checks and balances in government, as delineated in the Constitution of the United States, was set down by Locke. And his conception of naturally arising human rights underpinned the American founding fathers' use of rights as the basis around which the American state was to be constructed.

But in basing human rights around the individual, his property and his freedom, Locke gave secular intellectual justification to the invisible hand and the market mechanism that was subsequently to transform into a grim orgy of nation-state building and ethnic cleansing over the next 200 years. Locke also spurred a conception of 'rights' based around the white, male property owner – at the expense of any rights of community. The present western emotional fascination for individual breach of rights often masks the far worse systematic breaches perpetuated against entire peoples – such as the western blindness to the massacre of the Armenians – that are committed in pursuit of westernisation. All this can be traced back to Locke.

He argued for a toleration that allowed the government to stand elevated above and apart from a multiplicity of competing religions. Roman Catholicism, however, which carried the potential of a return to a sacred community, collective values and rights, was just too threatening, he felt. It should be outlawed as inimical to the state. And neither did Locke's toleration extend to those who lived outside this self-defined natural human condition of empirical rationality and individual self-awareness: these were the enemy to be crushed.

The Debris of History

This was a concept of toleration that polarised humanity between those within civilisation, and those beyond civilisation's frontiers, to whom neither toleration nor protection were to be extended. It is this concept that gives legitimacy to western exclusion of Islamic fighters and political leaders from the protection of international law and which denies them their rights. The germ of this contemporary approach was embedded in the thinking of America's founders from the start. It exposes the latent hostility against the idea of communal religiosity, inherited from the puritan struggle, a prejudice that still underlies secularised western society.

Hobbes had identified the very raison d'être of the state in terms of such implicit hostility – 'spun' as a demand for the emancipation of individuals from the fear of 'divine violence', which had so scarred Europe during its civil and religious wars. Hobbes' social contract, and Locke's view of the self-conscious 'Self' and individual natural rights, defined 'freedom' as it has come to be known in the modern world.[7]

In short, from the outset the western nation-state was conceptualised around the Protestant 'spin' of 'divinely inspired violence' versus 'the individual as victim', and the pursuit of individualistic 'rights', and it was on these notions that its legitimacy depended. It is plain that this represented the 'victor's narrative' of history. It was the triumph of the Protestant ethos translated into state-building. In the contemporary era these ideas were extended to embrace a further 'right' of the 'international community' to intervene in other states, by force if need be, to protect individual rights.

Not surprisingly, Hobbes' and Locke's legacy is the pole of legitimacy around which western states have grouped to protect themselves, with the contemporary spectre of 'divine violence' appearing afresh in the shape of armed Islamist resistance, as well as the acts of a minority who adopt the al-Qa'eda 'shock-and-awe' mobilisation tactics.

But let us now return to Paul Klee's Angelus Novus. It is not divine 'rage' exploding in retaliatory anger that is at work here. What grips the angel, against his vain efforts to remain stationary, and propels him – still casting his eyes rearwards at history's mounting wreckage – is the wind of secular 'progress'.

A second look at Benjamin's account shows that what the angel contemplates 'fixedly' is one single catastrophe. Whereas we humans, blind to the reality, perceive only a chain of historical events, the angel sees but a single catastrophe, which keeps piling up wreckage, and hurling it at his feet. It is the catastrophe of so-called 'progress', whose tragedies he contemplates; but despite his wish to stay – to awaken humanity to this disaster and to make things better – the rush of progress simply sweeps him away in its tide, leaving his warnings unspoken.

Benjamin's is not a story of divine anger; it is an account of humanity, heedless of the mounting wreckage of history around it, held fast in the grip of the drive for 'progress'. It is a single catastrophe that is invisible to humans because of their insistence on seeing the wreckage not as wreckage but as a natural 'Darwinian' evolution of 'events': history on its march towards its culmination.

In the last chapter, we argued that Islamist movements such as Hamas and Hesballah ground their resistance on human values. And, as Mesha'al said:

> We, like all human beings, love life, but we love life based on dignity and on principles. So, when we say, as Palestinians, as Arabs, as Muslims, that in order to free our people from injustice and occupation we are ready to die, we say this not because we hate life, no, but because we want to die so that the rest of our people can live in freedom and dignity. It is a matter of some people sacrificing themselves so that the rest of the people may live. It is because we have a responsibility – not a hatred of life, or a death wish.[8]

We also argued that Islam recognises these values as being essential values. The respect of man, his dignity and his life, are all aspects of Islam; they are not viewed as means to an end. Hamas defines resistance not as a means to a pragmatic end of 'gaining power', but in terms of a universal Islamic view that places certain values ahead of politics. Hamas mounts resistance in order to force Israel and the West to acknowledge these principles. They do this not out of recalcitrance but because they believe that any attempt to resolve the conflict that does not pay regard to the principles of justice and equity will fail. Islamists are using resistance to challenge the prevailing paradigm based on instrumental thinking. They are using it, as Mesha'al suggested, to force behaviour change on Israel.

Hesballah adopts a culture of resistance, we argued, not just to defend its people but to invert the priorities in their lives: to elevate key principles above pragmatism; to re-politicise culture as a platform from which 'to do political things', and to invert the western privileging of the individual above the collective. It is also about setting a model for behaviour change.

It acts as a 'reminder' to the West of old truths 'that everybody knew', as the Qur'an points out: that humans need to conduct themselves with justice, respect, equity and compassion.[9] As Islamists look at the wreckage of the last two hundred years of history – with its genocides, massacres, ethnic cleaning and wars – they are demanding a right to return to 'old truths'.

But as with the angel of history's attempt to bring a halt to the unfolding catastrophe of secular modernity, their 'reminder' too goes unheard. Hubris simply hurls new tragedies at the angel's feet.

This is not 'divine' retaliatory rage: it is human voices echoing the angel's despair. Hamas leaders do not receive directions from God, but they understand that in God's final message to humans, he demanded that they behave to each other differently. Resistance represents a refusal to 'normalise' injustice. It is a refusal to continue quiescent.

The Meaning of Resistance

The object of mainstream Islamist resistance is not to resolve matters by force, but to reveal and expose the underlying causes of the wreckage piling at the angel's feet; to sensitise the consciousness of people who are able to hear, and to find a route back towards a different way of living. It is about defining the future therefore, and not about resentment – although plainly resentment amongst some small groups at the mounting wreckage has edged them towards an eschatological view.

Our Iranian cleric, with whom we introduced this book, summarised the purpose of martyrdom and resistance thus:

> When our essential values and principles are at stake, or are infringed, we offer our human body as a sacrifice; its spirit, nevertheless, remains to preserve these values.
>
> It is this language of values, drawn from the repository of human experience, that establishes a universal relationship between us and thinkers in the world. If we wish to understand why language is being misused, we have first to look at the definition of man himself. If we wish to correct

language, we have first to begin from agreed and common concepts. Until this is done, no dialogue will be successful.

How is it possible to discuss these deep and profound values with someone who does not have a moral conscience; or one who has utterly eliminated rationality from his calculations? In my opinion, a dialogue about ethical values with a person who believes that force and power are the most important values is irrelevant. Peace and justice can only be axioms for someone who recognises them as being definite and ultimate.

To summarise, I believe that in order to have successful dialogue with the West, we first have to look at the meaning and concept of moral values. We have to show that in the current western usage, concepts such as freedom, justice and welfare have little reality or moral value; and if we want to understand and put meaning to these words, we must begin by redefining man and his values. In this dialogue, the ultimate arbitrator is reason. Final judgment must be passed by man's intellect, and man's conscience should be the foundation by which these concepts are understood.

We believe that rather than holding dialogue with politicians and biased persons, we should engage with just minds and address the consciences of the western world. I believe that if we combine our efforts, take the time to create a common dictionary of these concepts, there would be many who want to listen.

I believe that we need clearly to express these values and their accompanying ideology. Unfortunately the monopoly of the western media does not allow us to do that.

Resistance emerges as a tool to expose the essence of the conflict; to call attention to 'forgotten' principles. This resort to resistance is the reflection of a true paradox: the need to adopt resistance in order to provoke and to bring about real dialogue. It is not just the monopoly of the western media that is the problem as the cleric inferred. The problem is deeper: language has been misused in the West for ideological purposes: it has been shaped to ridicule Islamism as a reactionary instinct that is either resistant to, or is culturally incapable of, attaining modernity.

Language has been the object of an effort designed to foreclose on debate and thought by promoting the conviction that when Islamists speak they have nothing to say, or that when they do speak, what they say either is nonsense or deceit. If Islamists cannot be heard against the overwhelming clamour of denigration, resistance becomes the inevitable result of western policy. It propels resistance into becoming the tool to emancipate humanity from an ideological manipulation that helps to render invisible the wreckage of history.

Hobbes' formulation in *Leviathan*, we suggested earlier, can best be described as victor's 'spin'. In his assembly of a narrative from the Thirty Years' War, he paints a picture of the individual living in fear for his life from fanatical religious violence. He picks up the commonplace of conflict – that its victims are mostly vulnerable individuals – to assemble a justification for a social contract between individuals and strong government.

It is an ideological operation that implies an essential opposition between a vision of religiosity lived as a sacral community – and the interests of its members as individuals. This hides the true basis of conflict as being between the Catholic community on one side, and Protestants on the other. The Protestants 'won', and not surprisingly Hobbes spins Protestant individualism as a principle standing in opposition to the collective. This device is used to justify the individualisation of society, and to substitute a sovereignty of government for that of God.

That Hobbes' narrative was an ideological operation is clear from the title of his book, *Leviathan*, which in the Bible, is an aquatic monster, possibly a crocodile, a whale, or a dragon. It was a symbol of evil to be ultimately defeated by the power of good.[10] Rendered invisible in this confection is the basis for the war: it was one of Protestant 'divinely' inspired violence as well as Catholic.

Both sides to the conflict were using religious principles as the justification for violence. To portray the Protestant success as having been a struggle against 'divine' violence was an ideological 'spin'. It also throws into question whether the western preoccupation with 'divine violence' has any real meaning: both Hobbes' nation-state and Locke's natural human rights were derived from Protestant thought – as we have seen.

Locke's definition of the 'self' as naturally self-aware, conscious of pleasure and pain, capable of happiness or misery, and so concerned primarily for itself – a 'tabula rasa' at birth inscribed with ideas deduced from direct sensory experience – stands in direct opposition to the Islamists' conception of the 'essence of man'.

Both reflect religious insights: is it appropriate to see the defence of these religious insights, Islamist resistance, as 'divine' fury, but the systematic use of violence on behalf of Locke's insights as no more than a 'legitimate' use of force? Are they not both rooted in religious insight?

The angel's fixed stare, centred on a single catastrophe, which humans pass over as the natural casualties of evolution, reflects the continued invisibility of the systemic violence that was associated with the comfortable life that Locke was outlining to the English and to the American founding fathers.

Nationalism and the Transformation of Secular Morality

Benedict Anderson has argued that the dawn of the 'age of nationalism', which Hobbes and Locke symbolise, marked also the dusk of religious thought: 'The century of the Enlightenment, of rationalist secularism, brought with it its own modern darkness.'[11]

'The disintegration of paradise ... nothing [more than the prospect of void] makes mortality more arbitrary ... nothing makes another form of continuity more necessary.'[12] In short, and as Hobbes recognised in his writing, 'security' and 'order' signalled – in the dusk of religious certainties – a human longing to fend off the yet more frightful 'disorder' that death represents.

What then was required was a secular transformation of mortality into continuity; contingency into meaning.

> If nation states are widely conceded to be 'new' and 'historical', the nations to which they give political expression always loom out of an immemorial past, and still more important, glide into a limitless future. It is the magic of nationalism to turn chance into destiny. With Debray we might say,

'Yes, it is quite accidental that I am born French; but after all, France is eternal.'[13]

In the absence of a religious consciousness, we are, as Professor Eagleton has pointed out, 'riddled from end to end with the scandal of our own non-necessity'. Since this is a potentially debilitating condition, nationalism as an ideology exists to convince us that we are needed – that we serve some end. It is required, more importantly, to imbue life with a sense of purpose beyond living for life's sake.

In this way the nation-state substitutes a sense of national continuity for the vanished afterlife. The state picks up on functions that once were the province of the sacred, and the nation takes up the 'legitimacy of purpose' that was earlier attributed to God.

Nationalism becomes a symbolic edifice of transcendental qualities:

> The nation is immortal, indivisible, invisible yet all-encompassing, without origin or end, worthy of our dearest love, and the very ground of our being. Like God, too, its existence is a matter of collective faith. There would not be a nation unless we believed that there was.[14]

The violence that preceded the nation-state does not cease once the state is founded. It is simply folded into the new entity: what was formerly 'violence' is assumed into the army and the security forces as 'legitimate force'. Its frightening and disruptive qualities are co-opted by the official and the familiar. The new order comes to take the violence that had been external and threatening and to place it – its institutionalised violence – at its heart, as the very symbol of nationalist pride and sovereignty.

This legitimacy of purpose to state action has caused the consequences of systemic state-institutionalised violence to be lost to vision, while subjective violence and natural disaster increasingly becomes an obsessive public preoccupation.

In the present post-political era, which aspires to rise above old ideological divides in a world of self-pacified docility created in a harmony of lifestyle pleasures, and with the future being nothing but an extension of seeking comfort and security, any violence that threatens the vulnerability and safe administration of life is perceived to be frightening, whether it is a naturally occurring disaster or violence exercised by the 'irrational other'.

In these societies, caring, anxious westerners are often disposed to define themselves as being opposed to all violence, suggesting that there is no such thing as good or bad violence. They are ready, however, to endorse the violence perpetuated by the armed forces of the state, viewing this as purposeful and legitimate. They see its legitimacy deriving from its necessary contribution to harmony and order. Harmony here becomes an ideal that stands above concerns about the violence deployed in its realisation.

This means that, in the name of progress, free market reform and the spread of democracy, genocides, massacres and ethnic cleansing are easily overlooked and quickly forgotten. There is, as Terry Eagleton noted, something pathological about the western rage for nation-state building: it conceals a ferocious inner compulsion which is the opposite of freedom. Fundamentalism is one name for it; in the desire for absolute security, cities are shattered and blameless civilians become victims.[15]

The liberal turns curiously illiberal and uncaring towards the vulnerable victims of modernisation projects, in sharp contra-distinction to a caring preoccupation with the victims of natural disasters. But the 'other' that exists outside the natural order, as Locke suggested in his essays on tolerance, cannot in any way be tolerated as soon as he or she becomes intrusive. The over-reaction seems to reflect the fear of the crumbling of the protective symbolic 'walls' that keep others at a proper distance. Western tolerance seems inversely related to the extent of 'safe distance' between the westerner and the 'other'.[16]

In the years since Edward Said published his classic work on western orientalism, the West has elevated orientalism into something far more serious than a tool for the 'domestication' of Islam – as Said identified its purpose. It has become an inexorable and self-fulfilling project: the war on terrorism has transformed Said's orientalism from its Euro-centric purpose to make Muslims more docile, into a new paradigm that redefines Locke's clear frontier between 'civilisation' and a new 'barbarism'.

'New Orientalism'

This 'new orientalism' has given birth to a different set of political tools – no longer simply the tools to impress upon the colonised the 'fact' of their cultural primitiveness, but to sharply delineate civilisation. One Israeli politician likened Israel – as the symbol of western civilisation – to a 'villa', an oasis of civilised life, transported to the jungle's edge.[17] With Hamas in control in Gaza, an Israeli journalist suggested, the jungle's tentacles, its creeping undergrowth, were encroaching on the garden wall. If one was very quiet, his imagery seemed to imply, the murmuring of the creatures of the jungle could clearly be heard beyond the villa wall. The 'other' was encroaching both on safe distance and on 'tolerance'!

As these Islamist 'new barbarians' are defined as living beyond the 'garden walls', beyond the scope of civilisation, civilised rules need no longer apply to them: if 'they' win elections, they still cannot be part of 'us', the civilised West. Office-holders and parliamentarians can be abducted and interned without a murmur; members of 'barbarian' movements can be arrested and taken away for imprisonment and torture in other countries; and barbarian leaders, whether or not legitimately elected, can be assassinated at the pleasure of western leaders.

Violence practised by the nation-state is the 'legitimate' response of civilisation, but violence used by non-state actors is a 'threat' to civilisation. The 'barbarians' do not possess resistance movements in the lexicon of 'new orientalism'; they are not fighting for their liberation; and they are not fighting oppression. To admit this would be to admit that the West is an oppressor; and that cannot be. Leaders such as Mr Blair describe such allegations as 'false grievances', and insist that British Muslims denounce such imaginary grievances. Muslims may try to say that they are fighting for their homes and their lands, but this not true. Their real motivation is 'extremism'.

Those who adopt armed resistance – defined now as 'terrorists' – face a double proscription: not only are they placed beyond the frontiers of civilisation but, undeserving of having civilised standards applied to them (such as respect toward elected representatives), they are to be excluded from international law too.

If the West does not apply civilised standards to them, and is prepared to use unrestrained military force against them, is it any surprise that a minority have responded in kind? In this way, 'new orientalism' has proved to be self-fulfilling. It has fuelled radicalism and given space and oxygen to those minority Sunni Salafi movements that argue that accommodation with the West is impossible and that there is little choice but to burn down the system – those remaining colonial remnants – to cleanse by violence and allow an Islamic state to emerge from the ashes.

A distinction has to be made here between the mainstream Islamist perspective of resistance centred on exposing the roots of conflict and a refusal to permit the 'normalisation' of injustice, and that of those who deny the possibility of accommodation with an entrenched West. This tiny element, which believes in 'imploding' the whole colonial edifice by acts of outrage, is really doing little that differs from what western policy-makers have attempted – although the former would bristle at the parallel.

A Wind Named Progress

Milton Friedman's advocacy of a 'tabula rasa' being brought about in the collective mind of a nation through massive shock and disorientation – that wipes the mind clear of past patterns of economic and social behaviour, and allows new patterns to be burnt onto 'clean' brains – is conceptually close to the ideas of al-Qa'eda.

The angel of history however looks on. And as he surveys this 'war on terror' new wreckage piling at his feet, his fixed stare must reflect deepening concern, as well as despair. As he looks for causes for this latest accumulation, he must reflect how some humans, who have embraced secular progress as an article of faith, still seem driven by a compulsive need to demonstrate the non-necessity of religion to human well-being.

We have seen in the Enlightenment philosophies that shaped the last two centuries that this drive had its roots in a Protestant religious rebellion that coincided and was connected with two powerful processes: the rise of new technologies such as printing, as well as free market capitalism.

Although rooted in a puritan reinterpretation of the story of the Patriarch Abraham, this impulse eventually was transformed into a secular instrumentalism founded on the secular 'faith' in progress and the free market mechanism through the works of writers such as John Locke, Thomas Paine and Hobbes.

These new 'faiths' essentially transcended the boundaries of their puritan genesis to make religion a secondary or derivative aspect – until their more recent conflation with American Evangelicalism. In its secular version, religion became a subsidiary aspect of human life that would disappear or become a cultural 'background' to a person's choice of lifestyle. Once poverty was eradicated, as education diffused secular ideas of progress and science, and as the free market brought material prosperity and consumerism to all, individuals would 'rise above' their traditional instincts and culture. The world would become more peaceful and harmonious.

True believers in these articles interpreted the collapse of communism as a sign of an inexorable trend, and neo-liberals greeted the few years of American supremacy that followed as a new epoch in history. Underlying this article of faith was a determination to prove that religion in the shape of the 'old' religion, the religion of community, of intuitive revelation, of living as God demanded of humans, was a 'non-necessity' to modern life. The Protestants had 'won' an earlier struggle to prove the 'non-necessity' to live life as a community based on religious principles, and now their successors intended to see through the birth-pangs of a new era in which the old 'regressive instincts of religion' were to be completely overlaid by the supremacy of science and market freedom.

At the very moment of this triumph, it seems, a recrudescent religiosity emerged – not in the shape of the quiescent 'old enemy' of Catholic Christianity re-awakening, but in an Islamic renaissance.

It is hard not to see, in the passion for proving that Islamist extremism is the main threat to freedom, anything other than an obsessive drive to foreclose on the possibility of an historical explanation for the Islamist revival. In its dismissal of rational analysis, which its use of derogatory language is intended to bring about, it exposes where fundamentalism truly lies.

Explanation is taken for appeasement and exculpation. Reasoned accounting masks deceit and the 'truth' hiding beneath. Islamist resistance is just some surreal and transient explosion of resentment and anger. All attempts to assign a cause to this growing resistance are rejected, or claimed to be no more than envy of American 'freedom'.

These articles of faith – pressed to an extreme that involves loosing a form of terror on the humanity that it seeks to redeem – suggests a ferocious inner compulsion which is the very opposite of freedom. Paranoia is often a protest against insignificance – the 'scandal' of our own emptiness. Hollowness is potentially a debilitating realisation, particularly when pointed up by an adversary long thought to have been rendered impotent:

> Like the tragic protagonist, [a paranoiac] can glide through some invisible frontier at which its 'everything' collapses into nothing. Yet even this is not an absolute limit. For it is also possible ... to 'will' such nothingness, which is what we know as evil.[18]

Is this the wind named 'progress' blowing so strongly that the angel's wings were unable to unfurl, thus sweeping him forward despite his will?

Walter Russell Mead in *God and Gold* quotes G.K. Chesterton noting: 'cows may be purely economic, in the sense that we cannot see that they do very much beyond grazing grounds, and this is why a history of cows in twelve volumes would not be very lively reading'.[19] Russell Mead continues:

... cattle are all equal; bulls may vie for dominance of a particular herd, but there are not oppressed races or castes of cows stewing over their historical grievances and plotting to overthrow bovine tyrants. The Guernsey cows do not envy the Angus; the oxen are not agitating for their right; the Herefords to not resent the special status of the Brahmin, and the Texas Longhorns do not frighten and offend the rest by their unpredictable displays of unilateralism in their foreign policy.

'This is all very soothing', Russell Mead suggests, 'but how much like cattle do people want to be?'[20]

The thrust towards secular utopia of the last two centuries contained within it a contradiction: it was essentially a deformed version of those very religious impulses that ultimately it sought to show were empty of meaning. Its mission was to demonstrate that empirical thinking, science and the market mechanism were in themselves sufficient to ensure human happiness.

A Faith in Secularism

Secularism emerges, not so much as a worldview, but as political doctrine. In this sense, a secular state is one that banishes religion from public life while leaving people to believe what they like. Secularism of this kind is consistent with religious belief. American Evangelicals can ally themselves with the objectives of militant free marketeers as they share a close identification with the Abrahamic model, perceived as making the right decisions in a series of personal choices during a person's life, economic success as a mark of God's grace, embracing change, believing in America's divine mission in the world and an uncompromising opposition to the idea that any religion other than Protestant Christianity is true.

The political aim of this utopia was an end to political divisions and social antagonisms, and the secularisation of politics. Modern life was to be the more secure for having been perfectly de-politicised and for being lived as an ambient milieu of comfort and safety. But in pursuing this utopia, humans end up in a supervised world in which they all live painlessly, safely – and tediously.

> We are left with a humanity that has joined the cows, and like the inhabitants
> of John Lennon's imagined utopia, has nothing to kill or die for. The world
> turns into a big mall, and we go shopping: for ever. Nietzsche called the
> inhabitants of this peaceful shopping paradise the 'last men' and devoted
> some of his harshest polemics to the kind of human being who would be
> satisfied by this type of world.[21]

The greatest loser, paradoxically, as these articles of faith are
pursued, is actual life itself: the radical pursuit of secularisation
and neo-liberal economics transforms life itself into an abstract
anaemic process.[22]

What makes life worth living is the awareness that there is
something for which it is worth risking one's life – as the Islamist
leaders keep reminding us. Perhaps then, it is no surprise that an
Islamist resistance that keeps recalling 'old truths' and principles
for living has caused such a rage of rejection at any suggestion
that this resistance may have something to say – that it can offer
insights and the possibility of historical explanation for the
wreckage confronting the angel of history. Perhaps this rage also
confirms that Islam has become one of the few sites from which
to make this historical explanation?

In Chapter 3, we saw how a concept of 'defence of Islam'
emerged after the Prophet's death by about the eighth century.
This did not mean, however, that the Prophet was not himself
directly involved in fighting on behalf of His message. He was. As
we saw earlier, the Qur'an did not put forward any philosophical
arguments for monotheism. Its approach was practical: human
behaviour had gone astray. There was spiritual malaise, chronic
and destructive warfare, and rampant injustice. Its call was to
change the way men behaved with each other.

The earliest community which formed in Mecca around
Mohammad and his teachings made no use of resistance, but
the migration, or hijrah, in 622 changed everything. The hijrah
was as symbolic of transformation and the embrace of change
to Muslims as the interpretation of the Abrahamic story was to
be for Protestants. It was a revolutionary step: the hijrah was no
mere change of address. In pre-Islamic Arabia, the tribe was a

sacred value. To turn your back on your blood group and join another was unheard of, but to become the head of a community not bound together by blood but by a shared ideology was an astonishing innovation. The Prophet's tribe vowed to exterminate the community at Mecca.[23] The community founded in Medina by a Covenant, was clearly founded more for armed resistance than for any other purpose.

The second part of Mohammad's life, from 622 until 632, was thus largely taken up with warfare, and marks a contrast with the Mecca period, where the predominant themes include the discovery of a transcendent God. This latter period was a period identified with striving in battle as the heart of the Prophet's mission.[24]

Many of the first believers were converted by the sheer beauty of the Qur'an, which resonated with their deepest aspirations, cutting through their intellectual preconceptions in the manner of great art and inspiring them, at a level more profound than the cerebral, to alter their whole way of life. It also transformed them through the activity of fighting on behalf of that message.

Therefore, when contemporary Muslims take up arms against oppression and injustice, identified in the Qur'an as the objects against which Muslims must fight, it is not, as often perceived in the West, an inherent contradiction with the spirit of religion. Provided that their intent is genuine, the Islamist resistance members are following in the footsteps of the Prophet himself.

The original importance attached to the well-being of the Umma was so central to Islam that if their community was humiliated by apparently irreligious enemies, or beset by injustice, a Muslim could feel that his or her faith was in jeopardy. Every effort had to be expended to haul politics back on track, or the whole religious enterprise would fail and life would be emptied of meaning.[25]

The purpose of Islamist resistance, we have argued, is to do what the angel of history was attempting to do, before another blast of modernity swept him aside peremptorily and dismissively. Islamist resistance is not therefore the irrational, incomprehensible rage of 'divine capriciousness'. It is a genuinely emancipatory violence intended to expose the essence of the issue and to call humans to a fundamental change of behaviour. It is, we have argued, no more the savagery of 'divine violence' than the systemic violence, practised as 'legitimate force', that has been embraced by the West in pursuit of its articles of faith: both have roots in religious insights.

We have also argued that the reaction of the West to Islamist resistance has been a drive to foreclose any possibility of historical and rational explanation of resistance, and to close down the means of communication. We have argued that these actions expose the hollowness of secular modernity's purpose to complete the Protestant victory over religious community by demonstrating the non-necessity of religion to human welfare. We pointed out the contradiction between this object and secular modernity's own roots in Protestant themes. The emptiness, we suggested, stemmed from the purposelessness of the anaemic life to which this path had led.

In the next chapter, we shall examine how 'instrumental language' and the American development of its concept of power and politics have combined to create an entire way of thinking that we link to the particular wreckage of the last few years looked upon with despair and helplessness by Klee's angel.

9

THE NATURE OF POWER

'You spoke to the leaders of Hesballah?'
'Yes.'
'And to Hamas?'
'Yes.'
'And they said that they wanted democracy?'
'Yes.'
'And you believed them?'

This exchange occurred during a discussion we had with a member of a well-respected Washington-based foreign policy 'think-tank'. The biting scepticism of these words was deliberate, pernicious and by no means unusual: such expressions of dubiety are intended to imply the breathtaking naivety of actually believing what Islamists say.

It represents the ideological conviction that Islamists have 'nothing to say' – and when they do speak, what they say is either 'babble' or deceit.

This manipulation is justified on the pretext that the language of the Islamists is shadowy, unreachable and coded, whereas that of the West is transparent, accessible and honest. When westerners say they support democracy, they mean it; but when Islamists say it, they're lying.

To which a Hamas leader on a separate occasion retorted: 'We must conclude from this attitude that when we say we are for democracy, and the West replies that we are lying – then conversely, when the West says it is promoting democracy: we shall know that it does not mean it.'

The idea that non-Western cultures are instinctual, introverted and ethnocentric has a long history in European colonial thinking.

As we saw earlier, European Great Powers deliberately tried to break up the Arab people when they drew new frontiers in the 1920s. The Great Powers feared any pan-Arab sentiment arising based on Islam that could threaten their interests in the region.

In order to prevent this, ethnicity – sometimes a concocted one – was used to define the unitary national 'family' at its core, and by playing off ethnicities against one another to facilitate a secularisation of society. Ethnic nationalisms were placed in competition to a transnational Umma. Colonial powers attempted to divide the Arab and Muslim world into ethnic enclaves that were given arbitrary and at times whimsical 'national' boundaries as imperial envoys played with their pencils over regional maps. 'Officially ordained' nationalism was from the start a conscious, self-protective policy, intimately linked to the preservation of imperial-dynastic interests.

In its North African colonies, France drew a legal distinction between 'Berber' and 'Arab'. By governing Berbers with 'customary law' and 'Arabs' with religious law, they turned Berber and Arab into mutually exclusive identities. Not surprisingly, who is a Berber and who is not – and what percentage of Morocco's population is Berber today – is now a profoundly political and divisive question, whereas it was not, before the French imposed this 'ethnicity'.

But having 'made' ethnicity a defining characteristic in the new world of Arab states – in the United States, the very ethnocentric-ity which the western powers had promoted was itself becoming viewed as a threat by some conservatives, to American values: this they concluded was the consequence of misguided western 'liberalism'.

Allan Bloom in his book *The Closing of the American Mind* – a critique of US university education written in response to the anxieties felt by conservatives at the 'lack of patriotism' demonstrated by young people during the Vietnam War – argued that this unwillingness to fight for the nation showed that western values were eroding among young Americans. The universities were devaluing the contribution made by western thinking.

This erosion was principally the result of a misconceived multiculturalism adopted by the universities: its purpose was to force students to recognise other ways of thinking: 'but if students were really to learn something of the minds of these non-western cultures – which they do not – they would find that each and every one of these cultures is ethnocentric', Bloom said.[1]

The idea that non-western cultures are instinctual, closed and 'ethnocentric' is rooted in the same ancient Greek inheritance that gave us Plato and Aristotle. The Greeks also gave us the word 'barbarian', because the uncivilised people on their shores were viewed as 'babblers' who spoke an incomprehensible language, who literally 'baba'd' or 'stammered' and so could not be understood.

The Greeks, foreshadowing western 'new orientalism', soon put this term to political use, accusing their Persian enemies of rejecting the values promoted by the city state, in which free citizens could live in peace and security, whereas the Persians lived as slaves to a tyrant: they were the 'barbarians' who lived beyond the boundaries of civilisation.

Americans' inability to view other cultures as anything other than instincts of tradition and of tribal ties that immobilise non-Europeans in their static societies was re-circulated in an up-to-date formulation by Popper. Simplistic versions of this narrative entered into general currency in western political circles, and have been absorbed by many US officials quite unconsciously. From these beliefs they see Islamist discourse as imprisoned in their regressive cultures, and one without substance or of significance in the modern secular world. Listening was not necessary, it was sufficient to 'understand' – from Popper – that these societies had only one ambition, which was to smother the freedoms of the 'open' societies.

When a US Federal Bureau of Investigation (FBI) counter-terrorism official was asked for his views on the content of an al-Qa'eda video, he responded with a shrug: 'It's the same old Jihadist rigmarole,' he said. 'Rigmarole' is a slang expression first used in the late 1770s that is derived from 'ragman roll', the name of a children's game filled with incomprehensible words; it did not matter what Ayman Zawahiri was saying on the video – he was a barbarian, he was babbling.

The conviction that Islamist language is empty of content has extended to such a degree that even the most basic characteristics of Islam are considered to have little real significance. When *New York Times* reporter Jeff Stein in 2006 asked a number of senior US officials and Congress-persons with a direct stake in counter-terrorism or policy in the Middle East whether they knew the difference between a Sunni and a Shi'i, not one could give even the sketchiest of answers.[2]

Referring to a case in which the bemused FBI counter-terrorism chief had been unable to answer a few basic questions about Islam, the reporter noted that the most senior official in the FBI dealing with Muslim affairs simply had brushed aside his deficiencies by asserting that these details were of little consequence – compared to the importance of his qualities of being a good manager.

In contrast, the head of the FBI's Security Branch, the vice-chairman of the House intelligence sub-committee, and the chair of the House sub-committee overseeing CIA activities, had all agreed that the difference between Sunni and Shi'i would be a good thing to understand, but conceded that they did not know what differentiated them, and had some difficulty in deciding whether Iran or Hesballah was Shi'i or Sunni.

This lack of knowledge was compounded by the strong American conviction that it was unnecessary to understand and know in detail the societies from which Muslims came, as the idea took hold that it was more important to understand the type of government – whether it was closer to a tyranny or a free society model. This typology was held to offer a better guide than knowing the traditions and thinking of a society.

This latter was, in any case, disdained by American conservatives as a 'liberal' failing of trying to understand the 'other', whereas conservatives such as Leo Strauss believed that humans were, in a particularly inescapable way, defined and shaped by the political system in which they lived. It was therefore sufficient to know its characteristics – 'open' or 'closed', 'transparent' or 'deceitful'

– to 'understand' the individual Muslim with whom the official was dealing.

Added to this was the widespread western conviction that Islamists in any case almost invariably do practise deceit when they speak – and that Islamists are trying deceive the West about their true intentions, which are widely construed as ultimately seeking the destruction of the West, whatever they may say.

Convictions of Deceit

The origins of these convictions of deceit also derive from classical roots and more particularly the reinterpretations of Plato's thought that witnessed a popular revival in the United States after the Second European War, by instrumentalist thinkers such as Allan Bloom and Leo Strauss. The barbarians lay beyond the frontiers of Greek civilisation, but Plato had argued that it was the nature of politics – of competing city states – to seek to undermine and to destroy their rivals. Plato wrote that subterfuge, and deceiving your rival regarding your intention to bring about an enemy's downfall, was an inevitable prerequisite of politics.

If city states therefore are always camouflaging their true motives – and their natural inclination was to conspire against their rivals – then little that those rival political leaders said about their intentions – and certainly nothing that the Persian barbarians in thrall to a tyrant said – should be taken at face value. This is what Plato was understood to have concluded.

In the last chapter, we described the West's elevation of this 'war of language' to new heights – to something far more sinister than making some rhetorical point about the regressive nature of 'closed' culture. This use of language represented a deliberate ideological operation designed to capitalise and draw advantage from the Popper paradigm. Its use follows him in defining civilisation in terms of the 'open' society and makes this synonymous with the American way of life, but it goes further in positing an existential war between 'civilisation' and a new barbarian 'enemy'.

The purpose of such language was not only to foreclose on the possibility of looking for a rational and historical explanation for resistance and to place Islamists outside the boundaries of civilisation where international law and conventions are held not to apply. It was also done with the motive of exploiting this demonisation of an enemy.

Standing behind the language was the ideological purpose of turning the 'war on terror' into an 'opportunity', in what Naomi Klein has identified in *The Shock Doctrine*, as a different genre of 'disaster capitalism'. Naomi Klein uses the concept of 'disaster capitalism' to describe the thinking that treats disasters, whether natural or man-made, as economic opportunities to acquire assets, to privatise and to restructure economies to the benefit of corporate America.

To a certain extent, Klein argues, it does not matter what causes disasters – whether they be naturally occurring ones or ones brought about by military action – what matters is that these opportunities occur, in order to pursue the neo-liberal agenda by exploiting the shock and disorientation which they temporarily bring. Klein illustrates this with examples going back over 30 years.[3]

John Gray has noted that American neo-liberalism is an ideology that originated on the left. He argues that it is too simple to view neo-liberals as reformulating Trotskyite theories in right-wing terms, instead he maintains that Trotsky's style of permanent revolution – that society as it exists is beyond redemption, and must be destroyed in order for a new world to come into being – has been reproduced by neo-liberal American conservatives:

A type of catastrophic optimism, which animates much of Trotsky's thinking, underpins the neo-conservative policy of exporting democracy. Both shared a view on the need to demolish existing institutions in order to bring about change. Both endorse the use of violence as a condition of progress, and insist that the revolution must be global.[4]

The purpose in using 'new orientalist' language therefore is multiple. It is a powerful tool to weaken and to erode the identity of Islamists – to portray them as so extreme, as so irrational and so deeply antagonistic to the West that no one would wish to identify with them, or even to meet them. But the war on terror was also conceived as an opportunity to extend American interests and to install western clients as leaders in key areas of the world. The 'exclusion' of Islamists from the civilised universal was necessary in order to give the administration of George Bush the widest scope to take advantage of this so-called 'war on terror'.

A Contemporary 'Inquisition'

We are not talking here about language as the medium of reconciliation and mediation, let alone to achieve a better understanding of the other. That only becomes available when the parties accede to a minimal respect and recognition of the other party. Language here is used deliberately to misconstrue, reducing the wide shadings of Islamism to a narrow 'thing': 'terrorism'.

It inserts Islamism into a hollowed-out meaning that is alien to its wider nature. In this context, language is itself a form of violent extraction of one element, violence, to mask the wider meaning and rich tapestry of thought on which Islamism is contingent.

This ideological operation has been successful partly on account of the focus on violence – any violence – feeding into a predominant western popular sentiment that 'all violence is bad'. This is of course a position which depends for its consistency on westerners' ability to mitigate and normalise western violence as a natural process of state institutions doing their legitimate best. In short, viewing violence as practised by the West to be legitimate to the point of not being counted as violence (e.g., Israel's systematic military action against Palestinians is legitimate because it is practised by an army and is seen as Israel defending itself), whereas Palestinian resistance is seen as terrorism and therefore illegitimate.

It has also been a successful strategy because dialogue is rarely, if ever, egalitarian. It reflects power relationships. It is vulnerable to the more powerful, or whoever controls more media, asymmetrically imposing a 'master-signifier' on the other. There is no way for the weaker party to argue rationally against this imposition – 'terror' as 'master-signifier' – for it is strictly an irrational imposition: it is not 'open' to debate. 'It is so', the stronger party insists, 'because I say it is so.'

We have returned to the issue of language because this adversarial use of it has drawn unexpected public support in Europe and the US because of a significant shift in thinking in the United States towards the view that 'liberalism' has been a contributory factor to Islamist extremism; that policy has been 'too tolerant'; that western nation-states need to become more 'intolerant' and more self-consciously identified with the state in order to find the resolve with which to the fight 'extremism' threatening their 'open' societies.

This shift in thinking, dating from the last European war, can be identified as a strong conservative counter-reaction to the forces that we identified in the last chapter that helped create the ominous spectre of secular nationalism, and to shape the constitution and institutions of the United States itself.

If the last 300 years of European history may be thought of 'Hobbesian' and 'Lockean', the last decades might be termed the anti-Hobbesian era: the blowback against 'liberalism', collectivism, and social-democratic rights-based politics. It challenges the basic 'liberal' premise of the natural goodness of humanity – drawn from John Locke.

Following Allan Bloom's argument that 'liberalism' had been responsible for opening young American minds to multiculturalism and thereby had undermined American values, now the argument was extended to suggest that the same liberal way of thinking had allowed western states to be too tolerant towards Islamism in the past – and that the price for this tolerance was the emergence of Islamist extremism.

Both arguments had their roots in the American conservative fascination with the demise of the inter-war Weimar Republic of Germany, which they attributed to liberal influences that had made it 'too tolerant'. As this tolerance had made the Weimar government vulnerable to Nazism, so too liberal tendencies had rendered the West vulnerable to Islamist extremism. In short, Islamism was a convenient stick with which conservatives could attack liberalism.

We are not attempting here any systematic account of the many influences that have shaped American thinking in this recent period – it is beyond the scope of this book – but we wish to look at one particular theme to draw out an important point that was touched on in the introduction – the nature of politics as it is today in the West, and its relationship to the Islamist understanding of the meaning of politics.

We noted earlier Allan Bloom's and other conservatives' concerns that young American protesters against the Vietnam War were showing a lack of 'patriotism', which he ascribed to 'liberal' policies introduced at American universities. For conservative thinkers centred at the University of Chicago – and in the post-war period a number of prominent conservatives were gathered there – this lack of patriotism had sinister overtones: they saw this as one more danger signal, among many, warning of the dangerous consequences that had flowed from Hobbes and Locke.

Hobbes, we may recall, laid the foundations for a concept of natural rights to emerge. We suggested that Locke extended this, and his ideas about government, rights, and of the self-aware 'Self' and human innate 'goodness' had huge influence on French and American revolutionary thinking. But the small group of philosophers and economists centred around Chicago University felt it was Hobbes and Locke who were responsible for unleashing the genie of 'liberalism'.

These thinkers believed that 'Lockean' politics had contributed to the French Revolution's unleashing of forces that had led directly to the nihilism into which the revolution finally had sunk. Similarly, one of the main intellectual progenitors of neo-liberalism of recent years, Leo Strauss, believed also that liberalism derived from Hobbes and Locke, who were the 'fathers' of nihilism, which, in a vicious circle, ends by consuming its own liberal authors. Strauss wrote in his book *Natural Right and History*: 'We must say that the founder of liberalism was Hobbes.'[5]

Strauss and colleagues of the Chicago School believed that the liberal Weimar Republic in Germany, from which Leo Strauss, a Jew, had been forced to flee, was also a victim of nihilism. And now he and his Chicago colleagues, including Allan Bloom, identified within the anti-war movement in the United States the same ominous symptoms of incipient nihilism carried to America by the germs of liberalism. The question that preoccupied them all was how America's liberal market polity could be protected from infection by nihilism.

In linking liberalism with nihilism, Strauss was following a path well trodden in Germany: Nietzsche and Heidegger both viewed nilhilism as the defining modern disorder, but it was his lifelong friend and mentor, Carl Schmitt, who seemed to Strauss and some of his Chicago colleagues to have some, but not all, of the answers.

The Chicago School and the Essence of Power

Carl Schmitt was born the son of a small businessman in Westphalia in 1888. He studied law in Berlin, Munich and Strasbourg, and became Professor of Law at Berlin University. He joined the Nazi party, and with Hermann Göring's assistance, was appointed Chief Jurist. His legal arguments for dictatorship were seen to justify the 'Führer' state. Schmitt presented himself as anti-Semitic; but despite his expressed views, the Nazis did not trust Schmitt: he was denounced as an opportunist and Catholic pretender. He lost his position as Chief Jurist, but retained his professorship. After the war and a period of internment he continued to exercise wide influence – receiving a continuous flow of visitors seeking out his ideas on the failings of liberalism and its incompatibility with democracy.

It was through his critique of liberalism, and his redefinition of the nature of power and politics, that Strauss' ideas had their influence: Schmitt and Leo Strauss were life-long friends. Schmitt supported Strauss for a Rockefeller Foundation fellowship, and Strauss remained an ardent admirer and scholar, who taught his works – many of which were translated and published by Chicago University Press and circulated among Strauss's so-called 'Chicago School' followers.[6] It was only in one important respect that their paths had diverged: Strauss, a Jew, left Germany for the US; and Schmitt, a devout Catholic, joined the Nazi party in 1933.

Schmitt's *Political Theology*, published in 1922, derived its title from his assertion that all significant concepts of the modern theory of the state are no more than secularised ideas originating from religious themes – an argument we too have made in earlier chapters. In other words, Schmitt argued that political theory traditionally has looked at the state and sovereignty through the same prism that theology views God – that is from ethical principles.

From this starting point evolved his *Concept of the Political*, published in 1932, in which he argued that this approach had been misconceived: politics was totally different from theology. Moral philosophers and theologians may be preoccupied with justice and equity, but politics has nothing to do with making the world fairer or more just – that is the task of moralists and theologians – politics for Schmitt concerns power and survival, and nothing more.

Distinguished from the jostling of party politics, the 'true' political represents the essence of power – it is power's identity. While churches are predominant in religion, or society is predominant in economics, the state is predominant in politics.

It was an attempt to define exactly what politics is: the political is the most intense and extreme antagonism, Schmitt wrote. War is the most violent form that politics takes, but even short of war, politics still requires that you treat your opposition as antagonist to everything in which you believe. It's not personal, you do not have to hate him, but you have to be prepared to destroy him if necessary. Schmitt challenged liberals to admit that politics was literally a 'matter of life and death'.

This distinction had to be taken to the limit, to the point of life or death, which is to say that the enemy is whomsoever is, in an especially intense way, something different and alien. Such an enemy need not even be of a different nationality: as long as the conflict is potentially intense enough to become a violent one between political entities, the actual substance of enmity may be anything.

This deliberate dichotomy between power and moral or theological objectives reflected Schmitt's belief that liberalism's basis in human rights and a preoccupation with self cannot provide a reasonable justification for sacrificing oneself for the state – in other words, the Vietnam protesters were acting exactly as Schmitt would have expected in the circumstances.

Schmitt's answer to liberalism was threefold: his first response was to set aside moral considerations from the issue of whether or not a citizen supports his state. It was not appropriate to invoke moral principles in order to achieve common national purpose. Unity was to be achieved by redefining politics as opposition to the 'other'. That is to say, a national unity was to be formed around opposition to an enemy – a stranger – and not from moral responsibility. National unity was no longer to be based on Locke's reasonableness and natural harmony of human innate goodness – it was to be achieved by having an enemy, and by demonising him thoroughly.

His second answer was to stress the importance of a government being able to take 'decisive action' unencumbered by doctrines of separation of powers; and his third response was for a government to make use of a 'state of exception', which, according to Schmitt, freed the executive from any legal restraints to its power that would normally apply. The use of the term 'exceptional' has to be underlined here: Schmitt defined sovereignty as being he who has the power to instigate a state of exception – thus expanding the scope for discretionary 'decisive action' open to the government.

It is not hard to see why such ideas might have attracted the interest of American conservatives preoccupied with their dislike of liberalism as the 'disease' of democracies, and shocked by the lack of patriotism shown by the anti-war protesters of the 1960s.

The lack of mass anti-war mobilisation in America against the 'war on terror', in comparison to the earlier huge protests against the Vietnam War, may be seen to represent, at least partly, the successful application of Schmitt's principles of demonising an enemy. Equally, memorandums by US special legal counsel arguing that the President's claim not to be bound by the Geneva human rights conventions in the use of torture, the 'Unitary Presidency' proposition that a President as Commander-in-Chief in a time of war cannot be bound by law, and legal criticism of the separation of powers doctrine as historically inaccurate and problematic for the 'war on terror', have all been seen by Professor of Law Scott Horton, among others, as based on the work of Schmitt.[7]

Schmitt criticised the liberal faith in rational discussion and openness as the basis of democracy: politics just was not like that.

Reality, he said, was real parliamentary party politics, in which outcomes were hammered out in smoke-filled rooms by party leaders. It was from this observation that Schmitt questioned the liberal doctrine of separation of powers as out of line with reality: the real 'separation' was that of the tension between the rulers and the ruled, which made the liberal doctrine of a triumvirate of powers a fantasy, he suggested.

Liberals and humanists, Schmitt was suggesting, are queasy at using power to crush alternative forces from emerging. Their optimistic view of human nature leads them to believe in the possibility of mediation and compromise, based on a better understanding of the 'other'. The conservative optic, however, dismissed humanism in favour of an emphasis on the role of power in modern society.[8]

This is where the essence of a nation-state's political identity lies, Schmitt claimed. And, in a further resonance with contemporary US conservative thinking, Schmitt argued that as long as people exist in the 'political sphere', they must make use of the distinction between friend and enemy. From the moment that the western nation-state lacks the capacity or the will to use this distinction, a people ceases to exist politically. If the people should no longer have the strength to act decisively to preclude any force arising that can contest its power, this may not be the end of politics, but it is the end of a weak people.[9]

The distinction between power and moral objectives, and Schmitt's insistence that the two should not be confused, meshed well with parallel thinking about American power in the twenty-first century. The New American Century Project, a conservative think-tank, insisted that America must maintain its absolute global supremacy. There was resonance between the Bush administration's claw-back of decisive executive autonomy of action – including a dictatorial use of American power at the global level – and a relative sidelining of Congress that echoed some of Schmitt's themes. But the essence of the neo-liberal project remained the overwhelming conviction that nothing could prevail against the overwhelming dynamism of liberal capitalism.

Divine Victory and the 'War on Terror'

The fusion of this realpolitik conservative thinking with the American evangelical right merely reinforced the latter's deeply held religious faith in America's divine mission in the world – paradoxically conflating Schmitt's ideas of power as the-means-to-an-end philosophy with a sense of the divine redemptive mission of America.

The idea of power as distinct from morality was taken up by Allan Bloom in 1968 with his translation and interpretation of Plato's *Republic*, which attempted to sweep away the cobwebs of Christian themes and moralising that he claimed to identify in earlier commentaries on Plato. Another pivotal figure was Albert Wohlstetter, who redefined American defence strategies on these lines, and Nobel Laureate Milton Friedman. Both were University of Chicago professors, but it was Friedman who would first take forward some of this conservative thinking into the practical realm of politics.

Friedman became an icon to neo-liberals, but was not entirely in their political camp, believing that smaller government and less spending was always better for the economy and that government should interfere as little as possible in the freedom of individuals and their efforts to build wealth and advance themselves.

These key figures of neo-liberalism represented instrumental-ist thinking coalescing around ideas that would help inoculate America from liberalism, and see its free market mechanisms – which represented the second strand to its planned containment of liberalism – being exported to the world in the style of Trotsky's 'catastrophic optimism'.

At the centre of this ideological project lay the 'war on terror'. The war on terror served to separate politics from the Lockean basis in rights, and to redefine it as an existential conflict with the enemy 'other'. And the 'war on terror' provided the means to recoup presidential powers and the 'opportunities' to intervene and re-make other societies.

It was a means-to-an-end instrumentalism: moral rules were seen only as tools: thus the moral code rising from a given population was simply the collection of rules that were regarded as useful to that population.

Milton Friedman paraphrased the instrumental 'realism' by explaining that he had no ideological love for free markets per se, and that he might as easily be a socialist, if socialism fulfilled the ends most people seem to want. Karl Popper added to this a belief that we should empirically measure all politics and verify whether they fulfil their goals, and try to come up with better ways to reach these ends.

This foray into the roots of contemporary American thinking about power is definitely not intended as a comprehensive account of political events in recent years in America, which are more complex. But this partial glimpse is intended to highlight what is at issue when Islamists ask, as our Iranian cleric did in the introduction to this book, about the prospects of Islamist leaders finding any understanding with western political leaders were they to agree to sit together to talk.

It is clear from the foregoing that the meaning of 'politics' for Islamists and for conservative Americans is at opposite poles of understanding. For Islamists politics is the servant to human values; for American conservatives, survival and power are the only values, and extension of the market mechanism is their expression. The philosophies suggest little in common. And the Islamist 'threat' may prove to be too good a tool in the conservatives' struggle against liberalism for them to relinquish it easily.

Shock and Awe

Viewed from this perspective, the language used to demonise Islamists may be viewed as pure instrumentalism – that is, language used not to communicate, but as a means to an end: to forge national unity by raising the spectre of fear of the 'other'. The enthusiasm with which political leaders resort to it, however, suggests a deep vulnerability, rather than the mere resort to 'realpolitik' to promote national 'determination'.

When Islamists refer to western ways of thinking as irreconcilable with Islamist thinking they are referring to this instrumentalist approach, by which they mean the western belief that human nature can be qualitatively changed by means of human action; that anything that can be conceived can be brought into being by means of money and power, without need for any deep understanding of the societies or people who are to be affected; that views sentiment, habit and custom as obstacles that should and must be overcome by means of the free market; that views each situation as a 'tabula rasa' onto which a blueprint for a new vision can be imposed by means of shock and disorientation; and, because it assumes that man and society always can be brought to a preferred template by these collective means, sees all as possible and prospects for progress unlimited.[10]

It is not hard to discern both the Christian themes as well as the conservative views on the nature of politics and power in this thinking. It is well illustrated in practice by the Chicago School's economic policies.

Neo-liberal economics as a potential antidote to the liberal culture of rights and social democracy inherited from Hobbes and Locke, and to capitalism's ills, had long been lurking in the wings of public policy. But it was only during the troubled years of the 1970s that it moved to centre stage.

The point of departure in this thinking was the role of shock and disorientation required to bring about economic reform. It reflected the conclusion that economic reforms do not normally come about by a natural steady piece-meal implementation and good management – the passive 'instincts' of social and cultural factors are powerful forces against change – *pace* Popper.

Milton Friedman's metaphor for the missing ingredient was 'shock therapy', which he deemed necessary to impose free market capitalist reforms. The psychiatrists who experimented with electroshock therapy in the 1950s and 1960s, Naomi Klein has written,[11] sought to disorientate patients and destroy their existing psychic structures. They imagined they could create a clean slate on which new, healthier structures could be formed. Friedman thought similarly in terms of economic reform: without some sort of traumatic event to destabilise social habits and institutions and disorient the population, Friedman believed his reforms would never be accepted.

The first such practical experiment took place in Pinochet's Chile in 1973 after a coup which had been strongly backed by the CIA and Secretary of State Henry Kissinger. In Chile, Milton Friedman's free market ideas were already well established before the 1973 coup, in part through the training programme for Chilean economics students at the University of Chicago. Friedman acted as adviser to Pinochet during the early period of his regime.

The stubborn instincts of Chilean society that resisted the political and economic transformation – communists, trade unionists and others – were dealt with through torture and massacre. Pinochet's Chile brought into play all three elements that comprise 'shock therapy': military shock from a coup d'état, economic shock of neo-liberal economic transformation, and social shock through torture, imprisonment and massacre.

In *Shock Doctrine*, Klein traces the neo-liberal experiments through Argentina, Thatcher's Britain, Bolivia, Poland under Solidarnosć, China, post-apartheid South Africa and Yeltsin's Russia, to the 'Shock and Awe' in Iraq and Paul Bremer's attempt to build a neo-liberal economic system from the ground up. Her primary aim is to show that these policies were never adopted democratically or peacefully, and to argue that they all have failed – just as the nineteenth-century massive social engineering undertaken to free markets failed by the end of the century – and for the same reason: they failed to meet longer-term human needs.

The adherents of neo-liberal 'transformations' preached similarly that shock would create a 'new Middle East', would resolve the Palestinian–Israeli conflict – 'the route to Jerusalem lay through Baghdad – would change the 'balance of power' in Muslim societies in favour of the western model; but the 'tabula rasa' was never achieved – and all that is left behind are societies in ruins – more wreckage piling up at the feet of Klee's angel of history.

Resisting the American Project

For Muslims, there is a direct line connecting the western thinking that endorsed the massive social dislocation, the distress and the political upheavals in nineteenth-century Europe with the effort to make markets free, to the rampage of nation-building in the twentieth century that resulted in massacres and ethnic cleansing, and to the thinking behind the tabula rasa 'reforms' in Chile in 1973 and the 'Shock and Awe' of Iraq in 2003.

When the Secretary General of Hesballah or Khaled Mesha'al calls on Muslims or Palestinians to unite in resistance against the 'American project', they are referring to this instrumental way of thinking that purposively excludes the moral dimension from its 'therapies' – therapies that are predicated on humans being 'shocked' into conformity with a free market template, followed by the imposition of local strongmen who are provided with economic and military assistance so that they can accumulate wealth, buy off or repress opposition, and inflict their own micro-shock systems on Muslims.

The pessimism expressed by Islamists concerning the possibility of dialogue between political leaders to resolve the conflict with the West stems from their perception that the West has been, and continues to be, held in the grip of 'scientific' instrumental thinking. They see little possibility of a change in western behaviour so long as this thought process remains dominant. Islamists perceive this way of thinking to be responsible for westerners' 'blindness' to the consequences. And therefore the West is unable to accept the consequences of their actions. The Armenian massacres, the ethnic cleansing of the nineteenth century, the 'scientific racism' and experiments of the twentieth and the 'shock' therapies of the twenty-first century – all are perceived to form a continuum of western thinking. And it is against that thinking that Muslims are mobilising. They are not mobilising against the West; or westerners; but in response to a noxious system of thinking.

But even were western political leaders to decide to sit down now and talk with Islamists, the problem of language would remain, for instrumental thinking has bled over into western use of language and into diplomacy. Schmitt argued that 'liberals' can, by definition, never be truly 'political'. Liberals tend to be optimistic about human nature; whereas all genuine theories presuppose man to be evil, he held. Their optimistic view of human nature led them to believe in the possibility of mediation and compromise, based on a better understanding of the 'other'.

Liberals believe in the possibility of reaching objective understandings that mediate between conflicting positions, but for Schmitt there was no such neutrality, since any understanding – even ostensibly a fair one – merely represents the victory of one political faction over another. Schmitt also dismissed pluralism as an illusion – as no real forces would ever allow other forces, like the family or the Church to contest their power. In short, the essence of politics is struggle – a type of warfare in which there are only enemies.[12]

Language and Meaning: the Legacy of Schmitt

Whether or not these ideas have been consciously absorbed, and whether or not diplomats have even heard of Schmitt, this type of thinking can be seen in the contemporary use of language and in 'negotiation'. It is not the language of mediation or of finding common ground, it is not about finding of a path to coexistence.

It is the language of 'instrumentalist diplomacy': states face demands to 'come clean' about past sins, they must prove their good intentions towards the West, they must be transparent and open themselves to international inspection. States are confronted with false choices: either to modify their 'disruptive' behaviour or to accept the consequences; states have to 'step up' to the modern world or face isolation. The 'axis of evil' must be overcome by the forces of 'freedom'. Movements must renounce violence and disarm. States must cooperate in the 'war on terror'. 'Bad actors' and 'terrorists' must be eliminated.

This is the disintegration of meaning: this type of exchange is one in which a choice is presented on condition that we make the right choice. Islamists are solemnly reminded that they can say 'no' – and remain locked into seventh-century Arabia – but to say 'yes' is akin to entering a totalitarian system of prohibitions. One of the strategies of totalitarian regimes and of modern 'instrumental diplomacy' is to have such a range of 'disruptive behaviour' encompassing human rights, fighting terrorism, drugs, money-laundering and lack of support for the policies of Israel that, if taken literally, everyone is guilty of something. But then full enforcement is discretionary. It is at the discretion of the 'international community' either to appear lenient, or condemn and isolate you. It is about power – not justice as the Iranian cleric pointed out – it says 'behave and comply', for remember that at any time we can ...

It illustrates the language of empty gestures, of offers made to be rejected: the false choices that are being 'offered' to 'bad actor' states are intended to imply that its people somehow are freely embracing the outcome of this false choice; or, worse, have already made a bad choice, by placing their reliance on a tyrant – in which case their fate is their own fault. In either case, it is a false 'choice' dressed up by the international community as diplomacy. What is lost and has disintegrated is the entire complex network of implicit unwritten rules that sustains communities that have to live in close juxtaposition with each other and are obliged to consider what they say and how to say it, if they are to jog along with the neighbours.

The combination of this instrumentalist thinking linked with instrumentalist language throws into question any outcome from talking – at least until there is the possibility of a shift in behaviour and language. Historically, such changes have come about, but usually only as the result of a failure or crisis. Failure, however, seems inevitable: shock therapy lies in ruins, and global capitalism is inherently unstable. A worldwide free market is no more self-regulating than the free markets of the past. It already contains structural disequilibrium that may prove too great to contain.

The abuse of language is a problem of real concern to Grand Ayatollah Fadlallah. Educated at Najaf – a member of the Najaf nexus, and a respected Islamist thinker – Fadlallah is one of only a handful of Grand Ayatollahs in the world, a position of leadership among the Shi'i, worldwide. As a part of the Shi'i

élite, he has hundreds of thousands of followers who subscribe
to his teachings, and he takes great care in his use of language.
Fadlallah said:

> We can talk about the differences between freedom fighters and terrorists,
> about legitimate resistance and illegitimate resistance, and we can
> participate in dialogues and in debates – but every religion condemns the
> killing of civilians. The West knows this. Yet the West does not take care
> in what it says or in how it uses and applies its categories, or whether it
> follows its own principles. Its greatest mistake is in using these terms too
> readily. It needs to be more thoughtful, more attentive, more discerning
> in its use of language.
>
> There is an emptying of meaning in language at work here. What we
> need to realise is that words do have meanings, and misused, they can
> lead to violence.[13]

It is not surprising that Ayatollah Fadlallah, and Muslims
generally, should feel so strongly about language. Islam is a
religion based on a text and on language. It was because of this
language of such beauty that many were persuaded to alter their
whole way of life as a result of its aesthetic impact alone.

One of the most dramatic of these conversions was that of Umar
ibn al-Khattab, who was devoted to the old paganism, passionately
opposed to Mohammad's message, and was determined to wipe
out the new sect. But he was also an expert on Arabian poetry and,
the first time he heard the words of the Qur'an, he was overcome.
As he said, the language broke through all his reservations about
its message: 'When I heard the Qur'an, my heart was softened
and I wept, and Islam entered into me.'[14]

The Qur'an was not a philosophical tract: its approach was
practical and, radical as this sounded, it insisted that its message
was merely a practical 'reminder' of what we all know. God had
not left human beings in ignorance about the way they should
live: he had sent messengers to every people on the face of the
earth. All had brought their people a divinely inspired scripture:
they might express the truths of God's religion differently, but
essentially the message was always the same.[15]

The authenticity of the message lay in the creation of a new literary form and a masterpiece of Arabic prose and poetry. It challenged those (in the celebrated challenge verse) who doubted its authenticity as the word of God to produce anything approaching its equal in the beauty of its language.

In short, Islam and the Umma were imaginable through a written script and sacred language. Every word of this language was held to have huge significance and the various accounts of the lives, events and sayings of the Prophet and his followers were intensely researched and studied. On occasion the desire to include every utterance of the Prophet recalled subsequently by his companions may have led to error. The point, however, was that language was revered not only for its literal meaning, but also for its esoteric content. The language remained potent with the prospect of further insights for the future – through contemplation on the deeper significance of the words.

Even for those who could not understand classical Arabic, the language functioned to bind together a community from the beauty of sound as symbols of meaning – a purity of universal symbolism – to which all would have access.

Qur'anic language – even classical language inaccessible to the majority – carried with it the concept of an idea foreign to the contemporary western world: the non-arbitrariness of the language. It was literally a manifestation of reality: a direct link with 'truth'. There was no sense of today's idea that one language or one manner of expression is as good as any other – so long as it serves a purpose.

The western evolution of language however has been as a tool – a redefinition of language away from symbolising knowledge towards an expression of 'power' as an end in itself. The discovery of 'scientific' manipulation of language by western commercial and advertising interests demonstrated the ability imperceptibly to manipulate and control human aspirations and to persuade them to endorse social systems – even ones that ran counter to their own interests.

This instrumental use of language has proved capable of creating and transforming people's needs and desires to the extent that they have demonstrated a willingness to substitute their own interests for a fictional vicarious happiness that is momentarily satisfied in the fulfilment of aspirations implanted into them.

Politically, 'scientific' management of language has given western states the ability to assemble a discourse that is at once controlled, selected and organised according to a number of procedures, whose main role has been to avert the power and dangers of language from those in authority. Political parties have developed their 'response' units, whose purpose is to discredit – often by personal attack – those who criticise.

Language and the Asymmetry of Power

The combination of power and an instrumental management of language to control the parameters of what is counted as 'acceptable' public discourse and to manipulate human needs, has led to the disintegration of the link between language, truth and meaning. It was to this that Ayatollah Fadlallah was pointing when he suggested that the West needed to pay heed to the meaning of words and their ability to cause violence.

Inevitably the response of Islamists to instrumental language is to avoid the pitfalls of direct asymmetrical engagement with a dominant West in terms of its access to media. They have learned from direct experience of the impossibility of fighting their position on the terrain of western media, and have looked to other ways to pursue this ideological war of language. The loser, in all this, as Ayatollah Fadlallah was suggesting, is any real sensibility to the consequences, or empathy for the victims, of such international power-plays. On the one hand there is the 'reality' of people in their day-to-day misery; and on the other hand, the 'Real' of the inexorable abstract of the 'narrative' of power that erases emotional understanding of its victims.

The reaction of Sayyed Hassan Nasrallah to western criticism is not to try to explain Hesballah to the West, or to try to conciliate the West: his response is to warn Muslims that they 'faced a serious challenge for the control … over our decisions and destiny', adding that 'they [the West] come ... with their media and funds to wage a direct war'.[16]

Hamas pursues its resistance by simply refusing to participate in discussions based on the demand for prior acquiescence to western norms and parameters. It understands well that to accede to western rules of the game effectively locks them into a process whose ends will be determined through the prism of western power interests, and will be controlled by western norms of legitimacy of the nation-state, its monopoly of violence and of western institutional structures. Hamas simply does not believe that a just solution can emerge from such a process – and therefore contests the western right to impose its rules of the game.

The only option for Islamists, it would seem, is one of resistance. It is possible to resist by insisting on distinct language, insisting on separate identity and by flatly refusing to pay attention to the false 'choices' that the West demands from them.

Dr Abdullah Kassir, the director of al-Manar satellite television station, which is linked to Hesballah, emphasised that language of demonisation emanating from the West and its media was not the result of ignorance: it was, he said: 'the use of new technology intended to invade our sphere. The distortions presented of Islam and of movements such as Hesballah were deliberate; and served the western purposes by implanting the feelings of Muslim backwardness, of demoralisation and defeatism.'

Kassir argued that movements such as Hesballah had to respond with 'resistance media'. He argues that the invasion of the global information sphere by those who use language and narratives of power and oppression can only be met by a 'media resistance' such as that waged by al-Manar during the Israeli war against Hesballah in 2006.

He emphasised, however, that resistance media could only be founded on a just cause, and from a base of popular commitment. In a situation of asymmetrical power:

> ... resistance media could only succeed in combating power and superior resources by its credibility and by respect for the intellect of its audience. It could not succeed by matching distortion by distortion, it had to be

objective, it had to refute the ideas of the enemy with our ideas, and build esteem and morale.[17]

Dr Kassir said that, paradoxically, media competition was their biggest ally: al-Manar had forced other media to respond to it by virtue of the quality of their output. He quoted the number of Israelis during the 2006 war who had said publicly that al-Manar coverage was more credible than their own media, who were making exaggerated and unsubstantiated claims.

Political leaders such as Sayyed Hassan Nasrallah do use language to disarticulate the western offensive, but they are also careful to direct their rebuttals at those who launch them – rather than at westerners as a whole. Sayyed Nasrallah is careful to leave the door always open to the majority of westerners who share the Islamist belief that language is of too great importance to be reduced to a tool of power-play.

This two-track policy of rebuttal and openness to discussion is not easy to achieve, and of course rebuttal risks ratcheting up passions caused by polarised language, and of stimulating a further cycle of escalation. This was the reason that Ayatollah Fadlallah so urgently called for the West to understand, and to draw back from, the risks of using such language. The danger of the use of language as an instrument to undermine and demoralise an adversary is that, when you do come to need language as a means of communication, it is no longer available – it has been emptied of meaning.

'We know that in war innocent people will die, because this is the nature of war,' Grand Ayatollah Fadlallah said. 'But this does not excuse responsibility or negate the requirement that we do everything that we can to save the innocent.'

We have argued in this chapter that the demonisation of Islamists in language was motivated by two principal ideological objectives: the first of these was to displace the Lockean legacy of liberalism and human rights as the pole around which national unity was gathered – and to substitute fear of an enemy 'other' as the element that binds together the American national 'family'. Second, we have argued that the 'war on terror' served as the ideological tool to further American conservatives' aim to contain and weaken 'liberalism', which they perceive as the Achilles' heel of market-mechanism democracy.

We have argued that the 'war on terror' served this latter objective of weakening liberalism in two distinct ways: the prosecution of the war around the globe gave the United States the justification to increase its reach into other societies and regions, and to use this opportunity to shape these regions to its interests. And, second, the 'war on terror' provided the opportunity to widen the scope for decisive action wielded by a President enjoying greater powers that would be less constrained by the doctrine of separation of powers, and which would take advantage of the principle of legal exceptionalism.

The third strand to the containment of liberalism – apart from displacing the idea of human natural 'goodness' as the accepted premise of politics, and of restoring the capability for decisive unconstrained action to American leadership – was neo-liberal market reform, which by weakening or destroying social and cultural continuities was intended to strengthen an atomised self-reliant individualism and to deal a death blow to collectivism.

We argued that the consequence – beyond the short term – of pursuing these policies was failure: we suggested that the radical remodelling of the world, suddenly, by an act of human intervention, as a neo-liberal free market, was an illusion that has already collapsed – leaving only ruined societies in its wake. We have argued that the free market is neither self-regulating, nor does it contain any inherent mechanism within it, that naturally brings about a tendency toward equilibrium; rather, it contains forces leading to mounting imbalances that ultimately threaten its collapse – unless this prospect is recognised sufficiently early for it to be reformed first. The problem facing the United States is that it has modelled itself on ideas and thinking from the seventeenth and eighteenth centuries that are not adequate to today's world and which are being repudiated by a majority of the globe.

The other consequence of this policy has been the loss of language as a medium for expressing meaning, and we noted the corrosive effect of instrumental thinking in both language and diplomacy on the unwritten principles and conventions that underlie traditional understanding of the need for coexistence between peoples based on courtesy and respect. We warned that when western states find that they again need these conventions and principles, they may no longer be available.

What is inexplicable in all this has been that European leaders have been such enthusiastic collaborators in an ideological operation, one of whose primary objectives has been to dismantle liberalism and social democracy. The legacy of this collaboration has been to plant the seeds of the neo-liberal hatred for multiculturalism and of a nationalism defined in opposition to the 'other' into a Europe in which 20 million Muslims live.

In the next chapter, we conclude with a look at what all this might mean, and consider what those living in western societies might do to help step over and beyond the wreckage lying at the angel of history's feet.

10
THE LIMITS TO THE PRESENT

J.M. Coetzee, the celebrated South African writer, in a metaphor for his own society described the tribulations of a minor magistrate, a responsible official moderately corrupt but not brutal, serving out his days at the Empire's edge, adjacent to some barbarian tribes who visit his town only for trade or medicine.[1]

At the outset, the magistrate is confronted by Colonel Joll, a bureaucrat sent by the Empire's secret service, who claims that the barbarians are preparing to mutiny. The colonel leads an expedition in search of rebels and returns with a group of nomads in chains, terrified and mute. Although the magistrate argues that the barbarians are harmless, the prisoners are tortured in accord with that 'modern psychology' which is the mark of the security services in our time. The possibility that the barbarians may be innocent of any revolutionary plans is brushed aside by the colonel in his description of how he conducts an interrogation: 'First, I get lies, you see – this is what happens – first lies, then pressure, then more lies, then more pressure, then "the break", then more pressure, then the truth.' Or, as the Magistrate sardonically restates the torturer's creed: 'Pain is truth; all else is subject to doubt.'[2]

Unable to control or manage events, the magistrate tries to dissociate himself from the colonel – even as, in honesty, he has to admit to being a product of the same colonial identity. Not that he becomes a critic of imperialism or a romantic defender of barbarians; he simply wants to continue his slothful ways, spending time in 'old recreations': keeping a barbarian girl 'for my bed' and reading the classics in the evening.

The barbarian captives are broken by torture and released. One of them, however, an impassive girl with straight black eyebrows and glossy black hair remains behind and is taken in by the magistrate, who attempts to nurse her wounds and, in the end, decides to return her to her tribe out of confused feelings of guilt at the colonel's brutality.

Back at home again, the magistrate is charged with treason and 'consorting with the enemy'. He is imprisoned in the same barracks room in which the barbarians were interrogated. He is reduced, through humiliation and torment, to a subhuman level. And, as he later reflects, he learns the great lesson of the twentieth century:

> When the torturers first brought me back here ... I wondered how much pain a plump comfortable old man would be able to endure in the name of his eccentric notions of how the Empire should conduct itself. But my torturers were not interested in degrees of pain. They were interested only in demonstrating to me what it meant to live in a body – a body that can entertain notions of justice only as long as it is whole and well; but which very, very soon forgets them when its head is gripped and a pipe is pushed down its gullet and pints of salt water are poured into it ... they came to the cell to show me 'the meaning of humanity', and in the space of an hour they showed me a great deal.[3]

The point about J.M. Coetzee's novel in which the South African coloured and black populations were the barely disguised 'barbarians' living at the edges of the white Empire, was – as Professor Eagleton describes in another context – a story in which 'reason on its outer edge is demented because it seeks to possess the whole world, and to do so, must override the recalcitrance of reality'. But it is the very reality which it seeks to override, ultimately that 'kicks back inconveniently at reason's own paranoid projects'.[4]

Old psychic structures have not been wiped clean, the Middle East has not been 'shocked and disorientated' into becoming a pro-western satellite, and global capitalism is showing renewed signs of its innate tendency to disequilibrium and crisis.

Terry Eagleton suggests that it is only 'sane to acknowledge such madness; and lunatic to imagine that such madness could ever simply be bullied into reason'. The differences between the present

Colonel Jolls and the Islamist 'barbarians' are never destined for dialogue, but for psychological war until exhaustion intervenes. It is clear that Joll believes, in common with many of his modern counterparts, that barbarians only conspired or babbled – unless brought to truth with the clarifying purity of intense pain.

Finally, of course, reality does intrude on Joll and the Empire – through resistance to its special rights for 'white men'; and through resistance to the racialism of its fusty club for the 'civilised' that excludes 'those' barbarians, massing beyond the garden wall.

Today's gathering forces of reality striking-back are also a challenge to the comfort of the many western 'magistrates' for whom, too, the Colonel Jolls are a troubling intrusion, but who avert their gaze, preferring to console their conscience in other ways and spend time in old recreations.

As reality begins to dawn in Coetzee's metaphorical Empire, the magistrate does not begin a journey 'to defend the cause of justice for the barbarians'.[5] But in the end, in its confused way, an 'act of resistance' does take place. And it is an act that comes not from the barbarians, but symbolically from within the heart of Empire: the magistrate, who accepted his identity as a part of the Empire, nonetheless sets out on the long journey to return the abused barbarian girl to her tribe – a small act of kindness; but to Joll and his colleagues, an act of subversion of far greater consequence. It symbolises an act of censure from directly within the elite – a crack, a small but threatening fissure in collective resolve.

Resistance From Within

This was Coetzee's point: the magistrate was not a particularly moral person, he was no ideologue, and he was certainly no revolutionary opposed to the Empire – he was too set in his comfortable ways to welcome radical change. But his quiet questioning of the sense and rightness of what was being done in Empire's name, and his instinct that something was badly awry, was in this small expression of doubt, sufficient to open a fissure.

In the introduction to this book, the Iranian cleric was quoted as saying that the Islamist and the western views of what constitutes the essence of man were now too far apart to allow for dialogue between politicians to be of use until at least two things had happened: first, that the 'scales' begin to fall from western eyes with regard to the wreckage wrought over the last 300 years by instrumental 'scientific' thinking; and, second, that western thinkers began to consider how it was that this thinking could have given rise to such a catalogue of tragedies, ranging from genocide, to racial science and today's 'shock doctrine', while remaining genuinely – and the cleric emphasised 'genuinely' – convinced that they were acting in the best human interests.

Today it seems faintly absurd to recall the racial 'science' of the nineteenth century, when an anthropologist such as John Beddoes could compile an index of 'nigresence', cataloguing the inhabitants of the British Isles by their racial features. Initially anthropologists had conceived the 'lower classes' as being literally racially distinct from the middle and upper classes; the Irish, too, were interpreted as literally 'dark'. John Beddoes' study showed that 'nigresence' was increasing in the British lower classes owing to the presence of Irish immigrants, whom he described as 'Africanoid'.[6]

While we might grimace at such absurdities now, are they so very different – in their complete disregard of the human distress and misery of the victims of such 'science' – from the contemporary social 'science' that saw Pinochet's experiments in Chile in 1973 in the name of neo-liberal economics, or the destruction of Iraq, 30 years later, carried out in the name of America's vision of democracy. How did 'science' and empiricism become so warped? What was it about Protestant and secular modernism's obsession with proving its utopia, and demonstrating the non-necessity of collective religion, that it should induce western mass amnesia for 300 years to the consequences in terms of human suffering?

The cleric urged the West to reflect on these things. He argued that what was required, above all, was thinking about the processes of thinking. From such a reflection, he hoped that it might prove possible to find common ground on what does constitute the essence of man and his values, and from that base to examine the past.

In a similar way, we noted Michel Foucault's thoughts that the West needed to consider that its narrative increasingly roused hostility in much of the world – and that Muslims had simply stepped over it and beyond it, in defining their future. He argued that any civilisation faces episodes in its history when it needs to re-energise itself – in order to step beyond the constraints of established ideology – and to reason afresh.

J.M. Coetzee in his account of an Empire held fast by its belief in special rights for 'white men', illustrated so piercingly how renewal begins: this improbable revolutionary, the magistrate, begins to entertain doubts about the necessity or the value of treating the neighbouring tribes as barbarians threatening the Empire's existence, and who can only be persuaded to 'come clean' about their antipathy toward the Empire under the purifying experience of pure pain. J.M. Coetzee suggested that these few 'doubts' and a reasoned questioning of the colonel's mindset, in itself, marks no less than the onset of change.

The magistrate did not join the barbarians, he did not 'go native' and take up arms against the Empire; but he began, after a long period of pleasurable somnolence, to start to think critically again – and crucially made his symbolic act of human solidarity.

Foucault and the Essence of Change

This act entails, Michel Foucault suggests, discovering the resources to escape the 'authority' and controlling influences of a dominant paradigm of thinking and allowing it to lead to areas where critical thought is called for. I believe that we have to refer to much more remote processes if we want to understand how we have been trapped by our own history.[7]

Foucault suggests that an individual can only escape from this 'blackmail' of entrenched thinking and history by a 'change that he himself will bring about in himself'.[8] The essence of this change was to have 'the courage, the audacity to know'. Thus Enlightenment must be considered both as a process in which men participate collectively and as an act of courage to be accomplished personally.[9]

Foucault takes as an example Gregor Mendel's discovery of genetics in 1865:

> People have often wondered how on earth nineteenth-century botanists and biologists managed not to see the truth of Mendel's statements. But it was precisely because Mendel spoke of objects, employed methods, and placed himself within a theoretical perspective totally alien to the biology of his time.

His work suggesting that hereditary traits constituted a completely new biological object, was ignored and excoriated until the beginning of the twentieth century – when it was rediscovered. At that point, reconciliation became possible:

> Mendel spoke the truth, but he was not '*dans le vrai*' [within the 'true'] of the contemporary biological discourse: it simply was not along such lines that objects and biological concepts were formed. A whole change in scale, the deployment of a totally new range of objects in biology was required, before Mendel could enter into 'the true' and his propositions appear, for the most part, exact. Mendel was a true 'monster', so much so that science could not even properly speak of him.[10]

And at his death his papers were all burned.

In the real South Africa – as opposed to Coetzee's metaphorical setting of Empire – there was also resistance. There was armed resistance led by the African National Congress (ANC) and there was the unarmed 'resistance' of the trades unions, the religious movements and activists. But there was also another less obvious entry into this process. It was an intrusion that, in combination with the other constituents, and despite its unexpectedness, nonetheless played a key role, in Foucault's language, of 'change that he himself will bring about in himself'.

The 'white elite' remained gripped in the ideology of special rights for white men, despite the growing resistance, both armed and unarmed. But a few leading 'white' businessmen from within the circle of the elite tentatively began to question the 'shelf-life' and the rationale of their own peoples' creed of preserving 'special rights'.

They queried what the world might look like in their grand-children's day, and began to question and to criticise – but from a platform within and as a part of the inner circle. They saw that recalcitrant reality could only be postponed for so long. They recognised resistance. And they saw the ANC as a reality that would not disappear by labelling it as 'terrorist'.

They began to say these things, and they began to link up with activists outside of the elite who had been saying these things for a very long time. The activists, like Mendel, had spoken the 'truth'; but it had not been in the 'true discourse' at the outset. What they had said, like Mendel's genetic theories, initially had provoked only anger and outrage. But the Oppenheimers and the Anglo-Americans – like the magistrate, improbable revolu-tionaries – began their small but symbolically important 'acts of resistance'. The fissure opened.

They pursued their quiet 'acts of resistance' in the understanding that societies can become captives of their own historical outlook and way of thinking – of persisting with claims to 'special rights' for the white man in South Africa in a region that had long since won its independence from such notions.

These businessmen saw that reality in the shape of resistance could not be annulled for ever, and that only by making a challenging critique of this rationale internally, and by refusing to submit to a certain state of will that makes us accept someone else's authority, could the 'blackmail' of petrified categories of thinking be broken. It was, then, from within, from inside the bastion of the white 'establishment', that a mobilising of resistance was launched that triggered change.

Foucault foresaw that beginning a critique inevitably encounters difficulty in breaking through the 'limit-attitudes', the constraints to thinking, imposed by years of conditioned thinking, of settled conventions and of the almost imperceptible conforming influence of institutions and of the workplace. He emphasised that any act of freedom, of protest, however, must involve the deliberate 'transgression' of limits.[11]

The establishment South African businessmen who 'transgressed' the accepted norms of the white conservative elite to which they belonged helped their society step beyond its own limits and constraints. They helped move it beyond the 'bloody' future of civil conflict that so many had foreseen for South Africa.

We are not here suggesting that the situation of South Africa is a direct parallel to the situation of Islamism today. That is not the case; but what we are seeking to illustrate is the type of process that Foucault may have had in mind when he spoke of what he had witnessed in Iran, and its implications for western thinking. It is the 'processes' of the South African rupture with the past – rather than the political situation itself – that may serve as a parallel.

Those in the West who share the magistrate's anxieties about what is being done in the name of Empire, and who are troubled by Colonel Joll's limited views about the correct handling of the barbarians, can also do something about it. The improbable magistrate and the arch-establishment South African businessmen raised their voices in criticism of the prevailing orthodoxy of 'normalisation' of injustice: that is, they stood for refusal, rather than normalising the behaviour of the Colonel Jolls to make it part of the ordinary flow of things – the humdrum of perfectly de-politicised politics. The magistrate made his act of human solidarity, and the businessmen became a part of the 'resistance' of activists and their social movements. But most of all they questioned.

Political 'Sensibilisation'

W.G. Sebald, who wrote about Jean Améry's confrontation with the trauma of the concentration camps, picks up on the resentment discernible in many of his works. Améry justified this emotion as essential to a truly critical view of the past: it was the spur of resentment that nailed everyone to his ruined past.[12] The sensitisation of consciousness – and the critical view of the past to which it opens the door – is what provides the goad, in response to which the political steps forward to new thinking, as the Iranian cleric hinted.

But the emotions of resentment and the sensitisation of conscience are hard to access in today's self-pacified, lifestyle politics that no longer posits struggle in an increasingly administered and anaemic existence. It is not easy to re-politicise politics or to re-politicise culture in an era in which most people in the West live pleasurably, painlessly and safely.

In this sense, it is possible to share the cleric's pessimism about outcomes from political dialogue, while still seeing that a sea change of different thinking and new language could come about if those living in the West were to mobilise and to criticise – not simply for the sake of 'being critical', but simply by asking incessantly what now is the purpose of western power and what exactly are the values on which it now stands?

It is no longer the case of being on the wrong side of the 'true' discourse, as Gregor Mendel found himself to be in the second half of the nineteenth century: in the rapidly unravelling project of fashioning the Middle East and the emerging global order in the western image, the 'limit-attitude' of contemporary western security thinking mirrors, as Jean-Paul Sartre might tartly respond, thinking of the Colonel Jolls of an earlier era:

> He has already lost but doesn't realise it; he does not know that the 'natives' are false 'natives'. He has to make them suffer, he claims, in order to repress the evil they have inside them ... How come he cannot see his own cruelty now turned against him? How come he cannot see his own savagery as a colonist in the savagery of those [whom he] oppresses? The answer is simple: this arrogant individual, whose power and authority and fear of losing it, has gone to his head, has difficulty remembering he was once a man.[13]

What *Resistance* Has Shown

Islamist resistance was jolted into existence by the trauma of social engineering, ethnic cleansing, political disruption, repression and massacres that were the direct consequence of the western experiment in exporting to Muslim societies its vision of economic market-based life, freed from social and political control. The enforced westernisation and secularisation of Turkey, and the brutality of its nation-state building have come to symbolise the worst aspects of secular modernism. This is the first argument of *Resistance*.

The second argument is that the western myth of the free market acting to reconcile the self-interested, individualistic choices of men and women, operating through the invisible hand to produce the optimal human welfare – is simply irreconcilable with Islam and poses an existential threat to it. It was a vision built on the myths of an invisible hand and of a spontaneous order emerging naturally from the 'disorder' of selfish competitive contention. The western nation-state, human rights doctrine and the institutions of western democracy are all derived from these same myths.

Resistance's third theme has been that underlying this conflict are differing religious insights – and that Christian religious themes underlie western thinking on economics, on the nation-state and on the principles around which society is organised. It is therefore fundamentally a conflict touching on profound religious sensibilities, which subsequently synthesised into secular modernism.

It is not, however, a straight confrontation between Christianity and Islam. The Anglo-Saxon tradition, which America embodies, originated from the long-running struggle between the personalised, free-enterprise and Abrahamic embrace of change associated with Protestantism versus the community-based religiosity of Catholicism. These same originally Protestant themes can now be observed reflected in western language towards Islam.

A fourth theme has been that, at bottom, the dispute comes down to two opposing views as to what constitutes the 'essence of man'.

Resistance has argued that, in evolving an Islamist ideology, something important happened. Islamists, who had been constrained by western instrumentalist 'scientific' thinking along with most people in the nineteenth and early twentieth centuries, suddenly broke free. This was the crucial importance of the Iranian Revolution: it freed Islamists from self-imposed constraints resulting from an hegemony of instrumentalist thought. This is the fifth main argument.

The ideology that evolved is dynamic and substantive. Islamism is acquiring 'open' society characteristics associated with a dynamic and evolving matrix of thinking, whereas the West is acquiring some of the characteristics of a 'closed' society. This represents an inversion of the popular western perception, and is the sixth major theme of *Resistance*. Islamist social and economic components are the ideological re-politicisation of culture and of politics. They are the instruments of political mass mobilisation, rather than life-choices marking the personal domains of an individual.

The Islamist system makes little sense, however, if analysed simply as a competitor to western systems and judged by its efficacy in meeting these norms. Islamist economics can only properly be understood against the aspiration to regulate the personal within the context of a collective and just society.

Unlike the western project, the Islamist one is not utopian: it represents a system that is predicated on a realistic view of human nature. It does not aim to transform humans through human action, but believes that behaviour is influenced by the experience of living in a just and compassionate community, and by humans behaving with each other, as God directed.

The seventh argument of *Resistance* is that mainstream Islamist resistance is an expression of the human spirit in adversity, and represents a natural evolution from events that can be explained and understood historically.

Resistance is a means to facilitate political solutions through helping to correct asymmetrical imbalances, and by forcing the West to acknowledge the importance of key principles as necessary to any solution. *Resistance* distinguishes between the emancipatory resistance of movements such as Hamas and Hesballah, the 'burn-the-system-to-build-anew' philosophy of al-Qae'da and the eschatological leanings of some Salafi groups. It argues that the failure of the West to make this distinction empowers the more extreme movements at the expense of the mainstream.

Resistance maintains as its eighth theme that Islamist resistance is no more 'divine caprice' than the systematic violence deployed by western states as 'legitimate force'. Both have roots in religious insights. It argues that the reaction of the West to Islamist resistance has been the drive to foreclose any possibility of historical and rational explanation of resistance, and to close down the means of communication. This represents the re-emergence of old Protestant and secular themes to demonstrate the non-necessity of religion lived communally for contemporary humans.

The ninth argument is that the demonisation of Islamism is not the result of a poor understanding of Islamism, or a 'legitimate', but ultimately flawed, exercise of judgement. It represents a deliberate ideological operation, one of whose objectives has been to weaken liberalism everywhere, to strengthen America's scope to take 'decisive action'; and another of which has been to justify greater American intervention in the Middle East in pursuit of the neo-liberal agenda. Islamists were, in a sense, pawns to these strategic conservative objectives focused on securing an irreversible defeat of liberalism and entrenching American global hegemony.

And the tenth argument of *Resistance* is that the pursuit of these objectives has been a failure that is ascribed to a way of thinking that has strewn its wreckage across 300 years of history, and which in recent years has added another astonishing mound of debris in the Muslim world – a legacy that will haunt the West for years to come.

Glimpses of the Future

The arguments posed in *Resistance* suggest that we may stand at another key moment in history: it was such tragedies, then spawned by the nineteenth- and twentieth-century drive for nation-state building, and the then fashion for free market trans-formations, that first gave birth to Islamist resistance and to the Iranian Revolution. The experience for Muslims of the last 30 years – of western ideology, military occupations and attempted 'shock' transformation – seems an eerie repetition of the twentieth-century disaster, but in a more concentrated form.

This new act in the long-running play of the Euro-American utopian project is likely also to yield profound consequences – even if it is too early to identify these potential outcomes clearly.

There are, however, important differences with the earlier round in the 1920s: in that round, Sunni Islam was shocked and disorientated. The collapse of the Caliphate dealt a psychological blow to a narrative that was already on the defensive, and whose scholars were at work trying to tailor Islamist identity to western thought. Marxism was eating at the base of the Umma, and secularist rulers were emptying culture and tradition of its Islamicate content.

This was, we may recall, a moment just past the high-water mark of the hegemony of western 'scientific' instrumentalism and of that particular phase of free market ideology. The tide was already on the ebb: the nineteenth-century free market social-engineering projects in Europe had brought unrest and political dislocation – extending even to the brink of revolution – into Europe's Great Power societies, a process that was overtaken, and taken in other directions, only by the even greater upheaval of the First European War. By the 1930s, western capitalism had capsized into the Great Depression and further social dislocation.

The present act of a drama which is still unfolding appears to follow the pattern of the last century in one important aspect: America and its allies pursued their project with the same venomous convictions and, on this occasion, with the extra ingredient of overt Protestant millenarianism mixed in. But on this occasion, they met increasingly organised resistance, resistance that seems – so far – to be succeeding.

One clear difference between then and now – apart from the earlier lack of any resistance – is that in that earlier era, the case for mass industrialisation and commercialisation was in the ascendant, and seemed virtually unanswerable, whereas in the present era, its credibility largely has vanished.

In other respects, however, the parallels with early twentieth-century history seem ready to play out in line with that earlier episode: social unrest is mounting in Europe and America, and the long-expected financial and economic crisis in America and

Europe is gathering pace. As before, this combination portends severe political disruption. It also suggests that we stand at the brink of significant change – and the accompanying distress that change often brings in its wake.

In one respect, it is possible to see an inversion of roles between these two phases in respect to, on the one hand, the situation and condition of the European peoples and, on the other hand, the state of their Muslim counterparts living in the Muslim world. In the last century, it was Muslims who saw their social and political continuities and structures severed, whose society was individualised and who were politically anaesthetised. It took time to emerge, but ultimately resistance and an Islamist confidence and self-esteem returned. Islam has passed through the shadows and emerged as a revived and dynamic force in opposition to neo-liberalism.

Curiously, the impact of neo-liberalism pursued in America and in countries such as Britain, has left their own citizens in much the same state as Muslims in the wake of the great secularisation and modernisation projects of the last century: it has weakened and severed social, trade and professional structures; it has individualised society, weakened the working and middle classes, broken up capacity for community self-regulation and eroded community support systems. It has left Europeans and Americans alienated, living with an economic pain that is experienced as a private and isolating affliction, and with little political recourse against an elite of entrenched interests – much as Muslims found themselves in the post-Caliphate era of enforced westernisation.

This represents an inversion of roles between the two peoples: European citizens seem to be experiencing now, as a result of being the subject of the renewed neo-liberal experiment, something of what Muslims felt in the last century – although plainly Europeans have not been subjected to the horrors of massacre and ethnic cleansing as part of the current experiment. It would be interesting to speculate – but beyond the scope of this book – whether the European peoples' response to this will, like that of the Muslims, be one of political renewal and protest.

In terms of Muslim societies, the act of course is far from over. The western project may be in disarray, but the West remains hugely powerful in military terms. Its 'grand narrative' may no longer retain its hold or have legitimacy for a majority of the globe, but the prevalence of 'firepower' over moral authority is a reminder that imperial powers have never relinquished power readily or easily.

It seems likely that the West will be preoccupied with its economic crisis in coming years and, inevitably, this is likely to constrain domestic support for foreign policy interventions overseas. America faced a similar circumstance in the wake of the Vietnam failure, but instead of direct interventions to preserve American power from competition, resorted to encouraging proxy forces and promoting front movements in countries in Africa, for example, in order to pursue its Cold War against the Soviet Union.

In the Middle East, key strategic dynamic tensions, notably between an Israel apparently unable to make peace with its neighbours, and a resurgent Iran that challenges Israel's military domination of the region, will persist and threaten war. Equally, western political failures have left some Muslim leaders exposed and frightened: some are already responding by trying to rally the reactionary forces of radical Salafism into action – to contain Shi'i influence. This is already threatening sectarian instability in parts of the region.

But more significant in the coming next years will be the economic and social consequences of three separate but interlinked strands: one is the economic crisis that began in the West; the second is the rise in food prices, which has its own distinct structural causes – apart from the pressures of monetary inflation; and the third is the likelihood of continuing high energy costs that will affect all sectors of the economy.

This vicious combination of rising prices and economic crisis comes to a region whose social fabric already has been stretched transparently thin. In the West, Middle East economies are presented as having experienced the benefits of the globalised economy. This is a myth: the international super-rich of the region have boomed – that is certain – but the reality for the vast majority of its 400 million inhabitants has been a decade of steadily declining real incomes and vanishing middle classes.

Significant and growing proportions of Muslim populations now live in absolute poverty, while their elitist rulers have become hugely richer – and more detached from the communities from which they sprang – preferring to join the caravan of the super-rich, on its migrations around world resorts, where they can enjoy each others' company.

The rise in prices, coupled with lower employment, will add to the misery of the many Muslims who already live migrant-worker lives that more closely resemble indentured slavery than the western make-believe of the economic freedom of globalised capitalism. The soaring food price rises that have already occurred and will continue to occur in the next few years for those in absolute poverty mean starvation – not just 'belt tightening' – as many may assume. We may expect growing political radicalism and, as distress mounts, a turning to Islam.

The success of the Islamist movements largely will hang on their degree of success in offering a clear alternate economic and social vision from the western model for the distressed and poor in their societies. This is likely to be the defining ideological battleground of coming years.

The cocktail of continued US military presence in Muslim societies, of social and political turmoil resulting from economic and population pressures, and of the dynamics of strategic tensions reflected in the fostering of local proxy struggles is likely to be a potentially lethal one – this suggests a coming period of considerable fluidity, tension and change.

If the first act of the western project in the last century gave birth to Islamist ideology, it seems likely that the second act will bring major political change in its wake. It is possible that the disruptive, double-edged and potentially anarchic forces unleashed by economic dislocation will create dynamics beyond the control of any political movement; but whereas this represents a real risk, it is perhaps too pessimistic a scenario.

The key event that emerged from the Islamist revolution has been the freeing of thinking from its long tutelage to the tyranny of instrumentalism. 'We are free to reason anew', as the Hesballah leader noted. The last years have brought forth a stream of new ideas in the Muslim world as *Resistance* has sought to show over the last chapters. Raymond Williams concluded his *Culture and Society 1780–1950* with the comment that:

> There are ideas, and ways of thinking that have the seed of life in them, and there are others, perhaps deep in our minds, with the seeds of a general death. Our measure in recognising these kinds, and in naming them, making possible their common recognition, may be literally the measure of our future.[14]

The magistrate serving at the Empire's edge, troubled by what was being done in the Empire's name and recoiling at the warped human values of Colonel Joll, recognised and named these ideas – this demented way of thinking with its seeds of serial tragedy – and in his confused, but instinctively correct way, fought back with his small rebellious act of human solidarity. He returned the tortured and broken barbarian girl to her tribe.

The measure of our futures may depend on the extent to which others in the West prove ready to criticise – to make that small symbolic gesture of human solidarity like the magistrate – and to follow the South African businessmen who understood the need to recognise their situation, and like Plato's Athenian, work out how to haul politics back on to the safety of solid ground.

EPILOGUE

"Waiting for the Barbarians"

By the Greek poet C. P. Cavafy (1863–1933)

What are we waiting for, assembled in the forum?

    The barbarians are due here today.

Why isn't anything going on in the senate?

Why are the senators sitting there without legislating?

    Because the barbarians are coming today.

    What's the point of senators making laws now?

    Once the barbarians are here, they'll do the legislating.

Why did our emperor get up so early,

and why is he sitting enthroned at the city's main gate,

in state, wearing the crown?

    Because the barbarians are coming today

    and the emperor's waiting to receive their leader.

    He's even got a scroll to give him,

    loaded with titles, with imposing names.

Why have our two consuls and praetors come out today

wearing their embroidered, their scarlet togas?

Why have they put on bracelets with so many amethysts,

and rings sparkling with magnificent emeralds?

Why are they carrying elegant canes

beautifully worked in silver and gold?

    Because the barbarians are coming today

    and things like that dazzle the barbarians.

Why don't our distinguished orators turn up as usual

to make their speeches, say what they have to say?

    Because the barbarians are coming today

    and they're bored by rhetoric and public speaking.

Why this sudden bewilderment, this confusion?
(How serious people's faces have become.)
Why are the streets and squares emptying so rapidly,
everyone going home lost in thought?
  Because night has fallen and the barbarians haven't come.
  And some of our men just in from the border say
  there are no barbarians any longer.
Now what's going to happen to us without barbarians?
Those people were a kind of solution.

NOTES

Introduction

1. Hojat al-Islam Dr Mohammad Sobhani, interview with the author in Qom, Iran, September 2007.
2. Karen Armstrong, *Islam: A Short History*, London: Phoenix, 2001, p. 6.
3. Qur'an, 80:11.
4. Karen Armstrong, *Islam*, p. 5.
5. Karen Armstrong, *Holy War: The Crusades and Their Impact on Today's World*, New York: Anchor Books, 2001 edn, p. 67.
6. Jaques Rancière, *On the Shores of Politics*, London: Verso, 1995, p. 12.
7. Ibid., p. 1.
8. Walter Russell Mead, *God and Gold: Britain, America and the Making of the Modern World*, New York: Alfred Knopf, Random House, 2007.
9. Ibid., pp. 14–15.
10. A.T. Mahan, *The Influence of Sea Power upon History, 1660–1783*, Mineola, NY: Dover Publications, 1987, p. 63.
11. Walter Russell Mead, *God and Gold*, p. 228.
12. Jaques Rancière, *On the Shores of Politics*, p. 1.
13. Plato's last work 'Laws' involves a dialogue between a Cretan by the name of Clinias, a Spartan and an Athenian whose name is not disclosed. The dialogue concerns the nature of what constitutes the ideal legislation for an imaginary Cretian city. They discuss this from the standpoints of the different legal traditions in their respective states. In the discussion, Clinias remarks that the victory of the 'worse self' would mean the defeat of reason by pleasure – which he associates with the Athenian heritage. Giving one's life for one's city, Clinias states, is better than becoming a slave to pleasure.
14. Hojat al-Islam Dr Mohammad Sobhani, interview with the author in Qom, Iran, September 2007.
15. James Gordon Finlayson, *Habermas – A Very Short Introduction*, Oxford: Oxford University Press, 2005, pp. 3–5.
16. Ibid., p. 15.
17. Jaques Rancière, *On the Shores of Politics*, pp. 3–4.

18. Walter Russell Mead, *God and Gold*, p. 310.
19. Herman Melville, *White Jacket or The World in a Man-of-War*, Oxford: Oxford University Press, 1924 (first published 1850), p. 142.
20. John Gray, *Black Mass: Apocalyptic Religion and the Death of Utopia*, London: Allen Lane, 2007, p. 112.
21. Quoted by John Gray, in ibid., pp. 113–14.
22. William Dalrymple, 'Foreword', in Gerald MacLean (ed.), *Re-Orienting the Renaissance: Cultural Exchanges with the East*, Basingstoke, UK: Palgrave Macmillan, 2005, p. ix.
23. See Fatima Mernissi, *The Veil and the Male Elite*, New York: Basic Books, 1992.

1   In the Service of God and the Interests of the People

1. Quoted by Walter Russell Mead, *God and Gold: Britain, America and the Making of the Modern World*, New York: Alfred Knopf, Random House, 2007, p. 21.
2. Ibid.
3. Ibid.
4. Ibid.
5. Janet Afary and Kevin Anderson, quoting Michel Foucault, in *Foucault and the Iranian Revolution: Gender and the Seductions of Islam*, Chicago: University of Chicago Press, 2007, p. 15.
6. Hojat al-Islam Dr Mohammad Sobhani, interview with the author in Qom, Iran, September 2007.
7. Walter Russell Mead, *God and Gold*, pp. 243–45.
8. Walter Russell Mead, *God and Gold*, p. 53, quoting a reviewer of Macaulay's *History of England*.
9. Ibid., pp. 6–7.
10. John Gray, *Black Mass: Apocalyptic Religion and the Death of Utopia*, London: Allen Lane, 2007, pp. 33 and 117.
11. Justin McCarthy, *Death and Exile: The Ethnic Cleansing of Ottoman Muslims, 1821–1922*, Princeton, NJ: Darwin Press, 1995, p. 164.
12. Donald Bloxham, *The Great Game of Genocide: Imperialism, Nationalism and the Destruction of the Ottoman Armenians*, Oxford: Oxford University Press, 2007, p. 117.
13. Ibid., p. 35.
14. Ibid., p. 36.
15. John Gray, *False Dawn: The Delusions of Global Capitalism*, London: Granta, 2002, p. 18.
16. Ibid., p. 8.
17. By Caroline Finkel, among others: 'Myths of Ottoman Decay', an essay included in Gerald MacLean (ed.), *Re-Orienting the*

Renaissance: *Cultural Exchanges with the East*, Basingstoke, UK: Palgrave Macmillan, 2005, p. 155.

18. Donald Bloxham, *The Great Game of Genocide*, pp. 19–20.
19. Ibid., p. 1.
20. Ibid., p. 59, quoting Mark Levene, 'The Limits of Tolerance: Nation-state Building and What it Means for Minority Groups', *Patterns of Prejudice* 34(2): 21.
21. Edward Said, *Freud and the Non-European*, London: Verso, 2003.
22. Donald Bloxham, *The Great Game of Genocide*, pp. 110–11.
23. Edward Said, *Freud and the Non-European*, p. 43.
24. Walter Russell Mead, *God and Gold*, pp. 48–51.
25. Robert Fisk, *The Great War for Civilisation: The Conquest of the Middle East*, London: HarperCollins, 2005, p. 405.
26. Donald Bloxham, *The Great Game of Genocide*, p. 111.
27. Robert Fisk, *The Great War for Civilisation*, p. 452.
28. Ilan Pappé, *The Ethnic Cleansing of Palestine*, Oxford: Oneworld Publications, 2007, p. 12.
29. Ibid., p. 10.
30. Peter Balakian, *The Burning Tigris: The Armenian Genocide and America's Response*, New York: HarperCollins, 2003.
31. John Tirman, 'Ataturk's Children', *Boston Review*, December 1997/ January 1998.
32. Ibid.
33. Ibid.
34. Bobby Sayyid, *A Fundamental Fear: Eurocentrism and the Emergence of Islamism*, London: Zed Books, 1997, p. 59.
35. Andrew Mango, *Ataturk: The Biography of the Founder of Modern Turkey*, 1st edn, New York: Overlook Press, 2000.
36. Ataturk in a speech delivered in 1927; quoted in Bobby Sayyid, *A Fundamental Fear*, p. 59.
37. C.A. Bayly, *The Birth of the Modern World, 1780–1914: Global Connections and Comparisons*, Oxford: Blackwell Publishers, 2004, p. 17.
38. Karen Armstrong, *Islam: A Short History*, London: Phoenix Press, 2001, pp. x–xi.
39. Ibid., p. 6.

2   The Awakening of Resistance

1. Sayyid Qutb, *Milestones* (English trans.), Kuwait: Islamic Federation of Student Organisations, 1977.

2. Sayyid Qutb, *Islam, the Religion of the Future* (English trans.), Kuwait: Islamic Federation of Student Organisations, 1977, p. 61.
3. Ibid., p. 63.
4. Michael Bonner, *Jihad in Islamic History: Doctrines and Practice*, Princeton, NJ: Princeton University Press, 2006, p. 23.
5. Ibid., p. 100.
6. Ibid., p. 7.
7. Sayyid Qutb, *Milestones*, pp. 137–39.
8. Ibid., p. 100.
9. Ibid., pp. 110–11.
10. Sayyid Qutb, 'Hadhihi hiya Faransa', *Al-Risalah* 624 (June), 1945.
11. Sayyid Qutb, *Al-Islam wa-mushkilat Al-Hadarah*, Beirut, 1978, pp. 82–84.
12. Adnan Musallam, *From Secularism to Jihad: Sayyid Qutb and the Foundations of Radical Islamism*, Westport, CT: Praeger, 2005.
13. Sayyid Qutb, *Milestones*, pp. 16–18.
14. Michael Bonner, *Jihad in Islamic History*, pp. 143–44.
15. In conversation with the author, 2007.

3 Political Shi'ism

1. Sayyid Qutb, *Social Justice in Islam*, trans. T.R. Hamid Algar, North Haledon, NJ: Islamic Publications International, 2000.
2. Chibli Mallat, *The Renewal of Islamic Law: Mohammad Baqer as-Sadr, Najaf and the Shi'i International*, Cambridge: Cambridge University Press, 1993.
3. From 1954, Hesb al-Tahrir, which had been established in Jerusalem by Shekh al-Nabahani, opened offices in Iraq and influenced Islamist thinking with its avowed goal of taking political power with a view to restoring the Caliphate. Despite the Shi'i opposition to the earlier Sunni Caliphate, Shi'i Islamists were also members of the party.
4. Hesb al-Da'wa is the same party that plays a prominent role in Iraq today.
5. Baqir Sadr, *Falsafatuna*, Qom: Ansariyan Publications, 1959.
6. Baqir Sadr, *Iqtisaduna*, Qom: Ansariyan Publications, 1960.
7. Chibli Mallat, 'Muhammad Baqer as-Sadr', in Ali Rahnema (ed.), *Pioneers of Islamic Revival*, London: Zed Books, 2005, p. 261.
8. See note 2 above.
9. Jamal Sankari, *Fadlallah: The Making of a Radical Shi'ite Leader*, London: Al-Saqi, 2005, p. 71.

10. Mohammed Baqir Sadr, *Principles of Islamic Jurisprudence*, London: Islamic College for Advanced Studies (ICAS), 2003, p. 15.
11. Anthony Shadid, *Night Draws Near: Iraq's People in the Shadow of America's War*, New York: Henry Holt, 2005, p. 164.
12. CNN report: URL (accessed August 2008): http://www.cnn.com/2007/WORLD/meast/01/03/saddam.execution/index.html
13. Chibli Mallat, 'Muhammad Baqer as-Sadr', p. 258.
14. Ali Rahnema, *An Islamic Utopian: A Political Biography of Ali Shari'ati*, London: I.B. Tauris, 1998, p. 129.
15. Ali Shari'ati, *Collected Works*, vol. 2, p. 51, quoted in Ali Rahnema, An Islamic Utopian, p. 128.
16. Ibid., p. 130.
17. Ervand Abrahamian, *Khomeinism: Essays on the Islamic Republic*, Berkeley and Los Angeles: University of California Press, 1993, p. 47.
18. Ibid., p. 127.
19. Ibid., p. 126.
20. Musa Sadr, in a speech delivered in Beirut in May 1967.
21. Ali Shari'ati, *Collected Works*, vol. 16, p. 212.
22. Christian Bonaud, *L'Imam Khomeyni, un gnostique meconnu du XXe siècle*, Editions al-Bouraq, 1997, p. 20.
23. Mulla Sadra, *The Fourfold Journey*, 9 vols, ed. R. Lutfi et al., Tehran and Qom: Shirkat Dar al-Ma'arif al Islamiyyah, 1958–69.
24. Karen Armstrong, *Islam: A Short History*, London: Phoenix, 2001, p. 103.
25. Constitution of the Islamic Republic of Iran, Article 6.
26. Baker Moin, *Khomeini: Life of the Ayatollah*, London: I.B. Tauris, 1999, p. 276.
27. Jamal Sankari, *Fadlallah*, p. 181.
28. Michel Foucault, *Le Nouvel Observateur*, 16–22 October 1978.
29. 'Iran: The Spirit of a World without Spirit', interview by Claire Briere and Pierre Blanchet, in Michel Foucault, *Politics, Philosophy and Culture: Interviews and Other Writings 1977–1984*, trans. Alan Sheridan, ed. Lawrence Kritzman, New York: Routledge, 1990.
30. Ibid., pp. 250–60.
31. Fouad Ajami, *The Vanished Imam: Musa Al Sadr and the Shia of Lebanon*, Ithaca, NY: Cornell University Press, 1986, p. 90.

4 Social Revolution

1. Thomas Macaulay, *The History of England*, London: Penguin Books, 1986 [1880], p. 51.
2. Ibid., p. 52.

3. Walter Russell Mead, *God and Gold: Britain, America and the Making of the Modern World*, New York: Random House, 2007, p. 306.
4. Ibid., p. 15.
5. Ibid., p. 52.
6. Reginald Horsman, *Race and Manifest Destiny: The Origins of American Anglo-Saxonism*, Cambridge, MA: Harvard University Press, 1981, p. 22.
7. Ibid., p. 292.
8. Walter Russell Mead, *God and Gold*, p. 299.
9. John Gray, *Black Mass: Apocalyptic Religion and the Death of Utopia*, London: Allen Lane, 2007, p. 86.
10. Ibid., pp. 86–87.
11. John Gray, *False Dawn: The Delusions of Global Capitalism*, London: Granta, 2002, p. 213.
12. John Gray, *Black Mass*, p. 106.
13. Ibid., p. 147.
14. Johann Herder, *Philosophical Writings*, ed. Michael Forster, Cambridge: Cambridge University Press, 2002, pp. 380–82; quoted in Walter Russell Mead, *God and Gold*, p. 377.
15. John Gray, *Black Mass*, p. 147.
16. The Qur'an, 80:11.
17. Ibid., 76:8
18. Ibid., 9:103
19. Ibid., 59:7
20. Michael Bonner, *Jihad in Islamic History: Doctrines and Practice*, Princeton, NJ: Princeton University Press, 2006, pp. 28–29.
21. Ali Rahnema, *An Islamic Utopian: A Political Biography of Ali Shari'ati*, London: I.B. Tauris, 2000, p. 288.
22. Ibid., p. 285.
23. Ibid., p. 289.
24. Ibid., pp. 288–89.
25. Ibid., p. 279.
26. John Gray, *False Dawn*, p. 35.
27. 'Iran: The Spirit of a World without Spirit', interview by Claire Briere and Pierre Blanchet, in, *Politics, Philosophy and Culture, Interviews and Other Writings 1977–1984*, trans. Alan Sheridan, ed. Lawrence Kritzman, New York: Routledge, 1990.
28. Ali Rahnema, *An Islamic Utopian*, p. 286.

5 God Is a Liberal

1. Walter Russell Mead, *God and Gold: Britain, America and the Making of the Modern World*, New York: Random House, 2007, p. 192.

2. Ibid., p. 193.
3. Ibid., p. 303.
4. John Gray, *Black Mass: Apocalyptic Religion and the Death of Utopia*, London: Allen Lane, 2007, p. 5.
5. Ibid., p. 112.
6. Ibid., pp. 61–62.
7. Walter Russell Mead, *God and Gold*, p. 260.
8. Frantz Fanon, *Black Skin, White Masks*, London: Pluto Press, 1986, p. 18.
9. Ibid., p. 32.
10. Slavoj Žižek, *Violence*, London: Profile Books, 2008, pp. 24, 69, and his *Welcome to the Desert of the Real*, London: Verso, 2002, p. 88.
11. Slavoj Žižek, *Violence*, p. 69, quoting John Gray, *Straw Dogs*, London: Granta, 2003, p. 19.
12. Benedict Anderson, *Imagined Communities*, London: Verso, 1991, p. 19.
13. Anonymous interview with the author, Beirut, 2007.
14. Walter Russell Mead, *God and Gold*, p. 23.
15. G.K. Chesterton, *Orthodoxy*, New York: Bantam Doubleday Dell, new edn 1996 (first published 1908), pp. 146–47.

6 A Culture of Willpower and Reason

1. Albert Hourani, 'From Jabal Amil to Persia', in H.E. Chehabi (ed.), *Distant Relations*, London: I.B. Tauris in association with the Centre for Lebanese Studies, Oxford, 2006, p. 52.
2. Ibid., p. 64.
3. Augustus Richard Norton, *Amal and the Shi'a*, Austin: University of Texas Press, 1987, p. 7.
4. Rania Maktabi, 'The Lebanese Census of 1932 Revisited: Who Are the Lebanese?', *British Journal of Middle Eastern Studies*, 26(2), 1999, p. 219.
5. Elizabeth Picard, 'The Lebanese Shi'a and Political Violence in Lebanon', in David Apter (ed.), *The Legitimization of Violence*, London: Macmillan, 1997.
6. Chiclet is a brand of cheap chewing gum sold on street corners, often by children.
7. Souad Joseph, 'Politicisation of Religious Sects in Borj El-Hammoud', PhD dissertation, Columbia University, 1975, p. 210; quoted in Richard Augustus Norton, *Amal and the Shi'a*.
8. Mohammad Fadlallah, *Al-Islam wa Muntiq al-Quwwa* (Islam and the Logic of Force), Beirut: al-Mu'asasah al-Jam'iyah li al-

Dirasat was al-Nashr, 1976.

9. Musa al-Sadr in a sermon in 1975.
10. Timur Goksel, quoted by Hala Jaber, *Hezbollah*, New York: Columbia University Press, 1997, p. 28.
11. Michael Bonner, *Jihad in Islamic History: Doctrines and Practice*, Princeton, NJ: Princeton University Press, 2006, p. 100.
12. Sayyed Hassan Nasrallah in a speech given on 31 January 2007 in Beirut.
13. Alastair Crooke and Mark Perry, 'How Hizbullah Defeated Israel', *Asia Times*, October 2006, URL (consulted November 2008): http://www.atimes.com/atimes/others/hezbollah.html

7 Refusing Subservience

1. Edward Said, *Freud and the Non-European*, London: Verso, 2003, pp. 44–45.
2. Ibid., p. 46.
3. Nadia Abu el-Haj, *Facts on the Ground: Archaeological Practice and Territorial Self-fashioning in Israeli Society*, Chicago: University of Chicago Press, 2002.
4. Ibid., p. 74.
5. Herman Melville, *White Jacket or The World in a Man-of-War*, Oxford: Oxford University Press, 1924 (first published 1850), p. 142.
6. Benedict Anderson, *Imagined Communities*, London: Verso, 1983, pp. 13–14.
7. Ibid., p. 14.
8. Adalah, 'The Democratic Constitution', URL (consulted November 2008): http://www.adalah.org/eng/democratic_constitution-e.pdf
9. Marwan Dwairy, 'A Word from the Chairman', URL (consulted November 2008): http://www.adalah.org/eng/bill_of_right_dwairy.php
10. The head of the Israeli security services, as quoted in 'Rights Groups: Shin Bet Probe of Arab Group Undermines Democracy', *Ha'aretz*, 25 March 2005
11. Isaiah Berlin, *The Crooked Timber of Humanity*, Princeton, NJ: Princeton University Press, 1990, p. 246.
12. Khaled Mesha'al interviewed by Hugh Spanner in Damascus in June 2008 for the *Third Way*, transcript of full interview at URL (consulted November 2008): http://www.thirdwaymagazine.com/354
13. Ibid.
14. Anonymous prisoner.

15. Anonymous prisoner.
16. 'A quoi rêve les Iraniens?', *Le Nouvel Observateur*, 16–22 October 1978.
17. Frantz Fanon, *Racism and Culture: Towards an African Revolution*, London: Penguin Books, 1970, p. 35.
18. Frantz Fanon, *The Wretched of the Earth*, New York, Grove Weidenfeld, 1963, p. 16.
19. These were Palestinian refugee camps on the outskirts of Beirut where Lebanese forces allied with Ariel Sharon's occupation forces in Lebanon perpetrated a massacre of Palestinian refugees.
20. Anonymous prisoner.
21. Hugh Spanner interview with Khaled Mesha'al, May 2008.
22. Golda Meir, responding to questioning as quoted in news reports on 8 March 1969, URL (consulted November 2008): http://en.wikiquote.org/wiki/Golda_Meir
23. Khaled Mesha'al in an interview with the author, 2007.
24. Interview with Hugh Spanner in Damascus, May 2008.
25. A point made more recently by the British Parliament's International Development Committee report in January 2007 which noted that:

> while severe pressure has been placed on the Hamas-led PA to change its policies and accept Quartet principles, no comparable initiative has been taken with the Government of Israel to encourage it to put into practice agreements it has signed up to or to end clearly identified practices which are causing poverty and suffering in Gaza. (*Development Assistance and the Occupied Palestinian Territories*, Fourth Report of Session 2006–07, 24 January 2007, p. 28; URL [consulted November 2008]: http://www.parliament.the-stationery-office.co.uk/pa/cm200607/cmselect/cmintdev/114/114i.pdf)

26. That is, before Israel took the West Bank and Gaza Strip in the Six-Day War
27. Interview with Hugh Spanner in Damascus, May 2008.
28. Anonymous prisoner.
29. Interview with Hugh Spanner in Damascus, May 2008.
30. Khaled Me'shal in an interview with the author, 2007.
31. Ibid.

8   Resistance and the Normalisation of Injustice

1. Walter Benjamin, *Theses on the Philosophy of History*, New York: Schocken Books, 1968, Thesis IX.
2. Slavoj Žižek, *Violence*, London: Profile Books, 2008, p. 152.

3. Ibid., p. 167

4. Maximilien Robespierre, *Virtue and Terror*, London: Verso, 2007, p. 129.

5. John Gray, *Black Mass: Apocalyptic Religion and the Death of Utopia*, London: Allen Lane, 2007, p. 4.

6. Ibid., p. 184.

7. John Gray, *Black Mass*, p. 169.

8. Khaled Mesha'al interviewed by Hugh Spanner in Damascus in June 2008 for the *Third Way*, transcript at URL (consulted November 2008): http://www.thirdwaymagazine.com/354

9. The Qur'an, 80:11.

10. The Columbia Electronic Encyclopaedia, 2004, Columbia University Press, URL (consulted August 2008): http://www.reference.com/browse/columbia/leviatha

11. Benedict Anderson, *Imagined Communities*, London: Verso, 1983, p. 11.

12. Ibid., p. 11.

13. Ibid., p. 12.

14. Terry Eagleton, *Holy Terror*, Oxford: Oxford University Press, 2005, p. 94.

15. Ibid., p. 12.

16. Slavoj Žižek, *Violence*, p. 49.

17. D. Rosenblum, 'It's a Jungle Out There', *Ha'aretz* 16 June 2007.

18. Terry Eagleton, *Holy Terror*, p. 115.

19. G.K. Chesterton, *The Everlasting Man*, New York: Image Books, 1955, p. 137.

20. Walter Russell Mead, *God and Gold: Britain, America and the Making of the Modern World*, New York: Alfred Knopf, Random House, 2007, pp. 407–8.

21. Walter Russell Mead, *God and Gold*, pp. 407–8.

22. Slavoj Žižek, *Welcome to the Desert of the Real*, London: Verso, 2002, p. 88.

23. Karen Armstrong, *Islam: A Short History*, London: Phoenix, 2001, p. 12.

24. Michael Bonner, *Jihad in Islamic History: Doctrines and Practice*, Princeton, NJ: Princeton University Press, 2006, pp. 39–41.

25. Karen Armstrong, *Islam*, p. xi.

9 The Nature of Power

1. Allan Bloom, *The Closing of the American Mind*, New York: Simon and Schuster, 1987, pp. 39–43.

2. Jeff Stein, 'Can You Tell a Sunni from a Shiite?', *New York Times*, 17 October 2006.

3. Naomi Klein, *The Shock Doctrine: The Rise of Disaster Capitalism*, London and New York: Allen Lane, 2007.

4. John Gray, *Black Mass: The Apocalyptic Religion and the Death of Utopia*, London: Allen Lane, 2007, p. 123.

5. Leo Strauss, *Natural Right and History*, Chicago: University of Chicago Press, 1953, pp. 181–82.

6. Scott Horton, *The Return of Carl Schmitt*, 7 November 2007, URL (consulted August 2008): http://balkin.blogspot.com/2005/11/return-of-carl-schmitt.html

7. URL (consulted August 2008): http://en.wikipedia.org/wiki/John_Yoo

8. Alan Wolfe, 'A Fascist Philosopher Helps us to Understand Contemporary Politics', *The Chronicle Review*, 2 April 2004, URL (consulted August 2008): http://chronicle.com/free/v50/i30/30b01601.htm

9. This passage is drawn from Carl Schmitt, *Concept of the Political*, Piscataway, NJ: Rutgers University Press, 1976 (first published in German in 1927).

10. Jeane Kirkpatrick, *Dictatorship and Double Standards: Rationalism and Reason in Politics*, New York: Simon and Schuster (for the American Enterprise Institute) 1982, pp. 11, 17–18.

11. Naomi Klein, *The Shock Doctrine*.

12. Alan Wolfe, 'A Fascist Philosopher ...'.

13. Interview with the author, 2007.

14. Mohammad ibn Ishaq, *Sirat Rasul Allah*, trans. and ed. A. Guillaume, *The Life of Mohammad*, Oxford: Oxford University Press, 1955, p. 158.

15. Karen Armstrong, *Islam: A Short History*, London: Phoenix, 2001, p. 7.

16. Sayyed Hassan Nasrallah in a speech in Beirut on 9 March 2007.

17. Talk given by Dr Kassir at an international conference in Damascus in March 2007.

10   The Limits to the Present

1. J.M. Coetzee, *Waiting for the Barbarians*, London: Penguin, 1982.

2. Ibid., p. 5.

3. Ibid., p. 115.

4. Terry Eagleton, *Holy Terror*, Oxford: Oxford University Press, 2005, p. 11.

5. J.M. Coetzee, *Waiting for the Barbarians*, p. 108.
6. Quoted by Arun Kundnani, *The End of Tolerance*, London: Pluto Press, 2007, p. 12.
7. Michel Foucault, 'Qu-est-ce que les Lumières?', in Paul Rabinow (ed.), *The Foucault Reader*, London: Penguin Books, 1991, pp. 32–50.
8. Ibid.
9. Ibid.
10. Michel Foucault, *The Archaeology of Knowledge and the Discourse on Language*, New York: Pantheon, 1972, p. 224.
11. Michel Foucault, 'Qu'est-ce que les Lumières?'
12. Quoted by Slavoj Žižek, *Violence*, London: Profile Books, 2008, p. 160.
13. Jean-Paul Sartre, writing in the preface to Frantz Fanon's *The Wretched of the Earth*, New York: Grove Press, 2004, p. 1i.
14. Raymond Williams, *Culture and Society 1780–1950*, London: Penguin, 1985, end page.

INDEX